Tracking Loach

For *Núria*

Tracking Loach

Politics | Practices | Production

David Archibald

EDINBURGH
University Press

Edinburgh University Press is one of the leading university presses in the UK. We publish academic books and journals in our selected subject areas across the humanities and social sciences, combining cutting-edge scholarship with high editorial and production values to produce academic works of lasting importance. For more information visit our website: edinburghuniversitypress.com

© David Archibald, 2023

Edinburgh University Press Ltd
The Tun – Holyrood Road
12(2f) Jackson's Entry
Edinburgh EH8 8PJ

Typeset in 12 on 14pt Arno Pro by
Cheshire Typesetting Ltd, Cuddington, Cheshire

A CIP record for this book is available from the British Library

ISBN 978 1 4744 4211 4 (hardback)
ISBN 978 1 4744 4212 1 (paperback)
ISBN 978 1 4744 4213 8 (webready PDF)
ISBN 978 1 4744 4214 5 (epub)

The right of David Archibald to be identified as the author of this work has been asserted in accordance with the Copyright, Designs and Patents Act 1988, and the Copyright and Related Rights Regulations 2003 (SI No. 2498).

Contents

List of Figures	vi
Acknowledgements	viii
Introduction	1
1 Politics on-screen	22
2 Form	50
3 Team Loach	84
4 Performance	105
5 Words: Between script and screen	139
6 Politics beyond the screen	160
Epilogue: Revolutionary respair	177
Appendices	181
Filmography	187
Bibliography	190
Index	202

Figures

Cover: Filming the closing sequence of *The Angels' Share*.
I.1   Ken Loach talking to the actors whilst filming in the Highlands   2
I.2   Ken Loach and camera crew preparing to shoot the
      concluding sequence of *The Angels' Share*   10
I.3   Standing behind Ray Beckett's sound desk as Loach prepares
      to shoot a scene in the Caledonian Hotel in Edinburgh   17
1.1   Filming the gang arriving at Balblair distillery. The camera is
      normally placed on a tripod and positioned at Loach's and the
      cinematographer's eye level   24
1.2   The revolutionary militia fighters pose for the camera in *Land
      and Freedom*   32
1.3   Albert's 'meat and two veg' take a hammering as he walks
      back into history   46
2.1   The three boys raise their kilts when they are searched on
      their return to Glasgow   57
2.2a and 2.2b   Production designer Fergus Clegg's 'before' and
      'after' photographs of the whisky distillery shop   62
2.3   Filming the gang in a field overlooking the distillery. One of
      the few occasions when a stationary camera is placed below
      the standing eye-level of Loach and Ryan   67
2.4   The camera is placed on a platform to enable a better view of
      potential bidders arriving at the distillery   67
2.5   Albert prepares to fall backwards onto the train tracks   73
2.6   Notes on filming the snooker hall scene from Loach's
      shooting script   76
2.7   Editor Jonathan Morris at work on *The Angels' Share* auction
      scene   78

3.1	*The Ken Loach Collection* (Volume One) DVD cover	87
3.2	Eric Cantona casts a glance at his footballing self in *Looking for Eric*	93
3.3	The celebrated football scene from *Kes*, replete with on-screen scores	102
4.1	Crew call sheets make it clear that anything which might reveal aspects of the plot should be kept from the actors	117
4.2	Mo appears genuinely shocked as Albert smashes the whisky-filled Irn Bru bottles	119
4.3	Boom operator Pete Murphy hiding in plain sight on the set of *The Angels' Share*	123
4.4	Loach and Ryan discuss the logistics of filming through a hole in the wall	130
4.5	Loach and crew survey the set-up at the Caledonian Hotel	131
4.6	A brochure outlining the details of the rare Malt Mill is distributed to the auction attendees even though it will never be seen on-screen	133
5.1	Paul Laverty and Ray Beckett monitoring the action at Balblair distillery	143
5.2	Loach directs Paul Birchard as cast, crew and a group of journalists look on	148
5.3	Loach discusses shooting the snooker scene with the actors	151
6.1	Glasgow May Day Poster: illustration of Dave Johns as Daniel Blake, the film's eponymous hero, his left arm raised, fist clenched tight in defiance	161
6.2	Loach is the main attraction for journalists at the Cannes press conference	166
6.3	Loach and team receive a lengthy standing ovation at Cannes	168
E.1	Kim raises her fist aloft after emptying a handful of collectivised Spanish earth into her grandfather's graveside	180

Acknowledgements

In the first instance, I am grateful to Ken Loach for granting me access to follow his activity so closely. Few people would welcome a researcher looking over their shoulder as they go about their working routine, never mind a routine conducted on an intimate and personal landscape such as the set on which Loach creates his films. This book in its present form would not have been possible without his support. I owe much to Paul Laverty and Rebecca O'Brien, both for their role in facilitating this research and for giving their time so generously during it, and to Ann Cattrall, Jack Thomas-O'Brien and the other staff at Sixteen Films and *The Angels' Share* cast and crew who either facilitated interviews, participated in them directly, or assisted in multifarious ways to accommodate my numerous requests. Thanks to Sixteen Films for allowing me to reproduce the documentation pertaining to their work which features in the book. I am also grateful to the late Tony Garnett who spoke with me at length when he attended a Radical Film Network Scotland event in Glasgow in 2018. The staff at the British Film Institute Ken Loach archive were extremely helpful, both in providing access to the archive as it was taking shape, and in steering me through it on several occasions.

Ian Goode read the full final draft, highlighting moments of weakness and areas where the book might be strengthened, and David Martin-Jones, Karen Lury, Alistair Fraser and Amanda Gallacher provided valuable feedback on either chapters or sections of the book; I am grateful to them all for their insights throughout the long process of researching and writing. I am also grateful to students on the University of Glasgow's Theories of Authorship in Film course and on the Film and Television Studies master's programme as on both courses some of this research was presented while I was still thinking it through.

Gillian Leslie at Edinburgh University Press was very keen to publish this work and very patient in waiting on its arrival; I am extremely grateful to her on both counts. I am also grateful to the other EUP staff including assistant editor Sam Johnson, copy-editor Anita Joseph, who moved the book through the final process, and Simon Whittle for designing the front cover.

I had the opportunity to present preliminary research findings related to this work at several invited talks and thanks must go to the following: Michael Higgins (University of Strathclyde), David Martin-Jones (*Screen* Seminars at Glasgow), and Martin Cloonan, (International Institute for Popular Culture, University of Turku). I also presented Loach-related material at academic conferences as follows: European Network of Cinema and Media Studies (2012 and 2013); New Directions in Film and Television Production Studies conference at Watershed, Bristol (2015); and *Screen*, University of Glasgow (2017).

An earlier version of Chapter 3 was published as 'Team Loach and Sixteen Films: Authorship, Collaboration, Leadership (and Football)' in Ewa Mazierska and Lars Kristensen (eds) (2017) *Contemporary Cinema and Ideology: Neoliberal Capitalism and Its Alternatives in Filmmaking*, New York and London: Routledge; some exploratory thoughts on Loach and performance were published in 'Loach and acting: seven fragments', *The Drouth*, 2018 (60); and earlier ruminations on Loach and politics were sketched out in a short essay titled 'Revolution, my arse' which accompanied the release of *Three Films by Ken Loach:* Riff-Raff, Raining Stones, Ladybird Ladybird, British Film Institute, 2017.

The research was funded in part by the Royal Society of Edinburgh, The Carnegie Trust for the Universities of Scotland, and the John Robertson Bequest at the University of Glasgow, which also provided the research leave, an essential luxury, that allowed me the time to complete the monograph.

The photographs of the set of *The Angels' Share* and Loach at Cannes which appear in this book were taken by the author, bar two photographs in Chapter 2 which were supplied by *The Angels' Share* production designer Fergus Clegg. I am grateful to Fergus for his generosity in sharing this aspect of his work with me and for the permission to reproduce the photographs here. Thanks also to Lorna Miller, the artist who designed the Glasgow May Day Poster which features in Chapter 6, for permission to reproduce an image of the poster in this book, and to Jennifer McCarey at Glasgow Trades Council and Tommy Breslin at the Scottish Trades Union Congress for assisting in facilitating this process. Thanks, finally, to my mum, Ann Archibald. I owe her a great deal.

Introduction

17 January 2011. I am in a Glasgow hotel foyer, a stone's throw from the city's Buchanan Street bus station, pitching an idea to Ken Loach and his long-standing producer, Rebecca O'Brien. I outline that I am seeking access to observe the making of *The Angels' Share* (Loach, 2012), a film which they plan to shoot in Scotland in the ensuing months, adding that, as academic access to film production is extremely rare, it represents a unique opportunity to present a scholarly account of Loach's celebrated, but underexplored, working methods. During the discussion, O'Brien asks, 'What's in it for us, David?'

'The historical record,' I respond, somewhat off the cuff, and only partly in jest. Loach is seventy-five at this time, seemingly in the twilight of a long and illustrious career, and my reasoning is that they may weigh in this factor when deciding.

As the discussion continues, Loach and O'Brien indicate an eagerness for their work to be understood within critical frameworks which reach beyond the formal qualities of film or the specifics of film production. I reply that my plan would be to write a book-length account of Loach's methods, one rooted in film studies, but contextualised historically, socially and politically. The meeting concludes with a degree of uncertainty: 'We'll be in touch,' says O'Brien, before I depart the hotel.

As I saunter back to resume my teaching duties at the University of Glasgow, Loach telephones, advises that they have agreed to the request, and invites me to a production meeting later that week. He adds that he will shortly be participating on a BBC radio programme which will be broadcast live from a community centre near my home in Govan, and encourages me to invite any political activists I know to attend. 'It would be good to get their voices in too,' he says.

Figure I.1 Ken Loach talking to the actors whilst filming in the Highlands

Two days later, I am back in the hotel foyer, armed with tape recorder, notepad and pen, listening attentively alongside Loach and O'Brien as Michael Higson delivers a presentation on possible locations for the upcoming shoot. This aspect of my research is underway in earnest, yet I am uncertain as to how it will unfold, and to where it might lead.

I recount this episode as it outlines this book's genesis and general aims, whilst also revealing something of the filmmakers' desires and my methodological approach. The book's main title, *Tracking Loach*, refers in one sense to tracking *The Angels' Share*, however, the reach is broader, analysing this one film, and its production, within Loach's wider *oeuvre*, and within broader contexts.

What might it mean to track Loach more broadly? My main interest, it should be stressed, lies not in extensive biographical detail but in Loach's film and television work and its accompanying critical and political discourse.[1] If we understand 'to track' as 'to follow' or 'to trace' someone or

---

[1] For biographical details on Loach, see Anthony Hayward (2004). While throughout the book I use terms such as 'Loach film' and 'Loach set', this is shorthand and should not be taken to mean that I am ascribing full ownership in any artistic sense to the director nor subscribing to auteurist notions of filmmaking. A fuller and more precise account of the dynamics involved in the filmmaking process is developed in Chapter 3.

something then we might commence by tracing Loach's output from its beginnings. Following his appointment as a trainee television director at the BBC in 1963, his output included several television films in *The Wednesday Play* series, most notably *Up the Junction* (BBC, 1965) and *Cathy Come Home* (BBC, 1966), both undisputed landmarks, aesthetically and politically, in British television history.[2] From his cinematic debut *Poor Cow* (1967) through to *Sorry We Missed You* (2019), he has directed twenty-five feature-length fiction films that have garnered significant critical recognition. One signifier of Loach's cinematic success is that the Cannes Film Festival has screened more of his films in Official Selection than those of any other director. They also twice awarded him the Palme d'Or, world cinema's most prestigious prize, for *The Wind That Shakes the Barley* (2006) and *I, Daniel Blake* (2016). In addition to their critical success, the films' sympathetic depictions of the lives and struggles of working-class and marginalised people have regularly provoked public controversy: *Cathy Come Home* precipitated wide-ranging discussion on homelessness and *I, Daniel Blake* ignited major political debate on the Kafkaesque constraints imposed on the unemployed. What's more, when the films have focused on British foreign policy, they have received extensive press attention: the critique of Britain's role in Ireland evident in *The Wind That Shakes the Barley* (2006), for example, provoked significant discussion on the Irish War of Independence in the Irish press, and a ferocious backlash from the British right-wing press.[3]

Loach's career trajectory, however, has been neither smooth nor continuous. On the contrary, his television work's political radicality often prompted institutional conflict. For instance, the critique of both racism and charity in the *Save the Children Fund Film* (LWT, 1971), a documentary which was commissioned by the eponymous charity and scheduled for broadcast on London Weekend Television, appalled the funders,

---

[2] For a full filmography see pp. 187–8. I use the term 'film' even when discussing televisual outputs. This is in keeping with Loach's comments on *Up the Junction* (quoted in Fuller 1998: 14), of which he says, 'Our whole intention, at that stage, was to make films – not studio-based theatre.' John Hill also notes (2011: 104) that Loach and Garnett attempted to arrange cinema screenings of *Cathy Come Home*. Other critics, it should be noted, have situated Loach's early work firmly within the context of television: see, for instance, John Caughie (1980).

[3] See, for instance, the article by Conservative MP Michael Gove, 'A truly radical film would dare to tell the truth', *The Times*, 31 May 2006, https://www.thetimes.co.uk/article/a-truly-radical-film-would-dare-to-tell-the-truth-w3nf3xvbgj0 (last accessed 11 May 2020).

and following legal wrangles the film was consigned to the British Film Institute (BFI) vaults for decades.[4] Subsequent television documentaries focusing on British industrial relations also fuelled fractious disputes leading to delays to the broadcast of *Which Side Are You On?* (BBC, 1985), and to *Questions of Leadership* (Channel 4, 1983) not being broadcast at all.[5]

Although he has faced considerably less censorial intervention in cinema, the British film industry's parlous financial state ensured that, despite early critical success with *Kes* (1969), there were significant fallow periods in the 1970s and 1980s during which he struggled to secure film funding. Since the release of *Hidden Agenda* (1990), however, he has enjoyed a lengthy period of consistent activity which has helped cement his status as a leading international filmmaker, one who has successfully negotiated a pathway to direct films that, from a socialist, even Marxist, perspective, critique capitalism whilst operating within it.[6] In recent years numerous major international film organisations and film festivals have organised celebratory Loach retrospectives, including the British Film Institute (2011), the Irish Film Institute (2014), Karlovy Vary Film Festival (2016), Filmoteca de Catalunya (2018) and the International Film Festival of India (2019), or granted him prestigious lifetime or outstanding achievement awards, including the British Academy of Film and Television Arts (2006), the Berlinale (2014) and the scholarly body, British Association of Film, Television and Screen Studies (2018). At the time of writing (early 2022), Loach is eighty-five; with the global pandemic further threatening future output, it seems that we may well be approaching the denouement, if not quite yet at the final curtain, of one of cinema's most sustained and successful careers.[7]

In Hegel's oft-cited aphorism, the Owl of Minerva takes flight at dusk, surveying and comprehending what lies below her feet in the shimmers of the half-light. The tracking that takes place in this book involves analysing Loach's career from a similar crepuscular perspective: assessing his extensive body of work, whilst integrating insights gleaned from observing

---

[4] For more here see Matthew Hilton (2015).
[5] For further information see Julian Petley (1997).
[6] John Orr (2004: 303) suggests that Loach's success in the 1990s 'sparked a revival in the neo-Bazinian narrative of the British city' suggesting it influenced the production of *Secrets and Lies* (Leigh, UK, 1995), *Stella Does Tricks* (Giedroyc, UK, 1996), *Brassed Off* (Herman, UK, 1996) and *The Full Monty* (Cattaneo, UK 1997).
[7] In an email to the author (15 December 2021), Loach's long-term writing partner, Paul Laverty, indicated that they hoped to start shooting a new film, *The Old Oak*, in spring 2022.

the making of *The Angels' Share* and studying the BFI Ken Loach archive. In another sense, though, I have been tracking Loach since watching *Riff-Raff* (1991) in Glasgow Film Theatre on its initial release. Prior to this, I had encountered Loach's work via television, most memorably *Cathy Come Home* and *Kes*; however, *Riff-Raff*'s engagement with unorganised building workers' struggles resonated with my political sensibilities at that time and lodged the film deeply in my consciousness. I might now connect the term 'riff-raff' to sweepings or refuse, in this case supposed human refuse, and to the excluded and the disposable, which Nicolas Bourriaud (2016) terms the 'exform'. Then, however, the film's sympathetic portrayal of workers confronting life at capitalism's rough edges simply struck me as true to life, and an early scene in which Larry (Ricky Tomlinson) extemporises on the advantages of planned, socialist housing policies piqued my interest as to how films might advance radical ideas. My experiences working in an engineering factory on the banks of the River Clyde in the 1980s had fuelled an involvement in socialist and trade union activism, and, following this cinematic encounter, I sought out Loach's latest releases and examined his cinematic back catalogue. Engaging with film and television as a mature student in the mid 1990s precipitated an encounter with scholarly takes on Loach, on the modernist sensibilities underpinning his early television drama, and *Screen* debates over the film form he employed.[8] Moving into doctoral research and then teaching film and television studies in a university context, my interest in Loach underpinned the publication of journalistic and academic accounts of his work and, prior to commencing fieldwork on *The Angels' Share*, I had interviewed Loach on several occasions: in 1999, researching the Spanish Civil War in cinema, in a journalistic capacity on the sets of *Sweet Sixteen* (2002) and *Ae Fond Kiss . . .* (2004), which had both been filmed in Scotland, and also the Irish historical drama *The Wind That Shakes the Barley*, which had been filmed in Cork.[9] The journalism interviews were conducted primarily for mainstream British newspapers, but I had also written about cinema for *Scottish Socialist Voice*, the newspaper of the Scottish Socialist Party, which Loach has expressed support for.[10]

---

[8] I return to questions of film form in Chapter 2.
[9] The *Sweet Sixteen* interview was published in *The Sunday Herald* (2002) and *The Wind That Shakes the Barley* interview in *Cineaste* (2007) and *The Sunday Herald* (2006). On each of the occasions above, I also interviewed Paul Laverty on set and interviewed Rebecca O'Brien on the set of *The Wind That Shakes the Barley*. One chapter of my monograph, *The war that won't die: The Spanish Civil War in cinema* (Manchester University Press, 2012) analyses *Land and Freedom*.
[10] Uncredited (2011) 'Support the SSP', *Scottish Socialist Voice* (372) 20 April 2011.

Tracking Loach in this vein I had also crossed the path of Paul Laverty, Loach's principal screenwriter since the mid 1990s; in 1999 I interviewed him about being cast as a revolutionary fighter in the Spanish Civil War drama, *Land and Freedom* (1995), and on the sets of *Sweet Sixteen*, *Ae Fond Kiss . . .* and *Cargo* (Gordon, 2006) about his work on these films. In the autumn of 2010, following a lecture in which Laverty addressed University of Glasgow Film and Television Studies students, he indicated that Loach was planning to shoot another Scottish-based film that he had scripted, although he was characteristically tight-lipped about its content. This encounter sparked the idea of observing the film's production and, with Laverty's support and assistance, the meeting outlined above was arranged. Attending previous Loach sets, I had noted that individuals deemed extraneous to the shooting process were asked to leave the set immediately prior to filming itself commencing.[11] In my case, although permitted to observe the filming of exteriors in *The Wind That Shakes the Barley*, with *Sweet Sixteen* access was restricted to areas where the cast and crew assembled outwith shooting locations, and with *Ae Fond Kiss . . .* I was asked to leave a domestic interior just before shooting in that location began. On the latter two occasions, Loach and Laverty suggested that the tightness of the space meant that my presence might have negatively impacted the actors' performances. I had sensed, therefore, that Loach would be apprehensive about a researcher's sustained physical presence on *The Angels' Share* set and suspected that any access would be restricted. Consequently, even after it had been approved, there was an element of uncertainty attached to what would emerge when the fieldwork aspect of my research commenced. Indeed, I was only beginning to think through what 'fieldwork', in effect an ethnographic study, might entail in a film production context. Sarah Pink (2009: 44) highlights 'the impossibility of being completely prepared or knowing precisely how the ethnography will be conducted before starting'. I sensed that a rare opportunity had presented itself, and my approach was to grab what could be grabbed with a view to reflecting fully on its significance afterwards. I advance this brief autobiographical sketch and

---

In this article, which was also published as the foreword to the SSP's 2011 Scottish Parliament election manifesto, Loach states, 'A secure job, care for the elderly, a good education independent of private interests, a fully funded health service, decent housing – these are not unreasonable demands. But now they are revolutionary. The system cannot allow them', https://issuu.com/scottishsocialistparty/docs/socialist voice372 (last accessed 20 December 2021). I return to Loach's views on revolutionary demands in Chapter 1.

[11] Analysis of the set during filming is developed in detail in Chapters 4 and 5.

background detail for two reasons: firstly, to highlight the entangled relationship between writer and subject matter, and secondly to provide some contextualising background to the research itself.

Looking and listening

Between January 2011 and June 2012, I observed various aspects of the production of *The Angels' Share*, a process facilitated by O'Brien, with whom I spoke regularly throughout. In pre-production, this involved attending meetings to discuss locations, joining a 'recce', a survey of potential filming locations, in Glasgow and attending a casting session. During production, I spent approximately twenty days on set observing the shoot, and in post-production, visited the cutting room during the editing process and attended a private screening of a rough cut. Three factors, however, limited my capacity to follow every step of the process. Firstly, although most of the shoot took place during a period of the academic year which allowed me to attend, the necessity of conducting my own teaching practice during term time limited my availability. Secondly, consistent with Loach's desire that my presence did not impede the actors' performance, access was granted only to the filming of exteriors and larger interiors where my presence might be less intrusive.[12] Thirdly, with post-production occurring in London, observations here were restricted to half a day in the cutting room, and attendance at the aforementioned rough cut screening. Following the film's completion, I attended the 2012 Cannes Film Festival World Premiere and press conference, pre- and post-screening parties, and accompanied the film's entourage as it was chauffeured from La Croisette to ascend the Palais des Festivals' red-carpeted staircase.[13] Sixteen Films also supplied me with documentation pertaining to the film, including contracts, shooting schedules and various versions of the script as it developed, including Loach's annotated shooting script. Finally, I conducted extensive interviews with Loach and his collaborators.

Michelangelo Antonioni (2007: 78) contends that speaking with filmmakers about their films has limited value: 'I am convinced that whatever

[12] Access to these interiors allowed me to observe the filming of the sentencing at Glasgow Sheriff Court, the snooker hall exchange, the initial distillery visit, the whisky tasting in Edinburgh, the auction, and the exchange between Robbie and Thaddeus in its immediate aftermath.

[13] The Cannes activity feeds into my understanding of how Loach utilises festivals as a political platform, which I return to in Chapter 6.

a director says about himself or his work is of no help in understanding the work itself.' Film studies' origins as a text-based discipline, with the completed film the locus of criticism, also underpins a historical tendency to treat filmmakers' words with a certain uninterest.[14] In a different vein, John Thornton Caldwell, a prominent figure in film production studies, (2013: 162–4) cautions that academics 'fortunate enough to be embedded in a media company' should carefully negotiate 'managed top-down explanations of production'. I approached this research aware of such concerns, and particularly aware of the pitfalls of uncritically replicating interviewees' production narratives. I was cognisant that not only was I interviewing filmmakers about their work, but that many of them were also discussing their employer or business associate, as much as their collaborator. I contend, however, that there is significant value to be drawn from interviewing filmmakers, particularly away from the often carefully managed marketing process. The word 'interview' is etymologically connected with the French *entre vue* or 'see between', and the interviews complemented my participant observation, thereby contributing to the attempt to 'see between' the space of production and projection. For this research, I conducted interviews with Loach by telephone in August 2011 and in person after visiting the edit suite in early 2012, and with Laverty and O'Brien on several occasions throughout the filmmaking process and at Cannes. I also drew on interviews with Loach, Laverty and O'Brien that I had conducted on previous occasions, and subsequent email correspondence with Laverty about more recent plans. I also draw on interviews with twenty-four cast and crew members, conducted mostly during the shoot: in the spirit of Loach's words to me when he agreed to this venture, I was keen to get their voices in too. The crew members were as follows: Joss Barratt (still photographer), Ray Beckett (sound mixer), Karen Brotherston (make-up), Jas Brown (driver), Fergus Clegg (production designer), Paul Clegg (first assistant editor), Andy Cole (gaffer), Kahleen Crawford (casting director), Carole Fraser (costume), Peter Gallagher (line producer), David Gilchrist (first assistant director), Michael Higson (locations), Susanna Lenton (script supervisor), Eimhear McMahon (Sixteen Films staff member involved with multiple aspects of production) Campbell Mitchell (standby

---

[14] For instance, Barbara Klinger (2006: 73) writes critically about DVD commentaries, which are often delivered by directors: 'Viewers do not get the unvarnished truth about the production; they are instead presented with the "promotable" facts, behind-the-scenes information that supports and enhances a sense of the "movie-magic" associated with Hollywood.'

props), Jonathan Morris (editor) and Robbie Ryan (director of photography). I also interviewed the following cast members: Paul Brannigan (Robbie), Jasmine Riggins (Mo), William Ruane (Rhino), Gary Maitland (Albert), Roger Allam (Thaddeus), Charles MacLean (Rory McAllister) and Bruce Addison (unnamed auctioneer). Finally, I interviewed the late Tony Garnett who provided valuable reflections on his time as series editor and producer on Loach's early film and television work and an important historical perspective.[15] Eager to garner diverse perspectives, interviewees included several classified in the industry as 'below the line' workers, and these complement prominent production personnel views. In *Voices of Labor: Creativity, Craft, and Conflict in Global Hollywood* (2017: 2), Michael Curtin and Kevin Sanson suggest that in film culture 'Those we hear least are the voices of labor'. Situating their work within the context of broader labour studies, Curtin and Sanson focus primarily on industry working conditions, contributing to the valuable collection of scholarly work on labour conditions in the film industry and the erroneously termed 'creative industries' more broadly.[16] Although these matters arose occasionally in interview, I followed a different path, focusing on the participants' creative contribution and their thoughts on working with Loach.[17]

In addition, extensive periods of participant observation supplement the material which emerged from interview. Loïc Wacquant (2003: 5) describes ethnography as 'social research based on the close-up, on-the-ground observation of people and institutions in real time and space, in which the investigator embeds herself near (or within) the phenomenon'. Their aim, he continues, is 'to detect how and why agents on the scene act, think and feel the way they do'. My participant observation involved extended times spent on set in which, tucked away in a corner, I would observe, in real time, how the shoot developed. Often, this involved simply hanging around the film set, watching what was happening during and in between filming, and having occasional casual conversations with those

---

[15] This interview took place in 2018 when Garnett attended a screening in Glasgow of *The Big Flame* (Loach, UK, 1969), which he produced.

[16] See, for instance, Mark Banks and David Hesmondhalgh (2009) and Keith Randle (2015).

[17] I had speculated that questions related to finance might lead to some reticence to be open on the part of the interviewees, and avoided questions related to remuneration. I detected from several interviewees that the workers thought that, relative to a similar position in the industry, they were well paid, however, this is not a route that I pursued. Although Sixteen Films provided access to financial data, perhaps someone else might write 'The Workers' Share of *The Angels' Share*'.

Figure I.2 Ken Loach and camera crew preparing to shoot the concluding sequence of *The Angels' Share*

present.[18] John D. Brewer (2000: 10) cautions against ethnographic studies of people which lead to 'meaning being imposed on them externally'. The extensive period spent on set enabled me to develop a fuller picture of the filmmaking process without imposing any preconceived ideas. Participant observation was particularly valuable in allowing me to develop a greater understanding of how on-set working relationships are forged through specific human exchanges, and how this impacts filmmaking. For instance, how Loach as a director works with human agents, be they cast or crew, and how cast and crew bond together and develop a working relationship and ethos. It also enabled me to observe how Loach and the filmmakers utilise specific technology, for example camera and lighting equipment, how this impacts the completed film, and how the film takes shape as the script moves from words on the page to words spoken to camera. As part of what developed into a multimodal methodology, I also created an audio-visual record consisting of a series of still photographs and several hours of digital film footage. Shot on a deliberately unobtrusive, phone-sized digital camera, the footage functioned as a vital aide-memoir, allowing me to revisit my own audiovisual production archive whilst writing the book.

---

[18] During filming, I often positioned myself behind sound recordist, Ray Beckett, who had mastered the art of, as much as was practical, keeping himself and his equipment out of the actors' line of vision (see Figure I.3).

Entangled ethnography

As highlighted above, I was sympathetic to Loach's overall project and, cognisant of the danger that analysing a project which had my political sympathies might restrict my critical focus, considered striving to maintain some level of 'sympathising distance'. In doing so, I recalled a longstanding aphorism that 'critics and artists should walk on different sides of the street'. I was also acutely aware that I was entangled within it. My use of 'entangled' here is drawn from Karen Barad (2007: ix):

> To be entangled is not simply to be intertwined with another, as in the joining of separate entities, but to lack an independent, self-contained existence. Existence is not an individual affair. Individuals do not preexist their interactions; rather, individuals emerge through and as part of their entangled intra-relating.

Barad's work collapses any neat distinction which might be drawn between object and subject, researcher and research material, and has been influential in shaping understandings of how ethnographic encounters might disturb all participants.[19] Sevasti-Melissa Nolas and Christos C. Varvantakis (2018), for instance, suggest that entanglement

> conveys a meaning of bodies coming together, those of images, producers and consumers. It is a knotting and twisting of different modes of knowledge generation, and of the intersecting and enmeshment of media of production, representation and consumption of lived experience.

This book is evidence of how this research has altered my thinking, and one small anecdote indicates something of the opposite process. To justify my on-screen presence whilst filming the opening sequence in Glasgow's Sheriff Court, I was dressed as a journalist, and placed in the press gallery front row. There is a fleeting moment in the completed film in which the camera pans right across the courtroom and, for a few frames, my presence is evident on-screen. I make no claims, of course, for its critical significance, other than to offer it as a concrete, visible illustration of how entangled encounters change both researcher and research object. I was always cognisant, however, of the necessity of approaching the material with an open mind, and to be faithful to what I encountered, rather than what I hoped I might encounter.

---

[19] Writing on 'Gonzo' ethnography, an approach inspired by Hunter S. Thompson, Taylor R. Genovese questions whether 'intellectual or ethnographic distance is actually possible' (2019).

Ethnografilmic analysis

I have coined the term 'ethnografilmic analysis' to describe the process by which the ethnographic study of filmmaking influences analysis of the completed film, and film criticism more broadly. In Hortense Powdermaker's contemporaneous study of Hollywood in the 1950s, *Hollywood, the Dream Factory: An Anthropologist Looks at the Movies*, she notes (1951: 3),

> I went there to better understand the nature of our movies. My hypothesis was that the social system in which they are made significantly influences their content and meaning ... My hypothesis is hardly original, although it has not been applied before to the movies.[20]

Powdermaker's anthropological approach, grounded methodologically in the social sciences, has been pursued rarely in film studies, which originated in the arts and humanities. There has in recent years been an important growth of production studies of filmmaking, a subset of media industry studies and critical media studies.[21] John Thornton Caldwell (2013: 162) suggests that this work 'can provide rich insights that speculative theorizing misses.'[22] Yet contemporary production studies focuses primarily on filmmaking's industrial dimensions and studies of filmmaking's creative aspects are less common, not least because of problems of access.[23] In *The Making of Citizen Kane*, Robert L. Carringer details the pre-production, post-production and distribution of Orson Welles's celebrated debut, outlining the contribution of numerous individuals who shaped the film, including studio heads, the screenwriter and cinematographer, but also

---

[20] For further studies from a sociological perspective see also Margaret Thorp (1946).

[21] For further information here see Paul McDonald (2013); Timothy Havens, Amanda D. Lotz and Serra Tinic (2009); and Timothy Havens and Amanda D. Lotz (2012).

[22] As it draws more on social science methodologies, there has been some work in this area in television studies. For instance, Georgina Born (2005: 15), in her anthropological study of the BBC, including the Drama department where Loach began work in the early 1960s, points to some of the benefits of observing production processes when she suggests that 'Fieldwork makes it possible to explore the differences between what is said in publicity or in the boardroom and what happens on the ground in the studio, office or cleaning station. It is by probing the gaps between principles and practice, management claims and ordinary working lives – between what is explicit and what is implicit – that a fuller grasp of reality can be gleaned.'

[23] See, for instance, Sherry B. Ortner (2010) and John Thornton Caldwell (2008). One sub-field of film studies, that is the study of film festivals, has witnessed several ethnographic studies of specific festivals and the broader festival circuit. For an overview of both ethnographic film festivals and ethnographies of film festivals, see Aida Vallejo and María-Paz Peirano (eds) (2017).

the editors and master sound dubbers, roles that ordinarily fall outwith film studies' purview. Carringer examines the film's traces, including storyboards, shooting scripts and pertinent correspondence, to 'show that the collaborative process provides the best framework for understanding the remarkable achievement this film represents' (1985: ix). Other scholars have conducted retrospective studies of past film productions. Most notably, in *The Classical Hollywood Cinema: Film Style and Mode of Production to 1960*, David Bordwell, Janet Staiger and Kristin Thompson draw on Raymond Williams's insights on the relationship between individual outputs and their contextualised origins as they seek to argue that across Hollywood 'the concept of a mode of film practice can historicize textual analysis and connect the history of film style to the history of the motion picture industry' (1985: xvii). This influential book clearly posits an important connection between production context and text; however, as with Carringer's study, it lacks the insights gained from the presence of a researcher on the ground and in the moment. Perhaps not surprisingly, the in-person research that has been conducted into filmmaking has been conducted predominantly by anthropologists, including Tejaswini Ganti's *Bollywood: Inside the Contemporary Hindi Film Industry* (2012), Lotte Hoek's *Cut-Pieces: Celluloid Obscenity and Popular Cinema in Bangladesh* (2014) and Anand Pandian's *Reel World: An Anthology of Creation* (2015). Pandian's analysis of the work of Tamil filmmakers in South India's Kollywood, written, in part, in a form which seeks to convey something of cinema's 'creative and disruptive force' (16) also disturbs the binaries between creative and critical thinking and conveys formally the value of interdisciplinary approaches to the study of filmmaking. Lotte Hoek (11), for instance, suggests that anthropologists tend to pose different questions to film scholars, noting that the latter have their 'eyes often fixed on *the* screen rather than a multiplicity of empirical screens and all the extraordinarily less than ideal practices around them'. Ganti (21) develops further the differing approaches when noting, 'An anthropological approach to studying the mass media distinguishes itself from other approaches by its focus on people and their social relations, as opposed to a focus only on media texts or technology.'[24]

---

[24] Ganti (22) also advances an argument for the value of ethnographic approaches when stating their value 'both for understanding how media are produced in different cultural settings and for countering the ethnocentrism of much of the scholarship on culture industries and mass culture, which are mainly based on the study of North American and Western European media institutions and corporate capitalism'. This is particularly valuable given the current moves to decolonise film studies.

One of the few studies written by a film scholar which benefits from participant observation and does ask different questions than conventional screen-based film analyses is John Cook's research into the making of *La Commune (Paris, 1871)* (Watkins, 2000). Cook offers useful insights on how performance comes into being during the making of this experimental account of The Paris Commune; however, his rich study is limited to one journal article.[25] Perhaps the most notable book-length study of film production conducted by a film scholar able to observe the process at work is Sarah Atkinson's (2018) analysis of the work of director Sally Potter through a focus on *Ginger and Rosa* (2012). Notably, neither the name of the filmmaker nor the film itself features in the title, *From Film Practice to Data Process: Production Aesthetics and Representational Practices of a Film Industry in Transition*, thereby situating the research within digital film production studies in a manner which is not text-focused. Atkinson suggests that previous scholarly work in this area has focused on how the study of media industries might help develop knowledge of how textual products come into being. Atkinson seeks to reverse this, stating (9) '*by analysing how and why texts interact and come to be created, we can better appreciate how media industries operate*.'[26] My aim here is somewhat different: whilst hoping that insights into Loach's working methods might aid understanding of filmmaking processes more widely, I am cautious of over-extrapolating from one specific study. Awareness of the specificity of filmmakers' working methods cautions against collapsing difference, however, I do hope that further specific studies such as mine, and Atkinson's, may allow comparisons and wider understandings to emerge. Although, as this book's title might indicate, I explore broader political concerns, I am conscious of retaining focus on the film itself, examining how an understanding of how it comes into being might influence criticism of it and Loach's work more broadly.

Dorota Ostrowska (2010: 1) speculates on the reasons for the scarcity of on-the-ground academic research into film production, positing that different methodologies are required to conduct this type of work, and noting that it requires a conceptual shift away from traditional screen analysis. If we add to this the challenges of participant observation-based studies of

---

[25] John Cook makes direct comparisons between the work of Watkins and Loach: although there are clear differences in their working methods, they also share some commonalities, including employing non-professional actors.

[26] Emphasis in the original. Throughout the book, any additional instances of emphasised text in quotes are in the original.

filmmaking, not least, that it is difficult securing access to the production process, considerably time-consuming, and that writing about living and breathing people who you have been observing requires more delicacy than writing about completed films, then comprehending why research of this nature is scarce becomes clearer. In contrast to the relative absence of scholarship on film production, there is no shortage of popular commentaries on the filmmaking process, exemplified by Lillian Ross's *Picture*, an account of the making of the Western *The Red Badge of Courage* (Huston, 1951). Several filmmakers have also contributed accounts, for instance, Lindsay Anderson's *Making a film: the story of* Secret People, an account of the 1952 Ealing Studios' film noir directed by Thorold Dickinson, and Wim Wenders' *My Time with Antonioni*.[27] Yet Powdermaker's thesis, that ethnographic knowledge of film production might influence analysis, remains largely unexamined by film scholars. This book seeks to change that somewhat by illustrating how the study of Loach's filmmaking processes and working methods can open the films up to greater hermeneutic possibilities, and also how knowledge of production might influence wider discussion in film criticism and theory. My aim is not to elevate the study of production above the practice of criticism and theory, but to illustrate how the latter might benefit from insights gleaned from the former.[28]

---

[27] Recent years has also witnessed an exponential increase in commercial books detailing the production process of numerous blockbusters. The shelves of the film sections of popular bookstores are heavily laden with titles such as *The Batman Movie: The Making of the Movie*, *Harry Potter Page to Screen: The Complete Filmmaking Journey*, James Mottram's *The Making of Dunkirk* and *The Art and Making of Independence Day*. Whereas insights gleaned from critical journalistic accounts and from filmmakers themselves can illuminate our understanding of film culture, this growth in production-related literature is indicative of the commercial benefits of migrating film content to the publishing world, exploiting additional forms to maximise the accumulation of capital rather than the accumulation of knowledge.

[28] Born (2000: 424) suggests that television studies as a discipline 'historically positioned itself outside television' and that the task was 'to move inside television so as to engage critically and productively with the complexity of that situation'. That Loach has worked in both film and television in multifarious production contexts makes his work a particularly rich case study with which to move 'inside' film production; however, I hope that in providing detailed analysis of Loach's working practices, it will also prove of some use to television studies scholars.

Loach scholarship

Loach's work has received significant academic attention; most notably, the four-part television series, *Days of Hope*, provoked intense debate on realism and film form.[29] Subsequently, in addition to several book chapters and journal articles, three book-length academic studies on Loach's wider output have been published: George McKnight's edited collection *Agent of Challenge and Defiance: Films of Ken Loach* (1997), Jacob Leigh's *The Cinema of Ken Loach: Art in the Service of the People* (2002) and John Hill's *Ken Loach: The Politics of Film and Television* (2011). In addition, Bert Cardullo's *Loach and Leigh, Ltd.: The Cinema of Social Conscience* (2010), which focuses on Loach and his contemporary Mike Leigh, surveys their respective careers.[30] Leigh's book offers, as he puts it, 'a personal aesthetic history' (1) of Loach's work, one which 'refrains from judging his political beliefs' (1). Hill provides a highly impressive and comprehensive overview of Loach's career, describing him as 'probably the most distinguished English film-maker at work today' (2011: 1). In keeping with film and television studies' text-based origins, however, both Leigh and Hill concentrate on formal qualities and thematic concerns. There is consideration given to the institutional production context of Loach's work, particularly in relation to how this influences exhibition and transmission, and there are some references to Loach's particular filmmaking methods. Absent from the extant scholarship is detailed information about, and analysis of, these methods. In *Loach on Loach* (1998), Graham Fuller's interview-based book offers a popular account of the director's work which deals in more detail with his methods, including the use of location and linear shooting, the use of non-professional actors and the withholding of scripts from actors.

---

[29] The question of realism in the arts in general has been the focus of ongoing debate. Given the Anglo-American bias in English-language film and television studies, and the influence of realism, specifically, social realism, in British film and television then much of that discussion has focused on British audiovisual culture and the study of Loach's work has been central to that. Early debates in *Screen* in the 1970s over what was termed the 'Classic Realist Text' were significant in influencing the discipline's understanding of realism although the debate was characterised by a reductive formalism which effectively erased audience agency. For a useful summation, see John Caughie (2000).

[30] More poetic scholarly engagements with Loach's work have also emerged, with, for instance, Liz Greene's audiovisual essay, 'The Shipping Forecast: the audiovisual poetics of Ken Loach', which represents a welcome trend in film studies away from the dominance of the written word: https://vimeo.com/258107902 (last accessed 1 March 2018).

Figure I.3 Standing behind Ray Beckett's sound desk as Loach prepares to shoot a scene in the Caledonian Hotel in Edinburgh

Loach's working methods also feature in Anthony Hayward's biography of Loach, *Which Side Are You On? Ken Loach and His Films* (2004), which draws on numerous interviews with the director and his collaborators. Academic engagement with Loach's working methods, however, is minimal. As with the growth in production-related popular material in film generally, there have been several relevant publications: Simon W. Golding's *Life After Kes: The Making of the British Film Classic, the People, the Story and Its Legacy* (2006) offers a retrospective account of the production of *Kes*, the strength of which lies in the interview material rather than new knowledge of Loach's practice; considerably more insightful is Tony Garnett's *The Day the Music Died: A Memoir* (2016), which provides a valuable insider's perspective. There is also a growing body of audiovisual material, with *Loach on Location: Making Land and Freedom* (Boulting, 1995), produced by the BBC, an early example. In subsequent years, Sixteen Films, which Loach and O'Brien established in 2002, released *Versus: The Life and Films of Ken Loach* (Osmond, 2014); as the title indicates, this recounts the basis aspects of Loach's life, the films themselves and his cinematic methods. Broadly coterminous with the above, the BFI also released *How to Make a Ken Loach Film*, an interactive guide which provides glimpses into the director's practice.[31] In addition, *The Angels' Share* Blu-ray edition features

---

[31] The film is available at http://www.bfi.org.uk/news-opinion/news-bfi/features/how-make-ken-loach-film (last accessed 20 December 2021).

Distilling The Angels' Share (McArdle, 2012), an account of the film's production. While these popular resources do provide some useful background, my intention is to offer a more rigorous, scholarly engagement with Loach's method of filmmaking and to explore how this knowledge might influence new understandings of the work itself.

Certain Tendencies in Loach's Cinema

Through the various methodologies employed, fieldwork, archive research, textual analysis, and historical and socio-political contextualisation, I have developed what I am calling 'Certain Tendencies in Loach's Cinema'. This identifies fifteen tendencies which appear regularly, but not always, and at varying levels, in what we might call 'the Loach method', a working practice which was developed in the late 1960s and honed over the ensuing years.[32] In the following chapters, I show how these fifteen tendencies relate to work created throughout Loach's career and specifically how they function in *The Angels' Share*. They are as follows:

1. On-screen political engagement
2. Use of popular narrative forms
3. Realist *mise en scène*
4. Camera positioned as sympathetic observer
5. Maximising the use of natural lighting
6. Unobtrusive soundtrack (sometimes combined with recognisable pop songs)
7. Continuity editing
8. The importance of teams and leaders – on- and off-screen
9. Control of production
10. Realist casting
11. Pared-down film set
12. Linear shooting and withholding script from actors
13. Follow the writer
14. Screenplay as blueprint
15. Off-screen political engagement

I refused the use of the word 'taxonomy' as its structuralist underpinnings suggests a definitiveness that the films themselves would struggle free from: for example, *Sorry We Missed You* does not contain recognisable songs and any Loach aficionado would easily identify other exceptions.

[32] This title riffs on Francois Truffaut's 1954 essay 'A Certain Tendency in French Cinema', which was influential in establishing auteurism as the dominant approach in film criticism.

'Certain Tendencies', however, points to greater flexibility and fluidity: we might see a preponderance of these imbricated tendencies in relation to each of the films without seeing them all. There are an infinite variety of ways that this material could be organised; this narrativisation of the Loach method appears to be the most manageable way of communicating what I have observed in tracking the films over three decades and tracking one film in particular, *The Angels' Share*, being made.

In relation to this tracking exercise, there is nothing in my approach which is about hunting the object to foreclose interpretation. On the contrary, my hope is that this book might have some effect in focusing the lens through which Loach's work is viewed and might open the films up to new critical lines of flight. Despite my previously cited comments to O'Brien, the book does not offer 'the historical record' of Loach's working methods, or even of the making of *The Angels' Share*. Although the book presents a continuous narrative, it is one marked by significant gaps in the filmmaking process. Given the sheer volume of Loach's output, moreover, it would have been possible to write a book on each of these tendencies. Therefore, some aspects of Loach's method are identified but not dealt with in granular detail. Cognisant of the need to balance breadth and depth, I have focused on Loach's overall approach to cinema and politics and then on those aspects of the filmmaking process that I witnessed directly and which I thought it would be most valuable to write about.

Towards the conclusion of *The Big Flame* (BBC, 1969), an account of a defeated Liverpool dockworkers' strike, the judge sentencing the leaders of the rank-and-file strike committee to three years in prison comments,

> The doctrine of Marxism is not on trial here. Indeed, I know very well that this philosophy is favourably received in a number of our better universities. And insofar as it helps sharpen the wit and the intellect of students and helps rid them of this sort of distemper that seems to inflect the impressionable young today, well, it has its advantages. But when placed in the hands of determined working men this theory of social revolution becomes as dangerous as a loaded pistol in the hands of a criminal. It is the use, the practice, rather than the theoretical speculation, that we here are concerned with.

Similarly, although this book is informed by the work of numerous theorists and theorises its own object of enquiry, we are primarily concerned here with practice, that is, the methods employed by a socialist filmmaker who in a career approaching six decades has produced an outstanding body of work. In the chapters which follow, I flesh out the framework developed above, attempting to show how this work comes into being, and explore how this new knowledge might influence interpretation of the films.

Chapter breakdown

Indicating its centrality, politics is both the opening and closing tendency. In Chapter 1, I examine on-screen political engagement, presenting an analysis of *The Angels' Share*, contextualised within Loach's wider *oeuvre*. I also discuss Loach's engagement with Trotskyist ideas in the 1960s, explore how this influenced the films' political content in subsequent years, and offer a wider political critique of his work overall. This chapter takes a broad overview and does not specifically draw on the ethnographic work outlined above. I get to this in Chapter 2, in which I draw on interview material and film analysis to deal with questions of film form, suggesting that realism in Loach's work might be understood as a practice as much as an aesthetic. The focus here is on tendencies (2) use of popular narrative, (3) realist *mise en scène*, (4) camera positioned as sympathetic observer, (5) maximising the use of natural lighting, (6) unobtrusive soundtrack, sometimes combined with recognisable pop songs, and (7) continuity editing. In Chapter 3, I focus on tendencies (8) teams/leaders and (9) control of production, analysing Loach's status as the leading figure in what the director has termed 'Team Loach'. The chapter draws on interviews and observations, explores discourses around leadership and teams in a creative context, and connects this to the representation of teams in the films themselves. While academics have previously highlighted filmmaking's collaborative nature and, in some instances, the importance of teams in filmmaking, I lay out some of the specific dynamics at play on a Loach set. In Chapter 4, I develop this approach through analysis of Loach's directorial methods when working with actors. The chapter focuses on tendencies (10) realist casting, (11) pared-down set, and (12) linear shooting and withholding script, integrating observations from attending casting sessions and the shoot with analysis of the measures Loach employs to prevent the cinematic apparatus from impeding actors' performances. In Chapter 5, I focus on tendencies (13) follow the writer, and (14) screenplay as blueprint, starting by exploring the centrality that Loach places on the writer before moving to analyse how words come into being on set, in the gap between the screenplay and the finished film. In Chapter 6, I return to politics, moving beyond the screen to examine tendency (15) that is, how Loach uses the platform afforded by his films' success to intervene in contemporary political discourse. This begins with an analysis of the film's premiere and press conference at the 2012 Cannes Film Festival. I then turn to examine subsequent controversies on the international film festival circuit, and political interventions closer to home, noting how accompanying extratextual discourse arising from this activity might influence both press responses and frames for film analysis. Finally, in the Epilogue, in addition to pulling the various threads of my argument together, I also assess Loach's output in terms of influencing broader film culture and political discourse.

Some final comments on entanglement and methodology: in Lindsay Anderson's account of meeting John Ford for a book he was researching on the American director, Anderson describes how admiration for Ford and his films underpinned a developing tension in their relationship. 'I did not like being made to feel like a journalist,' he says, before adding, 'and I lacked the confidence to behave like a friend' (1999: 137). In conducting this research, however, establishing with Loach the affective bonds that might characterise a popular understanding of friendship was not my aim. For Aristotle, though, friendship is connected to a common understanding of *eudaemonia*, which might be understood as how best to live meaningful lives. From a socialist perspective, this is achieved through engagement in common struggle for human emancipation from capitalism.[33] This book, then, is written from the perspective of a critical friend and is offered here as an act of solidarity.

---

[33] When I spoke with Loach informally on set, our conversations tended to circle around the film itself, focusing instead on events in the worlds of football and politics, which appeared to be two of his favourite topics of conversation.

1

Politics on-screen

> When you're a worker it rains stones seven days a week.
> Jimmy (Mike Fallon) in *Raining Stones*
>
> Why can't you leave us, just once, with a smile, Ken?
> John Cooper Clarke[1]

10 October 1975. Margaret Thatcher stands to address the Conservative Party's annual conference in Blackpool's Winter Gardens. From the platform, the newly elected party leader rails against the dangers of socialism, and vehemently critiques those who challenge 'our heritage and great past'.[2] Following applause from the party faithful, she continues, 'There are those who gnaw away at our national self-respect, rewriting British history as centuries of unrelieved gloom, oppression and failure. As days of hopelessness—not Days of Hope.'[3] In directly invoking the title of the four-part BBC *Play for Today* series which was directed by Loach and broadcast earlier that year, Thatcher's speech indicates something of Loach's work's political content, and its capacity to unsettle the political representatives of the ruling class. Politics bookends the Certain Tendencies in Loach's Cinema, which I outlined in the Introduction, and this chapter explores the first of these, on-screen political engagement. It opens with a plot syn-

---

[1] Quoted in Tim Adams (2021) 'John Cooper Clarke: "There's three food groups I draw the line at – flapjack, falafel and tripe"', *The Guardian*, 19 September 2021, https://www.theguardian.com/food/2021/sep/19/john-cooper-clarke-poet-punk-manchester-ken-loach (last accessed 19 September 2021).

[2] Margaret Thatcher (1975) Speech to Conservative Party Conference, 17 October 1975, http://www.margaretthatcher.org/document/102777 (last accessed 1 February 2020).

[3] Ibid.

opsis of *The Angels' Share* before moving to interrogate broader political concerns in Loach's wider output and to consider how this film might fit within it.

The Angels' Share plot synopsis

Subverting two of the standard touristic signifiers of Scotland – tartanry and whisky – and with the leftfield addition of Irn Bru in bountiful supply, *The Angels' Share* (Loach, 2012) follows four young working-class Glaswegians, Robbie (Paul Brannigan), Mo (Jasmine Riggins), Albert (Gary Maitland) and Rhino (William Ruane), who receive community payback orders (Scottish legal terminology for non-custodial sentences which often involve unpaid work) for various criminal offences. Robbie has a particularly troubled past and criminal record, and narrowly avoids a lengthy prison sentence for a violent assault only because his partner, Leonie (Siobhan Reilly), is expecting a baby. The sentence is met with angry protests from members of a rival gang, led by Clancy (Scott Kyle), who attend court hoping to see their enemy sent down. Once the community payback programme commences, the supervisor, Harry (John Henshaw), takes a shine to Robbie and shares with him his love of whisky. Initially Robbie is repulsed by the taste, however, after the light-fingered Mo pockets a rake of miniatures during a distillery visit, he partakes of the whisky once more, becomes engrossed with its history, and rapidly displays an aptitude, or 'nose', for identifying the various blends and malts. The four young offenders form a friendship and start socialising together, playing snooker and participating in whisky-tasting sessions. At one such session in Edinburgh, they learn from whisky connoisseur, Rory McAllister (Charles MacLean), that an extremely rare Malt Mill whisky could fetch £1 million at a forthcoming auction in a Highland distillery. Coterminous with the group's developing appreciation of the amber nectar, Robbie's feud with the Clancy gang deepens, as does his troubled relationship with Leonie's father, Matt (Gilbert Martin), after the baby, Luke, is born. Eager to secure a safe and financially secure future for his new family, Robbie hatches a plan, and the gang don kilts and head to the Highlands to liberate the whisky. In the dead of night, they steal into the distillery and Robbie fills four empty Irn Bru bottles with Malt Mill, replacing it with whisky from a nearby cask. At auction the next day, a bidding war between shady whisky expert, Thaddeus (Roger Allam), and a US businessman (Paul Birchard) concludes with the American paying £1.15 million for the diluted cask. As

Figure 1.1 Filming the gang arriving at Balblair distillery. The camera is normally placed on a tripod and positioned at Loach's and the cinematographer's eye level

he samples his new acquisition, the successful bidder praises its qualities, to the relief of the gang who subsequently pose for photographs before the assembled audience. After the auction, Robbie arranges to sell three bottles to Thaddeus for £200,000 and the promise of employment. The four then return to Glasgow where, immediately following an altercation with two police officers, they inadvertently smash two bottles. They sell one remaining bottle for £100,000 to Thaddeus, who also secures Robbie employment at a distillery in Stirling, and Robbie surreptitiously deposits the final bottle in Harry's flat along with a thank-you note and journalistic evidence of their Highland escapades. The gang assembles once more to bid their farewells as Robbie, Leonie and Luke prepare to leave Glasgow in a camper van supplied by Robbie's new employer. The three remaining gang members decamp to the pub as Robbie and family depart in the camper van, which is seen travelling through the Scottish countryside as The Proclaimers' anthemic 'I'm Gonna Be (500 Miles)' blares over the credits.[4]

---

[4] There are clear parallels with the plot in *That Sinking Feeling* (Forsyth, 1978), which is also set in central Scotland. In this alternative comic heist movie, a group of working-class young people conduct a similarly daring raid, although in this instance the loot is ninety-three kitchen sinks.

Politics

This plot synopsis indicates that *The Angels' Share* is some distance from the more harrowing depictions of working-class life depicted in much of Loach's previous work, for example, tales of homelessness in *Cathy Come Home* (1966), domestic violence survivors in *Ladybird Ladybird* (1994) or unemployed Glaswegians enmeshed in poverty and hard drugs culture in *My Name is Joe* (1998). Indeed, the film's positive, upbeat content and conclusion fuelled significant press commentary, exemplified by Wendy Ide's review in *The Times*, which described the film as 'a feel-good caper comedy with more cheek than an army of Scots on a windy day'.[5] Paul Newland and Brian Hoyle (2016: 239) bracket *The Angels' Share* with *Looking for Eric* (2009), which featured fantasy scenes of footballer Eric Cantona, in what they identify in Loach's work as a 'move away from art cinema towards the Ealing comedy tradition'.[6] *The Angels' Share*'s tonal qualities and its somewhat fantastical narrative certainly invite reflection on the parameters of the social realist tag with which Loach's work is routinely identified.[7] The sympathetic portrayal of the four central characters and the narrative focus on Robbie's quest to secure employment, however, fit squarely with Loach's continued focus on the working class in general and on the role of work under capitalism in particular.[8] Here, the gang's heist, or 'job', counterposes the conventional exchange of labour which Robbie seeks in securing a 'job' with a local whisky company. This connection between criminal activity and work, coupled with the film's comic content, invites comparisons with *A Tap on the Shoulder* (Loach, BBC, 1965). Loach's first contribution to *The Wednesday Play* (1964–70), it featured a gold bullion robbery and, as John Hill notes (2011: 27), was described as a 'comedy thriller' in publicity materials, highlighting some ongoing thematic and formal continuities across Loach's long-standing career.[9]

---

[5] Wendy Ide (2012) 'Cuddlier Ken loses his Gorbals', *The Times*, 1 June 2012.
[6] In an analysis of the critical response to *The Angels' Share* and *Looking for Eric* in the British press, Carolyn Rickards (2018: 568) also suggests that '*The Angels' Share* evoked the gentle, nostalgic and collective British spirit associated with traditional media-mediated perceptions of Ealing comedies from the 1940s and 1950s.'
[7] I return to questions of classification and discussions of film form in Chapter 2.
[8] For an overview of the representation of work in European cinema, see Ewa Mazierska (2015), pp. 211–12 for a short analysis of *It's a Free World . . .*
[9] Loach directed an additional nine plays for the series, the last of which was *The Big Flame* (1969). Trotskyism has been a small but significant political force in British political life, however, its influence has waned considerably in recent years.

Loach's early output was broadly leftist in content, dealing with social problems facing working-class characters, such as abortion rights in *Up the Junction* (BBC, 1965) and prison life in *The Coming Out Party* (BBC, 1965); in the late 1960s, an engagement with Marxism, specifically with the ideas of Leon Trotsky, significantly shaped his subsequent output.[10] This emerges initially in *The Big Flame* (BBC, 1969) in which a Liverpool dock strike culminates in the declaration of a soviet. Significant here is the contribution of writer Jim Allen, an ex-member of the Trotskyist Socialist Labour League, who Loach credits as a major political influence.[11] Trotskyist politics are explicit in their second collaboration, *The Rank and File* (BBC, 1971), a dramatised account of a Pilkingtons glass factory strike. Reflecting on the dispute towards the film's conclusion, Eddie (Peter Kerrigan), a local union leader, delivers perhaps the most revolutionary declaration in British television drama history:

> Surely to God we've seen the futility of rank and fileism; that blind militancy will get us nowhere. The only question is one of political leadership and a foundation or the forming of a party that will lead the workers to power.[12]

Over a montage of monochrome photographs of children, Eddie continues, 'I go along with Trotsky: "Life is beautiful. Let the future genera-

---

[10] Loach states that he attended meetings of the Trotskyist Socialist Labour League but never became a member. (Hayward 2004: 109) In Tony Garnett's *The Day the Music Died: A Memoir*, he recalls organising a series of political meetings at his home which discussed Marxist ideas. The meetings are fictionalised in Trevor Griffiths' play, *The Party*, which opened at the National Theatre, London, in 1973 with Lawrence Olivier cast as a Trotskyist leader. In typical Trotskyist fashion Griffiths comments (1974: 51): 'The European and American proletariats... have been consistently and systematically betrayed by their leaders; and particularly by the Communist parties of the various European countries.'

[11] For instance, in interview in 1998, Loach states (Jones 1998): 'A lot of my way of looking at the world I got from Jim', https://www.independent.co.uk/arts-entertainment/how-we-met-ken-loach-and-jim-allen-1186744.html (last accessed 10 May 2020).

[12] In interview with the author, Loach comments, 'But the thing about the end of *The Rank and File* is that we had to smuggle those quotes on because when we first showed it to the hierarchy they said, "Well you can't say that, you've got to remove those quotes". It was perfectly innocuous about making life beautiful and they said "Yes, but look who said it." It wasn't the words, it was the man who said it. It was ridiculous. It was a funny story; we took them off on one version and sent that up and then shortly before transmission we said, "There's a problem with the one you have and we need to change the last reel" and out it went the next day. Shocking the bourgeoisie is the thing kids do when they're feeling mischievous.'

tion cleanse it of all the oppression, violence and evil and enjoy it to the full."[13]

In a 1980 *Cineaste* interview, Loach states, 'I was once close to a Trotskyist position, and remain to this day an anti-Stalinist socialist. However, I find the label "revolutionary" embarrassing. I don't want to be pigeon-holed as extreme left'.[14] In prefacing 'socialist' with 'anti-Stalinist', Loach distances himself both from the Soviet Union, and from the strand of pro-Soviet thought in the international labour movement in that period. Although Loach might then have found the label 'revolutionary' embarrassing, the term 'anti-Stalinist socialist', sits comfortably with a Trotskyist perspective. Reflecting on Trotskyism's influence some years later, he comments, 'When you look at the history of the labour movement over the last 150 years, what's not to agree with [in the Trotskyist tradition]?'[15] In the same interview, Loach reiterates the point about labels when he states, 'People don't understand it [Trotskyism]. It's a term of abuse.'[16] In a similar vein, in interview for this book, Loach refuses the label 'Marxist', arguing that it has been 'devalued', and is deployed as 'something for people to lob

---

[13] The quote is taken from Trotsky's final testament, which he wrote on his deathbed following an attack by a Stalinist agent. Trotsky's critique of the degeneration of the Russian Revolution under Stalin had led to his forced exile to Siberia in 1928 and then banishment from the Soviet Union the following year. Trotsky and his family settled in Mexico in 1937 during which time he continued to intervene in political affairs until his death in 1940. For the most comprehensive account of Trotsky's life and ideas, see Isaac Deutscher (2005), which contains the three volumes of his extensive, and sympathetic, biography.

[14] Quoted in Quart (1980: 27) Both Allen and Garnett remained committed to a Marxist perspective until their deaths in 1999 and 2018 respectively.

[15] John Rees (2016) 'Ken Loach talks Daniel Blake, Jeremy Corbyn and Leon Trotsky', *Counterfire*, 4 October 2016, https://www.counterfire.org/interview/18543-ken-loach-talks-daniel-blake-jeremy-corbyn-and-leon-trotsky (last accessed 28 December 2021).

[16] A useful example of how right-wing journalists have advanced Loach's association with Trotskyism and Marxism to negatively frame discussion of his work is evident in Dominic Lawson (2006) 'A hard-line Marxist distortion of history', *The Independent*, 10 May 2006. Here, writing on *The Wind That Shakes the Barley*, Lawson states, 'For many years, Mr Loach has been associated with the Fourth International, the Trotskyite movement formed during the Second World War,' and adds, 'I don't mean to suggest that Ken Loach's films can be dismissed simply because of his political opinions, but it is my observation that hard-line Marxists see historical truth as merely a convenient weapon in the class war.' Lawson's article, which is not burdened by analysis of the film itself, takes as its focus Loach's broader critique of British imperialism.

bricks at you with'.[17] In its stead, Loach states a preference for the term 'socialist', although he adds, 'I think it's impossible to make sense of what happens without an essentially Marxist analysis.'

Loach's connection with Trotskyism has been briefly noted previously (Hill 2011, McKnight 1997, Leigh 2002); however, this has focused on Allen's early influence and their cinematic collaborations: *The Big Flame*, *The Rank and File*, *Days of Hope*, *Hidden Agenda* (1990), *Raining Stones* (1993) and *Land and Freedom* (1995).[18] As I highlight in the chapters which follow, films are complex creations, influenced by the many hands involved in making them and the institutional contexts in which they are developed. Nevertheless, my contention is that Loach's engagement with Allen and Trotskyism in the late 1960s is critical to understanding his work.[19] Indeed, Loach suggests 'early involvement in the anti-Stalinist left was absolutely crucial for the way you see the world . . . So it's had a big effect on the subjects we've chosen.'[20] For instance, the question of labour movement leadership, a key Trotskyist concern, as indicated in *The Rank and File* quote cited above, also emerges in documentaries Loach both produced and directed in the 1980s: *A Question of Leadership* (ATV, 1981) and *Questions of Leadership* (Central TV, 1983, untransmitted).[21] In 'Manifesto: Towards a Free Revolutionary Art', which Trotsky co-authored with the surrealist theoretician, André Breton, they state (1938: 52), 'We believe that the supreme task of art in our epoch is to take part actively and consciously in the preparation of the revolution' *The Rank and File* certainly channels the manifesto's revolutionary spirit, resulting in Loach's most didactic work. Yet not all the films fit so comfortably, or obviously, with an overt political, never mind revolutionary, agenda: *Kes* (1969) for instance, which follows a Barnsley schoolboy destined for a life down the mines, is primarily praised for its poetics not its politics.[22] Of course, politics and poetics are always already entangled and intertwined in all artworks; that *Kes* and *The Rank and File* were produced in roughly the same

---

[17] Interview with author. All subsequent quotes from Loach in this chapter are from interviews with the author unless otherwise stated.

[18] Leigh and McKnight only mention Trotskyism in passing. Hill's monograph delves deeper but deals mostly with Allen's influence and their work in the 1960s and 1970s.

[19] Loach's association with Trotskyism, mostly from a position of political opposition, is offered in Alan Munton (2004).

[20] Quoted in Rees (2016).

[21] For instance, Trotsky (2002/1938) writes: 'The world political situation as a whole is chiefly characterized by a historical crisis of the leadership of the proletariat.'

[22] See, for instance, Dave Forrest and Sue Vice (2017).

period yet are quite strikingly different thematically and formally, indicates that Loach has adopted a pluralist approach in cinematically representing working-class life.

Lessons of history: Lessons of defeat?

Loach has spent most of his career in a period dominated by ideological retreat for the left and has produced significant work concerned with periods of revolutionary or transformative possibilities, but which did not realise their full potential. In *Left-Wing Melancholia: Marxism, History and Memory*, Enzo Traverso (2017: 34) cites Jules Vallès's description of the Paris Commune, the workers revolution which rocked Paris in 1871 but which was ultimately overthrown and mercilessly crushed, as 'La grande fédération de douleurs'/'The great federation of sorrows'. Traverso builds on this sentiment, suggesting (xiii) that 'the memory of the left is a huge, prismatic continent made of conquests and defeats'. Traverso advocates melancholia as a necessary corrective in rejecting the victory of capitalist ideology in the wake of the collapse of what he describes as 'State Socialism' (xx) in the Soviet Union and finds value in a depathologised melancholia that consciously nurses the 'open wound' Freud discusses in his 1917 essay 'Mourning and Melancholy'.

For Traverso, the open wounds of socialist defeat or capitalist injury operate as actually existing signifiers of capitalist damage and consequently resist its totalising ideological victory. Traverso quotes from Walter Benjamin's essay 'Left-wing Melancholy' in which he states, 'In its tenacious self-absorption it embraces dead objects in its contemplation, in order to redeem them' (1974/31: 47).[23] Whereas Benjamin holds out the prospect of revolutionary redemption, Traverso's advocacy of melancholy is connected to a perspective more ambivalent on whether alternatives to capitalism are realisable. Despite these misgivings, melancholy – palliative or revolutionary – is the prism through which Traverso addresses Loach's work, referring specifically to the 'melancholic gaze' in *Land and Freedom*, a cinematic engagement with the Spanish Revolution, the defeat of which foreshadowed the coming to power of Franco's fascistic dictatorship in 1939. Here, however, Traverso collapses the antinomy between mourning and melancholia; for defeat in *Land and Freedom*, whether that be the death

---

[23] Walter Benjamin (1974/1931) 'Left-Wing Melancholy (On Eric Kästner's new book of poems)', *Screen* 15 (2).

of the revolutionary fighter, Blanca (Rosana Pastor), or, by extension, the death of the revolution, is not wholly represented in a melancholic cinematic mode. This is evident in the film's conclusion when Blanca's coffin is lowered into the ground and the sounds of revolutionary Spain continue over a single cut which takes the viewer from 1930s Spain to 1990s England, and to the funeral of another of the revolutionaries, David (Ian Hart), who had travelled from Liverpool to join the Spanish anti-fascist struggle. Here, as his granddaughter, Kim (Suzanne Maddock), raises a clenched fist in socialist solidarity and reads a passage from William Morris's 'Join in the Battle', mourning is presented as but one stage of ongoing revolutionary struggle, and the old labour movement slogan, 'Don't Mourn, Organise', supplanted with 'Mourn and Organise'. Traverso notes that Gillo Pontecorvo, famed for, among other films *La battaglia di Algeri/ The Battle of Algiers* (1967) and *¡Queimada!/Burn!* (1969), never continued making films after the political defeats of the 1960s, arguing that he 'was a filmmaker of battle, not of mourning' (97).[24] In contrast, Loach has been a filmmaker of battle and of mourning. In addition to the defeat of the Spanish Revolution in *Land and Freedom,* there are other losses, political and personal: industrial disputes in *The Big Flame, The Rank and File, Days of Hope* and *Bread and Roses*; the Irish War of Independence in *The Wind That Shakes the Barley*, and the Nicaraguan revolution in *Carla's Song.* Astride these defeats sits the relative ideological and political victory of neoliberalism, and the weakening of both the labour movement and the socialist left. Raymond Williams suggests that the Welsh industrial novel was characterised by the 'pervasive sense of defeat' (1980: 222) which followed the 1926 General Strike. This notion of a sense of defeat as opposed to one communicated or articulated clearly or unambiguously is connected to Williams' concept of 'structures of feeling' in which, as he writes in *Marxism and Literature* (1977: 132), '"feeling" is chosen to emphasise a distinction from more formal concepts of "world-view" or "ideology"'. Loach's work, while underpinned by a firm socialist ideology, articulates this 'sense' or 'feeling' of defeat across a range of struggles, domestic and international, in the present and in the past.

Loach's engagement with the past might be viewed as a 'lessons of defeat' approach, one consistent with a Trotskyist focus on the proposition that workers are routinely betrayed by their leaders, and that ana-

---

[24] This is not strictly accurate; Pontecorvo did make some films after the 1960s, most notably *Operación Ogro/Eperation Ogre* (1979), although his output certainly diminished.

lysing these defeats will lead to alternative outcomes in future battles.²⁵ Reflecting on the Paris Commune, Kristin Ross calls this perspective into question (2015: 2): 'It is not at all clear to me that the past actually *gives* lessons' and highlights the dangers of simply mapping past events onto contemporary political and historical processes. She adds (2), 'Like Walter Benjamin, though, I believe that there are moments when a particular event or struggle enters vividly into the figurability of the present.' Rather than understanding Loach's cinematic engagements with history as primarily pedagogical and threnodical, we might, following Ross, view them as engagements with the 'afterlives' of these events.²⁶ Crucial here is the notion that every battle, every defeat retains an element of unextinguished possibility. It is not, then, simply a matter of being open to that moment of possibility returning, but to breathing life into the embers, rekindling it in the present. So, although *Land and Freedom* witnesses the defeat of the revolution, Kim's transformation recalibrates potential present and future anti-fascist and anti-capitalist struggle. By conjuring a new constellation, and in the spirit of Walter Benjamin blasting events out of their historical continuum, both present and past are reconfigured.²⁷ Cinema, particularly with montage's capacity to facilitate a Benjaminian tiger's leap, temporally and spatially, is the medium *par excellence* for undertaking this act. Contra *Land and Freedom*, which explicitly connects past and present, *Days of Hope* remains within the present of its fictional cosmos, that is, between the First World War and the 1926 General Strike. As the moment of its production was characterised by intense industrial unrest in Britain, however, past and present interweave in the world beyond the text. Loach's history films, then, oscillate between viewing the past as object from which lessons can be learned and as object which circulates in the present through its afterlives: raising consciousness of past struggles reaches towards a historical realignment, collapsing binaries across past, present and future.

---

[25] As I discuss in Chapter 3 in relation to teams, the role of leadership features prominently, both in Trotskyist discourse and in Loach's films across fiction and documentary. Notably, on *Land and Freedom*, the historical adviser, Andy Durgan, in addition to being an authority on the revolutionary dimensions of the Spanish Civil War, is also a long-standing Trotskyist. Moreover, the film's politics sit comfortably with even the title of some of Trotsky's extensive writings on these events, including 'The Lesson of Spain' (1936) and 'The Lessons of Spain: the Last Warning' (1937), in Leon Trotsky (2009).

[26] For more on the concept of 'afterlives,' see Kristin Ross (2002).

[27] See Walter Benjamin (2007).

Figure 1.2 The revolutionary militia fighters pose for the camera in *Land and Freedom*

The tales of labour movement defeat which Loach has focused on nationally and internationally are paralleled with tales in which working-class characters confront life under capitalism. Here, it is the consequences of defeat, of ongoing and intensified capitalist exploitation, which is depicted cinematically, encapsulated in the title of *Raining Stones*, a darkly comic account of unemployed workers Bob (Bruce Jones) and Tommy (Ricky Tomlinson) surviving the metaphorical stones which capitalism rains down on them daily. The result is often marked with personal tragedy: the death of workers in industrial accidents in *The Price of Coal* (BBC, 1976), *Riff-Raff* (1991) and *The Navigators* (2001); but also the death of Daniel (Dave Johns) in *I, Daniel Blake*, and the suicide of Liam (David McKay) in *My Name is Joe*. There is also a strand in the films which suggests that welfare institutions can function, as Gilles Deleuze would have it, as instruments of 'Societies of Control'. In *Cathy Come Home* and *I, Daniel Blake*, for instance, the welfare state, rather than caring for Cathy and Daniel, coercively creates what Deleuze describes as 'mechanisms of control that are equal to the harshest of confinements' (1992: 4). In repeatedly visualising harsh experiences of life under capitalism, Loach has been critiqued for pursuing a form of cinematic miserabilism, with Duncan Petrie (2004: 108) pointing to the 'sense of hopelessness and defeat that permeates Ken Loach's narratives of despair in *My Name is Joe* and *Sweet Sixteen*'.[28] Paul

---

[28] This is also a routine charge in popular film criticism of Loach's work. See, for instance, Tara Brady's review of *The Angels' Share* in *The Irish Times*, which sums up much of this position: 'Back in the day, rightly or wrongly, the Ken Loach brand was synonymous with council estate grit, miserabilism and getting a good metaphorical thump with a

Dave (2006: 162) connects this to a broader negative outlook, arguing that *My Name is Joe* is symptomatic of Loach's 'political pessimism', not solely for the possibilities of socialist change but 'for any social democratic, cross-class solidarity in the face of neoliberalism's impact on the most vulnerable sections of the working class' (162).

Dave's position places an excessive burden on one film's conclusion; moreover, as I discuss in Chapter 6, a critical perspective which views meaning as sealed hermetically within the text cannot grapple adequately with how the films operate with audiences. The films themselves, for instance, have acted as catalysts for broader political activity, most famously *Cathy Come Home* influenced the early stages of the British homeless charity, Shelter, and led directly to the establishment of another charity, Crisis, the following year.[29] My contention is not that the films must be interpreted alongside broader production and reception contexts, but that doing so creates a more holistic hermeneutic framework from which more holistic analyses might emerge. To return to the films for the moment, though, rather than being crudely bracketed as optimistic or pessimistic, they operate, to borrow from Traverso, as a 'barometer of left consciousness'.[30] If Loach's more personal films are characterised by recurring personal tragedies, these are connected to the history of defeats that the working class has suffered. From *Cathy Come Home* to *Sorry We Missed You*, however, tragic outcomes flow not from abstract personal decisions; viewers are not invited to judge characters' moral or ethical choices, but to question why capitalism forces individuals into such situations. As such, this is a cinema designed not to

thoughtfully worded socialist placard', https://www.irishtimes.com/culture/film/the-angels-share-1.1063293 (last accessed 18 December 2021).

[29] Referring to *Cathy Come Home*, Shelter's website states: 'Watched by over 12 million people, its Cathy impact ensured public empathy and support for Shelter from our very beginning', https://england.shelter.org.uk/what_we_do/history (last accessed 20 December 2021). For more on Crisis see https://www.crisis.org.uk (last accessed 20 December 2021).

[30] Film and television studies has itself retreated considerably from the leftism of the 1960s, 1970s and 1980s, although, as indicated above, there has been a certain uptick in relation to Marxist and radical film and criticism. For instance, in film studies see Ewa Mazierska and Lars Kristensen's edited collections, *Marx at the Movies: Revisiting History, Theory and Practice* (2014), *Contemporary Cinema and Neoliberal Ideology* (2017) and *Third Cinema, World Cinema and Marxism* (2020), and Mike Wayne (2019) *Marxism Goes to the Movies*. In addition, the development of the Radical Film Network, which brings together activists, filmmakers and academics, contains a strong Marxist current: see Steve Presence, Mike Wayne and Jack Newsinger (2020).

induce Aristotelian pity but to provoke collective anger and communal resistance.

It might be tempting to view the strident, revolutionary spirit evident in *The Rank and File* being gradually replaced by a more despondent cinema, one which highlights capitalism's deleterious impacts on working-class lives. It would be a cinema concomitant with the observation attributed to both Fredric Jameson and Slavoj Žižek that 'it has become easier to imagine the end of the world than the end of capitalism'. This might be discerned in the shift from *The Big Flame*, the aforementioned account of a major industrial dispute set in Liverpool docks, to *The Flickering Flame: A Story of Contemporary Morality* (BBC, 1996), a documentary outlining how the greatly weakened workforce struggles valiantly but unsuccessfully against their employer. *The Flickering Flame* laments the enervation of the worker's movement, and of socialist ideas; nevertheless, as the title signifies, the flame of resistance still burns. The ongoing possibility of struggle is also evident in *Raining Stones*, in which socialism is not foregrounded but haunts the Manchester-set film like a faint spectre. For instance, in one scene the camera follows Bob's movement through a working-class community centre before nestling on a poster in the background advertising a public meeting: 'World in crisis ... Is there a socialist alternative?' In the early 1840s, Engels published *The Condition of the Working Class in England*, his celebrated exposé of working-class experience under capitalism. Loach returns to Manchester, circa 150 years later, to offer a fictionalised, cinematic account of working-class life, one which clings onto the hope of socialist change in the bleakest of circumstances.

Loach has grappled with the idea that the socialism that he has articulated since the 1960s has waned in popularity. Thus, reflecting on *Save the Children Fund Film* in 2011, he states, 'It will be a great day when charities are replaced by a fair economic system and social justice based on common ownership. What we used to call socialism!'[31] Loach's use of the past tense here is significant. Yet, one ongoing consequence of the 2007/8 economic crisis has been an increased questioning of capitalism's legitimacy and viability, exemplified by the emergence of a raft of popular and academic books speculating on capitalism's potential demise.[32] This range of mate-

---

[31] Quoted in email from Sixteen Films' staff to the author in advance of a special May Day Scottish premiere of the film at Glasgow Film Theatre, May 2011.

[32] For instance, from socialist perspectives such as journalist Paul Mason's *Post-Capitalism*, and non-socialist perspectives, as with the economist Wolfgang Streeck's *How Will Capitalism End* and, indeed, books with a range of perspectives, *Does Capitalism Have*

rial itself speaks to the ideological crisis in contemporary capitalism, with Marxism having something of a small revival, both within and beyond academia. Against this shifting political landscape, Loach's cinema has been distinctive in its consistent dissensus from capitalist ideology.

Cracks in the system

In *Crack Capitalism*, John Holloway suggests that the task for the socialist left is, rather than simply preparing for one big revolutionary heave à la *The Rank and File*, to develop spaces, or cracks, of resistance within the current social formation, spaces in which the rules of capitalism are suspended, or capitalist ideology negated. Holloway (2010: 9) writes,

> The method of the crack is the method of crisis: we wish to understand the wall not from its solidity but from its cracks; we wish to understand capitalism not as domination, but from the perspective of its crisis, its contradictions, its weaknesses, and we want to understand how we ourselves are those contradictions. This is crisis theory, critical theory. Critical/crisis theory is the theory of our own misfitting. Humanity (in all its senses) jars increasingly with capitalism. It becomes harder and harder to fit as capital demands more and more. Ever more people simply do not fit in to the system, or, if we do manage to squeeze ourselves on to capital's ever-tightening Procrustean bed, we do so at the cost of leaving fragments of ourselves behind, to haunt. That is the basis of our cracks and of the growing importance of a dialectic of misfitting.

Loach's cinema operates as a crack or a rupture in capitalist consciousness in its cinematic depictions of the experiences and struggles of the working class and other oppressed groups, illustrating the personal instances where humanity 'jars increasingly with capitalism'. On occasions, this is the struggle of organised workers to improve working conditions (*The Rank and File, Bread and Roses*), broader struggles involving wars and revolutions (*Land and Freedom, Carla's Song, The Wind That Shakes the Barley*), the everyday struggle to survive capitalism (*Raining Stones, My Name is Joe, Sorry We Missed You*), and struggles against British state-sponsored loyalist death squads in the north of Ireland (*Hidden Agenda*).[33] In all instances, the focus is on specific individuals caught up in specific circumstances and the films have predominantly focused on working-class experience. There

---

a Future? by social scientists Immanuel Wallerstein, Randall Collins, Michael Mann, Georgi Derluguian and Craig Calhoun.

[33] The films in brackets are indicative rather than exhaustive.

is, however, an identifiable shift from organised labour (*The Big Flame, The Rank and File, Days of Hope*), to unorganised labour (*Riff-Raff, The Navigators, It's a Free World . . .*), to the working class without work (*Sweet Sixteen, My Name is Joe, The Angels' Share, I, Daniel Blake*). It is not, however, a straightforward linear trajectory, and contra Luke Davies' (2018: 145) assertion that the films focus predominantly on 'the lives of the out of work', *Sorry We Missed You* (2017) deals with the super-exploitation of an increasingly casualised workforce. In 'Fragments on Machines', Marx (1973/1858) envisages a future in which automation might facilitate working-class liberation; however, in *I, Daniel Blake* and *Sorry We Missed You*, technological innovations intensify the exploitation of the lead characters, unemployed carpenter Daniel and delivery driver Ricky (Kris Hitchen), respectively. In dealing with workers in both relatively secure and precarious employment, the films, then, reach beyond a singular experience of working-class life. The focus on class, of course, is not simply a moral question: for Marx (1968/1843–4: 3),

> A class must be formed which has *radical chains*, a class in civil society which is not a class of civil society, a class which is the dissolution of all classes, a sphere of society which has a universal character because its sufferings are universal, and which does not claim a *particular redress* because the wrong which is done to it is not a *particular wrong but wrong in general*. There must be formed a sphere of society which claims *no traditional* status but only a human status . . . which is, in short, *a total loss* of humanity and which can only redeem itself by a *total redemption of humanity*. This dissolution of society, as a particular class, is the proletariat.

Loach remains wedded to a conventional Marxist perspective, one which views the working class as the agent of change, in developing a cinematic depiction of, and for, a class which in its highest political expression seeks to abolish itself as it abolishes class exploitation.[34] Clive Nwonka (2014: 207) suggests that 'The films of Ken Loach during the early to mid 1990s represented the most explicit attempts to develop a Marxist analysis of class inequality as a political crisis in British cinema.' While I concur with this general claim, as I have outlined, the timescale is not restricted to the 1990s but stretches from the late 1960s to the present.

In addition to this class focus, several films positioned women as central characters (*Up the Junction, Cathy Come Home, Poor Cow, Family Life, Ladybird Ladybird, Bread and Roses*), although this focus is almost exclu-

---

[34] For instance, at the Cannes press conference, Loach discusses the working class as 'the agent of change' in classical Marxist terms. See Chapter 6 for more on this.

sively on working-class women and their struggles within and against patriarchal institutions, from the family to state institutions.³⁵ The predominant focus, however, has been on male figures (*Kes, Sweet Sixteen, My Name is Joe, Black Jack, The Gamekeeper, I, Daniel Blake, Sorry We Missed You*). This is even the case in *Carla's Song*, which despite the title focuses primarily on male bus driver George (Robert Carlyle) who falls for a Nicaraguan dancer, Carla (Oyanka Cabezas), and through this encounter learns something of the 1979 Nicaraguan revolution and US imperialism's determination to defeat the left-wing Sandinistas.³⁶

Several films have featured black characters or persons of colour: African liberation fighters in *Save the Children Fund Film*, building workers in *Riff-Raff*, cleaners in *Bread and Roses* and in *Ae Fond Kiss*... the narrative centres on a lower middle-class Glasgow Pakistani family.³⁷ The majority of the characters, however, across all class backgrounds, are white. *Save the Children Fund Film* deals most explicitly with questions of racism and imperialism, suggesting that racism cannot be resolved under capitalism. In one scene towards the conclusion, an off-screen narrator, Jim Allen, states,

> in the labour market, the colour of a man's skin is of no more importance than the hair colouring on cattle bred for the knacker's yard. Black sweated labour supplied raw cotton for the same employers who hire white sweated labour to work in the cotton mills of Lancashire.³⁸

---

³⁵ In his analysis of the television work of Jim Allen and Trevor Griffiths, Steven Fielding (2020: 240) suggests that although their workplace dramas focused on men, Allen 'gave women roles more significant than other, almost exclusively male, socialist TV writers'. Loach has also been accused of presenting women as stereotypical, perhaps most provocatively by Julie Bindel in *The Spectator* (2 June 2014) who in describing *Jimmy's Hall* as 'a load of old sexist shite' suggests that 'Loach is a man of the people, but only people with a penis': 'Dick-swinging filmmakers like Ken Loach constantly write real women and our struggles out of history', https://www.spectator.co.uk/article/dick-swinging-filmmakers-like-ken-loach-constantly-write-real-women-and-our-struggles-out-of-history (last accessed 16 May 2020). A critique of the representation of prostitution in Loach's work is also laid out by Kate Bradley on the socialist website RS21, 9 October 2019, https://www.rs21.org.uk/2019/10/09/ken-loach-sex-work-and-paternalism/ (last accessed 14 December 2021).

³⁶ George also illustrates a common narrative device in the films, which is to identify the audience with a naïve central character from which they will learn of the struggle from an outsider's perspective, a process also evident in *Land and Freedom* and *Route Irish*.

³⁷ Although, notably, this racism is brought into focus through an engagement with an analysis of Irish Catholicism, which has been a feature in numerous films.

³⁸ For more on this film, see David Archibald and Finn Daniels-Yeomans (2020). Allen is uncredited in the film, but Loach confirmed in interview that it is his voice which is heard in the film.

The film features several African revolutionary figures, including Ngũgĩ wa Thiong'o, author of the classic collection of essays *Decolonizing the Mind* (1986), indicating that Loach was addressing questions of decolonisation, indeed, anti-colonisation, decades before they became commonplace, even fashionable, and increasingly made safe, in English-speaking universities. One geographical area which is not foregrounded in current decolonisation discourses in British universities is Ireland, almost as if six counties of Britain's oldest colony did not remain under its direct rule. Loach, however, has for decades critiqued British imperialism's role in Ireland, chiefly in *Hidden Agenda* and *The Wind That Shakes the Barley*, but also in several other films, including *Days of Hope* in which a young Irish woman sings 'Down by the Glenside (The Bold Fenian Men)', a song long associated with Irish rebellion against British rule, to a group of occupying British soldiers. As such, just as Loach's work has identified how class and capitalism are entangled, the films also display a long-standing awareness of how colonialism and capitalism are similarly connected. In striving for a universalising commonality of working-class experience, however, in common with the quote from Marx above, the specificities of racialised experience under capitalism are in danger of being underplayed. Criticism that Loach's work neglected racial oppression emerged directly over the documentary *The Spirit of '45* (2013), which recounts the development and demise of the post-Second World War British welfare state, and of which Anna Chen writes, 'everyone featured in the film is white – it's as if people like me have been bred out of the working-class gene pool'.[39] If Loach's *oeuvre* was analysed through an intersectional lens, the class focus would emerge strongly; it would also identify those excluded, at least in part, via this approach.[40] For instance, although sexual and familial relationships feature prominently in the fictional films, only heterosexual relationships are on display. This flows primarily from a narrative approach aimed at encouraging audience identification with a 'typical' character through which to depict something of the universal and the total.[41] It seems, however, somewhat incongruous

---

[39] Anna Chen (2013) 'People of colour like me have been painted out of working-class history', *The Guardian*, 16 July 2013, https://www.theguardian.com/commentisfree/2013/jul/16/people-of-colour-working-class-history (last accessed 10 May 2020).

[40] Kimberlé Crenshaw coined the term 'intersectionality' in 1991 to attempt to theorise intersecting forms of oppression. At its weakest, and most liberal interpretation, intersectionality can be utilised to simply point to a list of forms of oppression; more recently, critics such as Ashley Bohrer (2020) have brought Marxism and intersectionality into a more fruitful analytical framework.

[41] It is indicative of the films' influence that they carry a significant burden of representa-

from a politically progressive twenty-first-century perspective: for even, if class is not viewed as just another identity, it is, nevertheless, marked by commonality and difference. Taken together, the films' politics might be viewed as oscillating arrhythmically between an ongoing exploration of how capitalism (and imperialism) impacts negatively on working-class lives, and occasional direct engagements with socialist ideas, both past and present. Sometimes, as with *The Big Flame* and *Land and Freedom* this is foregrounded, however, it mostly hovers inconspicuously – a cinematic socialist spectre, a reminder of what has been lost, yes, but which also holds out the promise of what is yet to come.[42]

Politics and *The Angels' Share*

How, then, might these broad political considerations find expression in *The Angels' Share*? As indicated above, class and work are central, although Robbie is not driven by a desire to overthrow capitalism, rather, he is desperate to secure gainful employment within it. That Robbie, and his foes, are embroiled in destructive and violent action exemplifies how the films refuse sanitised depictions of working-class life but visualise how workers struggle to forge meaningful lives under capitalism. To invoke Aristotle's notion of *eudaemonia* in this context, the film explores what it might mean to live a good life amidst poverty, insecurity and violence. In scene 43, which is included in the script, and in the shooting schedule (see Appendix I) but does not feature in the final film, Robbie attempts to make the peace with Clancy in a Glasgow tanning salon. Pointing to their commonality of experience, he says to his fierce rival (Laverty 2012: 162), 'Ah could be you. You could be me. One in a box . . . one in a cell . . . or we could just walk oot o' here . . . and live a life.' The film, then, is far from the revolutionary socialist didacticism of *The Rank and File*; but simply explores how to negotiate the quotidian pressures facing young working-class Glaswegians. Robbie's skills in identifying fine whisky, moreover, suggest that workers' tastes should not be restricted to the fortified wine, the excessive consumption of which lands Albert in court in the opening sequence. On the contrary, and in keeping with Kristin Ross's notion of 'Communal Luxury', work-

---

tion. Leaving aside the heteronormative and male focus, this might be viewed as concomitant with Friedrich Engels' suggestion (1977: 269) that realism implied 'the reproduction of typical people under typical circumstances'.

[42] My thinking here draws on the concept of 'hauntology': see Jacques Derrida (2006).

ers should aspire to life's finest offerings for them to be available in great abundance and distributed equitably.[43] In highlighting that Marxism is not a 'Theory of Everything', Terry Eagleton (2011: 34) suggests somewhat humorously that 'Marxism has nothing very interesting to say about malt whiskies'. But perhaps it does. Robbie's emerging appreciation of whisky's finer qualities exemplifies how working-class young people who have traversed unruly or criminal paths in their teenage years are full of untapped potential, not only capable of enjoying fine malts, but of creating lives other than the banal roles doled out to them under capitalism.

A life of labour

In Appendix 1 of *The Angels' Share* published screenplay (172), Laverty provides a brief note to contextualise the opening Sheriff Court scene:

> It has a Dickensian feel; obvious from the faces, pinched skin, hairstyles, tracksuits, accents, and general demeanour of the public that there is an enormous class difference on either side of the dividing wooden wall. It is clear many have never worked, and probably never will. Several have scars on their faces. Some look dozy from their methadone prescriptions.

The film opens, then, by visualising the consequences of long-term unemployment. When Robbie and the other accused appear in the dock, their faces often framed against a black background, it indicates not simply how they have been brought into conflict with the state apparatus, but also how capitalism is inscribed on their faces, with Robbie himself sporting a noticeable scar on his left cheek. In focusing on Robbie's quest for gainful employment, *The Angels' Share* is consistent with the labour movement demand of 'The Right to Work', a right which is enshrined in the Universal Declaration of Human Rights. This is hardly the most radical of proclamations, yet Loach argues that the demand for full employment is 'a revolutionary demand'.[44] In what sense might we regard this as revolutionary? This question takes us back to early twentieth-century labour movement debates over 'minimum' and 'maximum' demands. Put simply, minimum demands, such as a pay rise or a reduction in the working week, were reforms which capitalism could accommodate. In contrast, maximum demands focused on the immediate establishment of a socialist or communist state. Attempting to bridge these positions, Trotsky advocated rais-

---

[43] Kristin Ross (2015).
[44] See discussion of the Cannes press conference in Chapter 6.

ing demands which would be unrealisable under capitalism: posing these 'transitional demands', he argued, would help raise the necessity of social transformation in the working class.[45] Demanding the right to work in a context in which capitalism is unable to fulfil it can thus be understood as 'revolutionary'. This position, however, might be regarded as simply demanding the right to be exploited in the workplace. Marx's son-in-law, Paul LaFargue, for instance, advanced an alternative position in the pamphlet, *Le droit à la paresse/The Right to Be Lazy* (2011/1883), the title of which indicates an ongoing and alternative strand of revolutionary thinking related to work. In more recent years, Guy Debord became associated with the slogan '*Ne travaillez jamais*' or 'Never Work' which was famously inscribed on a Parisian wall, and in *The Revolution of Everyday Life* his fellow Situationist, Raoul Vaneigem, suggests (2012: 39), 'Today the love of a job well done and belief in the rewards of hard work signal nothing so much as spineless and stupid submission. And wherever submission is required, the stink of ideology hangs in the air, from the *Arbeit Macht Frei* of the concentration camps to the homilies of Henry Ford and Mao Tsetung.'[46] Vaneigem unhelpfully collapses the specificities of work in multiple social relations; nevertheless, his commentary is useful here in flagging an alternative position within the socialist tradition. It is certainly possible to critique *The Angels' Share*'s conclusion for acquiescing with capital by concentrating the narrative focus on Robbie's quest to secure employment, moreover, suggesting that this quest can succeed can sow illusions in capitalism's capacity to resolve the conditions facing the working class. A more complex reading might recognise Robbie's pursuit of work as an economic and social necessity under capitalism, at least for those without the economic resources to avoid it.

In the closing scenes of *Sorry We Missed You*, Ricky, suffering serious injury but facing mounting debts, is forced to continue his van deliveries despite clear risk to his person. In the concluding sequence, injured and barely able to drive, he responds to his son who is trying to persuade him not to drive for his own safety: 'I have got to go to work, I have not got a choice.' In the film, work represents no meaningful contribution to Ricky's individual personal development. Rather, indicative of the constraints to

---

[45] This text was also published as 'The Death Agony of Capitalism and the Tasks of the Fourth International' and was the founding statement of the Fourth International, which sought to unite the various anti-Stalinist communists hitherto organised as the International Left Opposition (1930–3) and then the International Communist League (1933–8) in opposition to the Soviet Comintern, or Third International.

[46] An image of the inscription appears in Guy Debord (2009: 84).

a life worth living that the casualised economy offers, it critiques the supposed freedoms enjoyed by workers under capitalism. Both films, then, present differing perspectives on the role of work under capitalism but present it, at least in the central narrative, as a necessity. This is disturbed somewhat in *The Angels' Share*, when the three other gang members head to the pub to 'get wasted', as Albert puts it. The refusal of Albert, Mo and Rhino to emulate Robbie's pathway to work undermines both the notion that the working class acquiesce in their own exploitation, and the narrative closure associated with Robbie and his family, creating a broader ambiguity. Despite this ambiguity, however, *The Angels' Share*'s focus on Robbie's quest indicates how the film might correlate with raising demands which capitalism cannot deliver, rather than narratives which demand its abolition, indicative of a what we might call an 'insider Marxism' which runs through Loach's work and to which I return below.

Scotland

The Angels' Share is the fifth film Loach has directed set in Scotland, all of which have been scripted by Laverty. The intersection of class and national identity features prominently in *The Angels' Share*, but also in their previous collaborations *Carla's Song, My Name is Joe, Sweet Sixteen, Ae Fond Kiss . . .*, and *Tickets* (2005), a portmanteau film with three directors, Loach, Ermanno Olmi and Abbas Kiarostami, with the Loach/Laverty contribution following a band of Glasgow Celtic fans travelling to a football match in Rome.[47] John Hill suggests that one reason underpinning Loach's attraction to working in Scotland was that it 'continued to maintain a consciousness of the politics of class, as well as the virtues of collectivism, that resonated with Loach's own political outlook' (2011: 183). These virtues feature strongest in central Scotland, specifically Glasgow, due to the city's industrial heritage, and Glasgow is the central location in all of Loach's Scottish-based feature films, bar *Sweet Sixteen* which was filmed predominantly around Greenock and Port Glasgow, twenty miles or so from Glasgow. Loach states in interview that one reason he returned to Glasgow was because 'that's where the mischief is', suggesting something of the irreverence and radicality with which the city is associated.

In the films, urban working-class life is brought into relief in several journeys to the Highlands, which feature prominently in *The Angels' Share*

---

[47] I return to matters related to filming in Scotland in Chapter 5.

and to a lesser degree in *Carla's Song* and *My Name is Joe*. For instance, in one scene in *Carla's Song*, George takes Carla, a refugee traumatised by her experiences in Nicaragua's revolutionary and counter-revolutionary conflicts, on an illicit double-decker bus trip to Loch Lomond.[48] As the couple sit atop a hillside overlooking the calm expanse of water, the camera pans across the (Scotch) mist-covered loch and George struggles to verbalise the location's pull. His inability to give voice to the landscape's sublime quality points towards an uncanny and impalpable magicality common to numerous films set in Scotland, from Hollywood ventures such as *Brigadoon* (Minnelli, 1954), Ealing Comedies like *Whisky Galore!* (Mackendrick, 1949), and the Scottish-produced *Local Hero* (Forsyth, 1983). *Carla's Song* remains firmly within a realist register, although as Carla and George's relationship is catalysed from a personal to sexual one during their trip, it suggests that the Highlands holds both restorative and transformative qualities. In the films, the Highland scenes also flag the disparity between Scotland's touristic image and the more typically urban environment of those living in the country's central belt. This emerges in the significant shift between city and country in *My Name is Joe*. Although set predominantly in Glasgow, lead character Joe (Peter Mullan), under pressure from a local drug-dealer, undertakes a drug run to the Highlands during which he stops off in Glencoe, buys a cup of tea, and observes a solitary bagpiper playing 'Scotland the Brave' as assembled tourists take photographs. The picture-postcard image is undercut when the female tea-seller says to Joe, 'Bonnie Scotland, eh?' 'Aye, Bonnie Scotland right enough,' he replies wryly.

My Name is Joe also invites commentary on broader aspects of the relationship between urban and rural life, past and present. Notably, just before this scene, Joe's friend, Sammy (Gary Lewis), discourages him from making the trip, and appeals to him to avoid those who are requesting his assistance, a local drug dealing 'clan', as he puts it. It is a pejorative use of a term for a social group generally celebrated in Scotland, at home and abroad.

Writing in the early twentieth century, the Scottish Marxist, John Maclean (1920) attempted to forge a connection between the Highlands' medieval social order and a future Scotland:

> The communism of the clans must be re-established on a modern basis ... Scotland must therefore work itself into a communism embracing the

---

[48] There are parallels here with how the film depicts Nicaragua as an unspoiled space, before US intervention in support of the right-wing Contras wreaks havoc.

> whole country as a unit. The country must have but one clan, as it were, a united people working in co-operation and co-operatively, using the wealth that is created. We can safely say, then: back to communism and forward to communism.[49]

The nature of clan society's class structure has provoked considerable debate. Neil Davidson, for instance, suggests that Maclean (and Marx) were mistaken in their analysis and that the clan system's mode of production was not dominated by any form of primitive communism but by feudalism. Indeed, he states that (2001: 317), 'If anything, the clans, far from being *opposed* to feudalism, were *representative* of its most extreme form.' *My Name is Joe*'s drug-dealing clan might be viewed as representative of capitalism in its most extreme form, far removed from the collective assembled in *The Angels' Share*.[50] The reference, however, points to another link between Scotland's Highland past, mythologised or otherwise, and its urban present. Reviewing *The Angels' Share* in *The Observer*, Philip French argues, 'You might infer here that the thieves believe whisky is part of the Scottish legacy that the boys' ancestors were robbed of when the Highland clearances took place.'[51] *The Angels' Share*'s modern-day clan of Glaswegian whisky-liberators may not be driven by a desire for historical revenge but their quest leads the group on a pathway into the past, and into history. In *Wanderlust: A History of Walking*, Rebecca Solnit (2000: 72) suggests: 'Just as writing allows one to read the words of someone who is absent, so roads make it possible to trace the route of the absent. Roads are a record of those who have gone before and to follow them is to follow people who are no longer there.' The road that Robbie's gang takes to the last part of Britain where capitalism was introduced, leads to an encounter with Highland inhabitants, past and present, and offers a critique of capitalism in present-day Scotland, one which flags how class inequality is entangled in the national question, expressed above all in the gang's engagement with Scotland's national costume.

---

[49] John Maclean (1920) 'All Hail, the Scottish Communist Republic' reproduced (1922) as 'All Hail, the Scottish Workers Republic!' available at https://www.marxists.org/archive/maclean/works/1922-swr.htm (last accessed 14 December 2021).

[50] I deal in more detail with the representation of teams in the films in Chapter 3.

[51] Philip French, '*The Angels' Share* – Review', *The Observer*, 3 June 2012. From the late eighteenth century into the nineteenth century, the Highland Clearances involved the often forcible removal of tenants from agricultural estates to make way for the more profitable farming of sheep. Some of those forced off the land relocated in towns which sprung up nearby, but most emigrated or relocated to towns and cities in central Scotland.

Tartan

Under the Proscription Act of 1747, introduced in the wake of the failed 1745 Jacobite rebellion, the British state forbade the wearing of tartan.[52] The act was repealed in 1782 following lobbying from the London Highland Society, which included numerous Scottish establishment figures and aristocrats who were incorporated into the British ruling class. Tartan was also appropriated by numerous British Army regiments, and its place in the higher echelons of British ruling class culture cemented when Sir Walter Scott persuaded George IV to wear a kilt on his 1822 state visit to Edinburgh, highlighting what we might call 'the plasticity of the plaid'. Jonathan Faiers (2008) points to this malleability when he suggests that tartan has the capacity to be both conformist and subversive. In early cinema, however, the emphasis was strongly conformist, and John Caughie (1982: 116) argues,

> It is precisely the regressiveness of the frozen discourses of Tartanry and Kailyard that they provide just such a reservoir of Scottish 'characters', Scottish 'attitudes' and Scottish 'views' which can be drawn upon to give the 'flavour of Scotland', a petrified culture with a misty, mythic, and above all, static past.[53]

Ian Brown (2012: 6) develops a more positive use for tartan in identifying within it a potential polysemy, which can 'represent an alterity that supports the unbuttoned, emotionally spirited and carnivalesque'. In combining the film's social concerns with the maladjusted way this Highland heritage fits the central protagonists, *The Angels' Share* both wears its tartan and critiques it. Commenting on the film, David Martin-Jones (2013) suggests that beneath what he describes as 'the kilted image of Scotland' there are 'forgotten young men whose homes are prisons, and whose lives evaporate into drink, drugs, petty crime and routine police harassment'. To develop further Martin-Jones's observation, the gang, particularly Albert and Rhino, are clearly uncomfortable custodians of their traditional national costume. In standard contemporary dress, the kilt is commonly worn with a Bonnie Prince Charlie – a black wool jacket, pristine white shirt and black bow tie. In this combination, the formal upper half's bourgeoise association negates

---

[52] For more on the history of tartan, see Ian Brown (2012).
[53] Caughie's essay was published in Colin McArthur (ed.) (1982) *Scotch Reels: Scotland in Film and Television*, London: BFI, an edited collection of essays which was highly influential in shaping understanding of how the imagery of tartanry is deployed in Scottish culture, often from outwith Scotland.

the kilt's free-flowing, carnivalesque qualities. With our gang, however, the black wool jacket is exchanged for blue-and-white tracksuit jackets, or in Mo's case, a denim jacket, signifying a distinctive and disjunctive, proletarian sartorial take. En route to the distillery, when one of a group of young female tourists asks Rhino if he is 'from the Highlands', he replies, 'Actually my great, great grandfather, he was, eh, Highland chief. This kilt is the tartan and I wear it with pride every time I put it on.' Amidst collective laughter, she asks, 'That's why you wear it back to front?' highlighting the group's inability to comfortably wear their ancestors' cloth and, by extension, their history. Jamie Chambers (2014) suggests that the kilt 'has a relatively complex significance within the film, acting as a conscious mask to an underlying class discourse, and thus a layer of self-reflexive inauthenticity'. This emerges when the gang arrive at Balblair distillery, the scene of the whisky auction, and Albert notes that his 'meat and two veg' have been suffering from considerable chaffing against the kilt. An additional contrast is added by the non-diegetic use of The Proclaimers' song with its prominent refrain: 'I would walk five hundred miles and I would walk five hundred more.' Solnit (2000: 29) suggests that walking 'shares with making and working that crucial element of engagement of the body and the mind with the world, of knowing the world through the body and the body through the world'. In Albert's case, his long walk through the Highlands, and into Scottish history (at least as represented by the signifiers of its past) rubs him up the wrong way, against the grain of history, against the twill of the kilt, with painful consequences. The gang's complex connection with Scottish culture and history is further signified when they arrive back in Glasgow and Albert roars

Figure 1.3 Albert's 'meat and two veg' take a hammering as he walks back into history

out a speech after being stopped by the police officers. As he raises his arms aloft, a whisky-filled Irn Bru bottle held tightly in his left hand, he exclaims, 'We shall not be moved! Billy Connolly! Robert the Bruce! Braveheart, ya bastards! Alex Ferguson! We are the fuckin' champions!' Albert's rant contains a curious blend of Scottish cultural heritage, circumventing comedy and football heroes via Hollywood cinema and medieval Scottish legends, exemplifying how this gang of working-class Glaswegians sit incongruously alongside dominant, touristic narratives of Scottish national identity, in turn, both sustaining and subverting Scottish stereotypes.

Marxism and happy endings

Laverty (2012: 7) suggests that *The Angels' Share* 'was an attempt to be realistic but also a little magical'. This apparent departure from the socialist realist norms is not entirely new in Loach's work; most notably it echoes Eric Cantona's fantastical appearance in *Looking for Eric*. *The Angels' Share*, however, falls closer to the comedy genre than *Looking for Eric*, even to the point of concluding happily, one of the features of Aristophanic comedy. In the upbeat, positive ending, Robbie, Leonie and Luke drive off into the distance with '500 Miles' playing one final time, and big smiles all round. Notably, the song's lyrics return to the question of work:

> But I would walk 500 miles
> And I would walk 500 more
> Just to be the man who walked a thousand miles
> To fall down at your door
> When I'm working, yes I know I'm gonna be
> I'm gonna be the man who's working hard for you
> And when the money comes in for the work I'll do
> I'll pass almost every penny on to you.
> (Reid and Reid, 1988)

In one sense, this expressed desire for employment and, in this context, its attachment to heteronormativity, supports a conservative reading of the film but a broader ambiguity is also in play. Discussing *Up the Junction*, Loach states, 'The idea of a story that is complete and resolved and too well worked out never feels right to me because it doesn't have any loose ends. It's just phony; life is full of loose ends.'[54] In *The Angels' Share*, the narrative threads are not seamlessly stitched: the futures of Albert, Mo and

---

[54] Quoted in Fuller (1998: 13).

Rhino are unclear and Robbie's dispute with Clancy is unresolved. The film closes, however, with the happy couple driving into the distance and, as such, leaves the film less open to charges of inducing political pessimism, and political paralysis which flow from the bleaker endings in films such as *Sweet Sixteen*. For instance, as outlined in this chapter's epigraph, John Cooper Clarke comments, 'We've always all liked a happy ending,' before adding, 'that's why I hate Ken fucking Loach. Why can't you leave us, just once, with a smile, Ken?'[55] Perhaps the working-class Mancunian poet missed *The Angels' Share*, for in its somewhat fantastic conclusion it allows for a different set of possibilities to emerge. Raymond Williams (1989b: 189) suggests that 'To be truly radical is to make hope possible, rather than despair convincing'. Despite Robbie's desire to seek employment and a safe nuclear family environment, that the film indicates that there is some form of hope in transforming Robbie's situation opens the door, even if just marginally, to wider social transformation.

One on hand, it is certainly possible to critique the film's conclusion for sowing illusions in capitalism's ability to resolve questions of unemployment. Yet, viewed within and alongside Loach's wider body of work other meanings emerge, returning us once more to the possibility of hope. Laverty often invokes the thinking of the North American historian Howard Zinn (2006: 270) who writes:

> To be hopeful in bad times is not just foolishly romantic. It is based on the fact that human history is a history not only of cruelty, but also of compassion, sacrifice, courage, kindness. What we choose to emphasize in this complex history will determine our lives. If we see only the worst, it destroys our capacity to do something. If we remember those times and places – and there are so many – where people have behaved magnificently, this gives us the energy to act, and at least the possibility of sending this spinning top of a world in a different direction. And if we do act, in however small a way, we don't have to wait for some grand utopian future. The future is an infinite succession of presents, and to live now as we think human beings should live, in defiance of all that is bad around us, is itself a marvelous victory.[56]

The hope in Loach's films often point to alternatives in the past but through their afterlives they remain connected to the present: perhaps if things had

---

[55] Tim Adams (2021) 'John Cooper Clarke: "There's three food groups I draw the line at – flapjack, falafel and tripe"', *The Guardian*, 19 September 2021, https://www.theguardian.com/food/2021/sep/19/john-cooper-clarke-poet-punk-manchester-ken-loach (last accessed 19 September 2021).

[56] For instance, *También la lluvia/Even the Rain* (Bollaín, 2010), scripted by Laverty, opens with a reference to Zinn.

turned out differently in revolutionary Spain then the youngsters represented in *The Angels' Share* might not be living such downtrodden lives. Is it stretching things to travel from the arid earth of the collectivised Spanish land depicted so powerfully in *Land and Freedom* to Robbie's search for work in *The Angels' Share*? Perhaps not if the open wound of defeat is seen as being inscribed on the bodies of Loach's working-class characters in the present, with the scar on Robbie's face an embodied signifier of 'the great federation of sorrows'. The film both catalogues the price of failure, whilst, simultaneously, holding out the possibility of change, suggesting that it might be located in the unlikeliest of sources.

The Angels' Share, then, although somewhat lighter and more fantastic than much of Loach's output, is a useful film in which to assess Loach's politics as it is paradigmatic of a pragmatic, practical Marxism focused primarily on exposing capitalism's limitations whilst haunted by the spectre of a post-capitalist, socialist world. It is this kind of reforming or insider Marxism which is dominant in Loach's *oeuvre* as he attempts to work within existing parameters, whether they be generic, industrial or political, critiquing and exposing them from within, and which, I hope to demonstrate in the next chapter, finds expression in the films' formal qualities.[57]

---

[57] Indicative of Loach's pluralist approach, he comments in interview, 'Not every film has to end with a fist clenched in the air.'

2
Form

> When you're young you pick ideas from all over the place, that's inevitable; but the biggest influences on us were things like *World in Action*, the hard-hitting current affairs documentary, but also Joan Littlewood was a big influence with things like *Oh, What a Lovely War!* where you'd have a concert party scene on stage but then the numbers of the dead running across it in figures across the stage so that you had the juxtaposition of drama and hard documentary side by side. And in things like *Cathy* and *Up the Junction* we nicked that idea. Brecht was also an influence in terms of the very pared down way in which he would stage things. The French New Wave up to a point.
>
> Ken Loach[1]

On one evening in 2012, I am sitting in a small, quiet hostelry in London. A long day editing *The Angels' Share* has just concluded and I am interviewing the film's director, Ken Loach. Towards the end of the interview, I seek his opinion on scholarly debates on his work's formal qualities. He replies that the audience he hopes to reach is the wider public and appears somewhat exasperated by academic responses which prioritise formal over thematic concerns.[2] This chapter does focus on Loach's film form; however, although I explore some aspects of formal classification, I am not primarily concerned with engaging with exhausted formalist debates on the progressive potential of varying film forms. The chapter covers Certain Tendencies in Loach's Cinema numbers (2) the use of popular narrative forms, (3) realist *mise en scène*, focusing on setting, production design, costume and make-up, (4) camera positioned as sympathetic observer, (5)

---

[1] Interview with author. All subsequent quotes from Loach in this chapter are taken from the author's interviews.
[2] See footnote 29 in Chapter 1 for more on these academic debates.

maximising natural lighting, (6) unobtrusive soundtrack and (7) continuity editing. The Oxford English Dictionary offers one definition of 'real' as 'actually existing physically as a thing', and I explore how real life 'things' – locations, people, clothes and so on – are utilised and transformed through the production process.[3] My focus remains on *The Angels' Share*, contextualising analysis of this film within Loach's wider body of fictional cinema, offering insights into how the aesthetics with which his films are associated are assembled, and exploring how Loach and his collaborators utilise discourses of the real when discussing their work. In doing so, I suggest that Loach's approach to realism might be understood as a practice as much as an aesthetic.

Loach and realism

In addition to the names identified in this chapter's epigraph, Loach has highlighted Italian neorealism[4], the Czech New Wave[5], filmmaker Peter Watkins[6] and artist William Hogarth as artistic influences.[7] These examples are drawn predominantly from the arts, however, the inclusion of the campaigning current affairs programme *World in Action* (Granada Television, 1963–98) highlights a direct documentarian influence.

In one sense, Loach's work stands in the early British documentary tradition, running from the formative work of John Grierson in the 1920s through to the Free Cinema Movement in the late 1950s. John Caughie

---

[3] OED Online, December 2021, https://www-oed-com.ezproxy.lib.gla.ac.uk/view/Entry/158926?rskey=Nwnpoj&result=3#eid (last accessed 8 December 2021).

[4] In *Acqua e zucchero: Carlo Di Palma, i colori della vita/Water and Sugar: Carlo Di Palma, the Colours of Life* (Kamkari, 2016), a documentary profile of the eponymous cinematographer, famed for his early work with Michelangelo Antonioni, Loach points to the emergence of Italian neorealism within the context of a wider anti-fascist movement in post-Second World War Europe and states, 'Maybe it's time we revived the ideas of the Italian neorealist cinema and we spread them across Europe.' The association with politics and film form here suggests that Loach views his own film form as embedded in post-war progressive politics, one which is anchored in a realist tradition.

[5] Loach has often cited *Ostře sledované vlaky/Closely Observed Trains* (Menzel, Czechoslovakia, 1966) as one of his favourite films. See, for instance, https://www.grandclassics.com/grand-classics-article/ken-loach-presents-closely-observed-trains (last accessed 9 October 2021).

[6] See *Culloden: Making Reel History* (BBC Scotland, 1996).

[7] See https://www.tate.org.uk/art/artists/william-hogarth-265/ken-loach-inspired-william-hogarth (last accessed 20 December 2021).

observes (2000: 115) that there is a 'complex history' which 'links the British documentary tradition to European modernism' and Loach's comments highlight that, although his work is understood predominantly within social realist discursive frameworks, his influences span documentarian and modernist traditions. Without collapsing the differences amongst this diverse assembly, a dominant commonality is an attempt to present the experience of oppressed groups in popular and/or realistic forms. John Hill suggests that

> The guiding impulse throughout much of Loach's work has been a pursuit of verisimilitude and authenticity in the telling of stories about ordinary people. As a result, it is the terms 'realist', 'naturalist' or 'documentary drama' that have most commonly been used to describe his work. (2011: 5)[8]

Since Hill penned these words, David Forrest (2019) utilises the term 'poetic realism' for the work scripted with Barry Hines, Jamie Chambers (2014) proffers 'brutal realism', and Nick Grant (2018) 'brutalism' as descriptors of Loach's output.[9] 'Social realist', however, is the generic tag with which Loach is most commonly understood in academic and popular writing: the *Guardian* columnist Steve Rose describes Loach as 'our social realist laureate', and David Forrest (2020: 8) suggests that 'Loach is the defining representative of the social realist tradition in Britain. As such, while they might not realise it, when critics speak of social realism in Britain they speak of Ken Loach.'[10]

Realism, certainly in the Marxist tradition, is not simply an aesthetic category, rather, it exemplifies a desire to illuminate social and power relations. Bertolt Brecht and György Lukács were key participants in debates on politics and aesthetics; however, whereas Lukács favoured an aesthetic

---

[8] Deborah Knight states explicitly, 'Loach is a naturalist' (quoted in McKnight 1997: 60). Caughie (2000: 102) states, 'In spirit and ambition if not in every aspect of its philosophy of form, Loach and Garnett can be placed in a Naturalist tradition.' The term 'docudrama' is identified with the work produced for television in the 1960s, most notably, *Up the Junction* and *Cathy Come Home*; criticism of these films was also embedded in discourses of the real, indeed, it was the blurring of fact and fiction in the films which fuelled critique from sections of the British press.

[9] Hines wrote, or co-wrote, *Kes* (1969), *The Price of Coal* (1977), *The Gamekeeper* (1980) and *Looks and Smiles* (1981). Grant suggests that Loach is 'trying to keep things brutally real in a harsh world'.

[10] Steve Rose (2021) 'Why is British cinema so reluctant to tackle immigration', *The Guardian*, 26 July 2021, https://www.theguardian.com/film/2021/jul/26/why-is-british-cinema-so-reluctant-to-tackle-immigration (last accessed 10 September 2021).

characterised by totality, Brecht was an eclectic pragmatist whose work was marked by fragmentation and interruption, designed to heighten spectatorial awareness. Despite their differences, both argued that political art was tasked with representing reality. For Lukács (1970: 34), 'the goal of all great art is to provide a picture of reality in which the contradiction between appearance and reality . . . is so resolved that the two converge into a spontaneous integrity', while Brecht argues (1977: 423), 'We must not abstract the one and only realism from certain given works, but shall make a lively use of all means, old and new, tried and tested, deriving from art and deriving from other sources, in order to put living reality in the hands of living people in such a way that it can be mastered.' As such, realism involves both politics and aesthetics, and scrutiny of Loach's work reveals a near six-decade-long experiment in producing work in multifarious institutional contexts which sympathetically visualise working-class experience in recognisable forms designed to impact a wide audience.

Loach's early television work, including *Up the Junction* and *Cathy Come Home*, is characterised by Brechtian-inspired experimentalism, including the juxtaposition of image and music, discontinuous editing and episodic narratives. That modernism had found a base at the BBC's Drama department in the early 1960s facilitated this period of experimentation.[11] A key influence here was the 1964 publication of Troy Kennedy Martin's 'Nats Go Home: First Statement of a New Drama for Television', which challenged the dominant tradition of simply filming plays for television, and championed a radical aesthetic.[12] So, although Loach's early television work is often discussed in terms of realism, this is related to subject matter as much as the documentary-style cinematography employed. Self-reflexive moments (actuality footage and on-screen captions) do appear in Loach's cinematic debut, *Poor Cow* (1967), however, these are increasingly dispensed with as his career progresses. The narrative in his second cinema film, *Kes* (1969), for example, although containing episodic and Brechtian elements, exemplified by the inclusion of a school football match the scores of which appear on-screen, is more linear than *Up the Junction*. Loach has suggested that the production of *Kes* was pivotal in transforming his filming style; it would be inexact to regard the post-*Kes* period as somehow fixed. Indeed, in interview in 1980, he suggests: 'I am also moving toward films which are more personal and

---

[11] For more on British television drama in this period see Caughie (2000).
[12] Kennedy Martin also co-wrote *Diary of a Young Man* (BBC, 1964), the television series on which Loach directed three episodes in the early days of his career.

grounded, where the politics lie in characterization rather than the power of its argument.'[13] In historicising Loach's output, an apparent contradiction emerges: in the wake of the radical political movements which marked the late 1960s – *Les événements* in France, civil rights movements in the US and Ireland, political turmoil across South America, developing revolutionary movements in the former colonial world – many politically committed filmmakers embraced experimental cinematic practices in terms of both production and exhibition.[14] Loach, however, traverses a different path as self-reflexivity is displaced by a more conventional self-effacing style in which political concerns are increasingly filtered through melodramatic narratives involving familial and (hetero)sexual relationships, most commonly male-centred, with comic moments interspersed throughout. While Loach in the *Kes* period onwards develops a filming style which utilises observational camera movement that has remained broadly consistent (discussed below), there are significant formal differences across the films as a whole: Brechtian experimentation in *Up the Junction*, long takes in *The Gamekeeper*, modernist dream sequences in *Fatherland* (1986), the upbeat montage sequence in *The Angels' Share* when our protagonists hitch-hike to the Highlands. These examples highlight that, contra any lazy assumptions that Loach's cinema is formally indistinguishable, despite their commonalities, there are significant visual and sonic differences, and criticism of Loach's work need be attentive to its elasticity and variety.

Popular narrative forms

While it might be tempting to consider *The Angels' Share* as something of an outlier in Loach's wider output, it contains three elements that Loach regularly employs throughout the fictional films: conventional narrative, melodrama and comedy. Conventional narrative has been critiqued as a far from radical, if not reactionary, film form, and filmmakers working against the artistic conventions of mainstream cinema often regularly utilise non-narrative forms, with the broader aim of challenging the power

---

[13] Quoted in Quart (1980: 29). In interview with the author, Loach also suggested that he views some of the early work as too polemical.
[14] For instance, Jean-Luc Godard moves into collective filmmaking and Fernando Solanas and Octavio Getino publish 'Toward a Third Cinema', which champions an alternative revolutionary cinema beyond both Hollywood and the arthouse circuit.

conventions of global capitalism.[15] In moving towards a more mainstream narrative approach, Loach has the same anti-capitalist goals but deploys different methods. Marx argues in *Capital* that 'all science would be superfluous if the outward appearance and the essence of things directly coincided'.[16] Following this line of thought in cinematic terms, it is futile to point a camera at the world with the aim of depicting it, to paraphrase Ranke, 'the way it really is'. Rather, Loach's narrative form is utilised to illustrate how capitalism operates in and through individual character's lived experience as it changes over time. As such, the films function not as single snapshots of working-class life, but as small, dramatised micro-histories of present and past experience.

As is evident from *The Angels' Share* plot synopsis in the previous chapter, the film follows a conventional narrative: it opens in a courtroom in which we are introduced to the central characters and their dilemmas, and concludes with them departing, with Robbie having resolved his central problem: how to secure a safe and viable future for his family. Elements of Robbie's violent past are revealed in flashback, and temporal shifts in the opening scenes cut between the court and Albert's previous drunken misadventures on a railway track; the narrative is otherwise linear.[17] Wyatt Moss-Wellington argues (2017: 51–2) that in *Land and Freedom*, *Carla's Song* and *Ae Fond Kiss . . .* the main characters' dilemmas are

> pegged to a concurrent dissonance in their moral self-concept. We observe the characters' attempts to resolve these dissonances with varying success, but importantly, the viewer is asked to experience the dissonance with them, and in so doing ask themselves difficult questions about the values their politics are predicated upon.

The same process is evident in *The Angels' Share* as narrative identification processes position the viewer with Robbie who regularly negotiates decisions about his future. Should he forsake his family in the face of threatened

---

[15] The critique laid at Loach's door during the *Screen* debates was that the narrative form he employed was inherently conservative.

[16] Karl Marx (1977).

[17] An additional scene in which Rhino is arrested atop a statue was shot during filming. In this instance, it was filmed as if shot from a security camera; it did not appear in the finished film. It features as scene 3 in the published screenplay but not in the deleted scenes in the DVD. The scene was shot at the iconic Duke of Wellington statue in Glasgow city centre. Footage of the filming of the scene in which local Glaswegians intervene in what they think is a real event was taken by a bystander and is available to view on YouTube: https://www.youtube.com/watch?v=AbonHOucBXY (last accessed 30 May 2020).

violence? Should he accept a bribe from Leonie's father to depart? Should he negotiate with Clancy?[18] These dilemmas draw on melodramatic conventions, which are also evident across much of Loach's *oeuvre*.[19] For instance, there is a focus on familial and sexual relationships in *Family Life*, *Ladybird Ladybird*, *Carla's Song*, *Ae Fond Kiss . . .*, fraternal conflict in *The Wind That Shakes the Barley*, and the use of death as a narrative device in *The Price of Coal*, *Route Irish*, *Riff-Raff*, *My Name is Joe* and *Land and Freedom*.

As previously outlined, *The Angels' Share* is tonally lighter than much of this work and contains significant comic material. In interview, Laverty comments, 'You could tell another tragedy but I was keen not to repeat *My Name is Joe* and *Sweet Sixteen*,' and cites the popular Spanish political comedy *El Verdugo/The Executioner* (Berlanga, 1963) as an influence.[20] Comedy features regularly across Loach's broader output, if not usually deployed as extensively as in *The Angels' Share*. There is a moment in *Raining Stones*, for instance, when a police helicopter monitors Tommy (Ricky Tomlinson) as he returns from a night on the tiles. Suddenly, he drops his trousers, points his substantial bare buttocks towards the police and roars, 'Do you know what you want? A fucking revolution!' Lightening the load of the often bleak situations that Tommy finds himself in, this scene illustrates not simply that comic moments can be located in dark circumstance but also that comedy can be a coping mechanism to survive life, under capitalism or otherwise.[21] It also illustrates that Loach's use of comedy often has direct political import, echoing Walter Benjamin's assertion (1999: 224) that laughter is the 'most international and revolutionary emotion'. This scene is also notable because, rather than advancing the nar-

---

[18] These dilemmas, as I outline in the previous chapter in the discussion of non-conclusive endings, are however, always only temporarily resolved.

[19] There is also a significant scene towards the end of the screenplay in which Robbie confronts Clancy, comments on their ongoing feud and threatens to kill him. In attempting to tie up the loose ends, which would allow Robbie and Leonie to, in this instance in a powder blue Volkswagen camper van, ride off into the distance, it stretches believability. Significantly, this scene does not appear in the finished film and the prospect of future conflict between the pair is left unresolved. The scene does appear in the DVD deleted scenes.

[20] Interview with the author.

[21] In addition, Loach has regularly cast comedians and stage performers as actors, including Chrissie Rock in *Ladybird Ladybird*, Ricky Tomlinson in *Riff-Raff* and Raymond Mearns in *Ae Fond Kiss . . .* . Continuing this trend in *The Angels' Share*, although we do not see him on-screen, the voice of established comic actor Ford Kiernan is heard in the opening scene in which the station announcer channels the spirt of the Almighty to warn Albert of the threat of an advancing train.

rative, it operates as a Brechtian-like episodic insertion, highlighting that, although Loach's narrative form became more goal-orientated over time, elements of the episodic form from the 1960s' work remain.

In *The Angels' Share*, Albert provides much of the humour. Embodying elements of the theatrical fool, his knowledge gaps span French painting (the *Mona Lisa*) to Scottish architecture (Edinburgh Castle), yet he also conjures the plan for the gang donning traditional Highland dress as cover for their forthcoming robbery. The kilts themselves provide comic material, for instance, when Albert's chaffed genitals cause him untold pain but light relief for the police officers who demand that the three boys raise their kilts when they are searched on their return to Glasgow. When one officer says, 'You want to get some cream on that,' it is the most notable of a string of Rabelaisian moments involving Albert, with his moist and malodorous woollen socks also making an unwelcome intervention when the gang reach the distillery. The film's most stomach-churning but comic moment, however, occurs when the badly hungover Dougie (James Casey) slakes his drouth by ingurgitating a whisky-saliva cocktail from a spittoon, the liquid leftovers from the four teenagers' whisky-tasting session. In much of Loach's work, comedy precedes tragedy, however, this process is largely reversed in *The Angels' Share*. Here, the darker plot points, for example, the flashback to Robbie's unprovoked and violent attack on a young man, make way for more comic elements as Robbie and the gang head towards the Highlands in pursuit of the whisky. David Martin-Jones (2013) states that *The Angels' Share* 'makes you laugh whilst also making you think'. The point, here, is that both laughing and thinking are embodied, cognitive activities. By deploying recognisable forms, popular narrative, melodrama

Figure 2.1 The three boys raise their kilts when they are searched on their return to Glasgow

and comedy, the films reach towards a wide, popular audience, to an audience whose lives mirror those who appear in the films.

Setting and design

Filming on location has long been regarded as a hallmark of neorealism, indeed several prominent Italian neorealist movement films were shot mainly in the streets, not least *Rome, Open City* (Rossellini, 1945). Similarly, since his early television work, Loach has utilised the possibilities afforded by the development of relatively lightweight 16mm cameras to move beyond the studio, a radical departure from the dominant forms in 1960s television drama. In interview, Tony Garnett suggests that the motivating factor in shooting on location is 'Truth. Why build a set when you can go to the place itself?'[22] Loach also discusses locations in similar terms when he comments, 'It's the streets themselves which give you the truth.'[23] Location shooting is integral to the approach, although not from the perspective of creating visually arresting cinematography. Indeed, as outlined below, locations are not filmed in a manner which draws attention to them, but neither are they simply backdrop to the action. In Loach's method of working, location filming functions as a space of site-specific performance in which both the space and the actor perform for the camera, thereby functioning as an authenticity signifier in two senses. Firstly, it signifies to the viewer that the action is taking place in a real location, whether that be a street in Glasgow's East End where young men confront each other with weapons, or a Highland field where the gang plan their caper. Secondly, it creates spaces of site-specific performance in which the desired authenticity of performance (discussed in Chapter 5) is augmented by the authenticity of space: verisimilitude during filming grounds the actors' performances throughout production.

Henri Lefebvre (1991: 93–4) suggests,

> vis-à-vis lived experience, space is neither a mere 'frame', after the fashion of the frame of the painting, nor a form or container of a virtually neutral kind, designed simply to receive whatever is poured into it. Space is

---

[22] Interview with author.
[23] Quoted in Graham Young (2014) 'Film Director Ken Loach dismisses Steven Knight's plan for sound stage in Birmingham', *Business Live*, 20 October 2014, https://www.birminghampost.co.uk/business/creative/film-director-ken-loach-says-7965069 (last accessed 18 December 2020).

social morphology: it is to lived experience what form itself is to the living organism, and just as intimately bound up with function and structure.

Following this line of thought, the location of filming is never free of meaning nor does it simply frame the performance. Discussing *Land and Freedom*, John Orr suggests that the 'Catalan landscape is little more than a functional backdrop with no visual identity' (2004: 304). I would contend, however, that in Loach's work the locations function in a manner more attuned to Lefebvre's thinking with power relations inscribed in the terrain in which filming takes place. Location shooting, then, is always already involved in concrete power relations which, in turn, are represented on the cinema screen. Specifically in *The Angels' Share*, no scenes are filmed within a studio: rather, the action occurs in existing buildings and locations, including courtrooms, houses, snooker halls, hotels, pubs, distilleries and on the streets of Edinburgh, Glasgow and the Highlands. For instance, the opening courtroom scene was shot in Glasgow Sheriff Court, the whisky-tasting sequence in Edinburgh's Caledonian Hotel, the scene in which Robbie and Thaddeus exchange the whisky in Ross's Bar in central Glasgow, and the snooker hall confrontation in Snook-A-Scene in the city's East End.[24] These locations, replete as they are with their own specific politics and ideology, work to ground the narrative, including its magical elements, in what we might call 'geographical realism' at the point of production.

In interview, locations manager Michael Higson outlines how the process starts when he receives the script several months in advance of filming. Higson suggests that, in keeping with all aspects of preparation on a Loach film, the process is more extensive than conventional film and television location shooting, with considerably more time allocated to location scouting.[25] Although Higson leads the process, Loach is involved

---

[24] I attended the technical recce during which Loach advises those in attendance on the aspects of the events that will be filmed in the location. Most of the discussion, at least in a group formation, centres on the logistics of what will happen in the scene. In the recce for the court scene, for instance, Loach leads the crew as they walk through position, discussing blocking, plans for shooting positions with Robbie Ryan, where the gang members will sit and so on. Also in attendance were court officials on hand to answer logistical questions from Loach: 'How many police officers would be expected to be there? How many cases might be heard in one morning?' and so on, thereby utilising their presence almost as unofficial consultants with the aim of ensuring that what is shot on the day would be in keeping with a normal day at court.

[25] Interview with author. Outlining the details of the additional time given to preparation, Higson also states: 'If I was working on a BBC job, I would get six or seven weeks' prep

heavily: 'Ken wants to see every option and he wants to know that every option has been looked at. There are no shortcuts. It's a much, much, much longer preparation time exactly for that reason.' Notably, Higson also utilises discourses of authenticity and realism: 'He wants the real thing; he wants complete authenticity, as accurate as possible.' Initial drafts of the script involved the auction taking place in Islay and as the Malt Mill cask had supposedly lain there for forty years, the aim was to secure a traditional-looking distillery.[26] Higson states: 'It was a very specific traditional kind of feel that he [Loach] was looking for.' As such, distilleries deemed to be too modern, ugly, industrial, or polished, were discounted and Islay became increasingly viewed as unsuitable and the script was amended to include a Highlands distillery. Higson then conducted an extensive survey of distilleries in mainland Scotland, factoring in the willingness of the distillery owners and management involved to be amenable to the process, and presenting the options to Loach via photographs and set visits. Again, he discusses the rationale behind Loach's decision-making in discourses of the real: 'Once he [Loach] sees it and he believes it, he believes its authenticity.' The script required two distilleries, one in which the auction and robbery occur, and one in which Harry leads the group on a tour. Balblair distillery in Edderton, a small Highland village in Ross-shire, was deemed suitable for the auction/robbery scenes. An old-fashioned, independent distillery, it possessed all the necessary locations for the shoot: dunnage in which to hold the auction, shop in which Robbie and Thaddeus have their post-auction business exchange, and a picturesque yard in which the attendees arrive and depart. The distillery which appears earlier in the film, however, is an amalgam of Deanston distillery and Glengoyne distillery, both of which are in central Scotland. In this sequence the gang's arrival and departure was filmed in Glengoyne, which contains elements of the picturesque, and when the gang retire for a post-tour whisky-sampling session the action was filmed in Deanston. Here, however, because the scouting never led to anything appropriate for shooting the whisky-sampling scene, relatively empty spaces within the distillery were converted into the shop that the gang visit after their distillery tour and in which Robbie first displays his talents for whisky tasting, and Mo her talents for whisky pinching.

for a six-week shoot. Whereas on Ken's prep, when the official prep starts, six weeks before the shoot starts, everything has been decided.' All other quotes from Higson in this chapter are from this interview.

[26] Information from draft scripts provided by Sixteen Films. See also the draft schedule in Appendix III, which illustrates that the action was initially planned to be shot in Islay.

In discussing the preparations for this sequence, we can see how locations interact with production design. Production designer Fergus Clegg suggests, 'If Ken could make a film without an art department, he probably would. I'm sure he'd be happy if he could find the location exactly as he wanted it.'[27] Clegg outlines, however, that existing locations are not fetishised but adapted to suit the film, a process which might involve constructing additional items or dressing the set with additional props. In preparing to shoot the distillery visit sequence, Clegg notes that significant work was required to prepare the set:

> In Deanston we were almost using it as a studio space in a way; we were using part of the architecture, the walls, the floor and the windows, but we were adding in walls and changing colours because it was just such a blank canvas ... You idealise a view of a distillery, but it doesn't really exist, so it's a composite of different elements, which is unusual because Ken can normally find a location which he's happy with in its entirety.

The extent of the transition is evident in two of Clegg's photographs taken before and after a near-empty room is transformed into one replete with stereotypical Scottish paraphernalia, from oak-coloured barrels to stag's heads.[28] In adapting the space, a false wall was built on the right-hand side, a side door added, and a wall at the end of the space which had double doors next to the window was constructed, highlighting that the reality of the situation is, on occasion, quite literally constructed.[29]

In creating this space, Clegg drew on the romantic associations attached to whisky:

> A lot to do with Scottish identity is this magical, mythical Scotland and part of that feeds into the Scottish whisky distillery. Some of it may be true, some of it may be imagined. But what you're doing is you're buying part of that imagery and you're using it as a brief for the design.

[27] Interview with author. All other quotes from Clegg in this chapter are from this interview.

[28] In interview, Clegg is eager to stress the important role in production design played by his predecessor, Martin Johnson. A long-standing collaborator, Johnson first worked with Loach on *Days of Hope* and they last collaborated on *Ae Fond Kiss . . .*, which is dedicated to his memory. Clegg worked under Johnson in the art department before stepping into his shoes on *The Wind That Shakes the Barley*. He comments: 'He (Johnson) talked me over the process which he'd perfected over the years, which is a very pared-down method, very low budget and with a very small department. It was basically me, him and a buyer, plus a construction crew. The unit has got bigger over the years which is something that we've always fought to try to prevent happening.'

[29] One particular attraction of this space is the large windows which allow natural lighting to be utilised. I discuss lighting in more detail later in this chapter.

Figures 2.2a and 2.2b Production designer Fergus Clegg's 'before' and 'after' photographs of the whisky distillery shop

The film's production design, then, lies somewhere between a functioning distillery and one which might be conjured into being in the tartan, or whisky, imaginary. An additional production design element emerges in interview when both Clegg and Higson note that Loach is averse to using intense colours and has a particular aversion to red: 'It's a colour that draws the eye,' says Higson, before highlighting the consequences for filming, 'red cars, old phone boxes and letter boxes have always got to go.' The interviews with Higson and Clegg reveal an unresolved tension between the real and the magical in which the real is neither fetishized, nor absolute, and is congruent with how *The Angels' Share* itself moves between both.

Costume and make-up

Filmmakers' attempts to construct a verisimilious aesthetic through appropriate costume is well established and several controversies have arisen on the use of costume deemed to be historically inaccurate or in some way inauthentic. Loach himself has been no stranger to such controversy, for instance, on the veracity of the badges on the soldiers' military uniforms in *Days of Hope*.[30] Given the immediacy and centrality of costume to a film's visual style, and perceived authenticity, Loach and his crew spend significant time working on this aspect of pre-production. In interview, costume designer Carole Fraser outlines that she will receive the script around four months before filming starts in order to fully research the characters.[31] In outlining how the cast are involved in the process, she states that they meet for an introductory meeting to develop a general sense of what costume might be relevant and, at a second meeting, cast members bring clothes that they might wear in different social situations 'so I can get an insight into what they wear', the rationale being, 'when I come to put them in a costume, they're not wearing something that is totally alien to them,' and that 'there's a fusion between their character and who they really are'.[32] Fraser suggests that providing costumes for *The Angels' Share*'s central characters was the production's greatest challenge because of streetwear fashion rules. When she notes that the actors 'keep us right', she alludes to the element of collective creativity involved in the

---

[30] See Anthony Hayward (2004: 139).
[31] Interview with author. All subsequent quotes from Fraser in this chapter are from this interview.
[32] I discuss this notion of 'fusion' between actor and character in Chapter 4.

process, and further exemplifies how the crew discuss their work in realist terminology.

Echoing the comments of Clegg and Higson in terms of the colour palette, she comments, 'We have restrictions in terms of colour. We like pale, washed-out colours; natural colours that look natural, with natural fabric. They just film better.' She adds, however, that, despite Loach's aversion to bright colours, she inserted splashes of red into the mix: 'If you look at all the Scottish Colourist painters, there are all these natural colours and then you'll get a wee hint of a burnt red and it just works. But I'm sure Ken doesn't miss a thing, I'm sure he's seen my reds in there. It's okay, they're not bright, not primary colours.' It is noticeable that the colour palette in Loach's other films tends towards blues and greys.[33] For instance, the lead characters in *Kes* and *My Name is Joe*, Billy and Joe, are often clothed in blue-grey, a choice which rejects a polarisation of light and dark through a more even distribution of tone, and which is expressive of the choices the characters must make in the difficult situations which they often find themselves in. The colour palettes in *The Wind That Shakes the Barley* and *Land and Freedom* stand out as green/brown and red respectively, both in terms of landscape and costume; however, these are atypical and related to the films' historical specificities in relation to military uniforms and landscape.

In *The Angels' Share*, aside from their tartan kilts, the central characters are routinely dressed in blue-grey. Supporting characters also normally wear various shades of blue-grey, but predominantly blue: Luke's baby-blue outfit; the darker blue uniforms that the gang wear when carrying out their community payback activities; when we first encounter Harry he is sporting a blue jumper and jacket, and Leonie wears a blue dressing grown in hospital. The costume colour palette also matches the overall production design: several locations have grey painted walls, for instance, the sheriff court and the hospital in which Robbie visits Leonie and his baby. In addition, the prominent vehicles that are used, Harry's van and the camper van, are also blue, the latter, approximate to the shades of Luke's baby-blue outfit.

Discussing costume in social realist cinema, Sarah Street (2001: 82) highlights that in *Wonderland* (Winterbottom, UK, 1999), 'Clothes are not used to create a spectacle in themselves but are used to support character and acting style.' While this resonates with *The Angels' Share* costume

---

[33] See Sarah Street (2018) for a broader discussion of the colour palette in British social realist cinema, including discussion of *Poor Cow* (Loach, UK, 1967).

design, one exception is the character of Rory McAllister, who in the whisky-tasting sequence, sports a pale blue shirt and tie, yellow waistcoat and tartan trousers, with a monocle adding an additional signifier of showmanship. In the auction sequence, he is once more attired in eye-catching tartan, this time kilted with a black blazer, sporting a pocket handkerchief, white shirt and a patterned red tie, one of the film's few flashes of red. Notably, McAllister's costume was provided by the actor who played him, professional whisky connoisseur, Charles MacLean, who dressed in his routine whisky-tasting attire. As such, although his costume functions to create spectacle, this remains within the realms of a realist aesthetic in that his costume is concomitant with his character.[34] Notably, however, Fraser highlights occasions when they depart from authentic costume if it risks disrupting other aspects of the film, outlining one instance in which a police officer was dressed in full kit, including body armour and utility belt. When they arrived on set, Loach suggested that they tone down the costume because the character, as Fraser puts it, 'looks as if he's about to go into combat and he [Loach] wants him to look more user-friendly than that'. As such, cognisant that this was inauthentic, the body armour and the utility belt were removed to maintain the film's lighter sensibility.

Cast members are routinely expected on set one hour in advance of shooting commencing to complete costume and make-up. In interview, make-up designer Karen Brotherston outlines that 'everything has to be really quite natural', and that, as with costume, the actors contribute to discussion of their own make-up and overall look, thereby granting them partial ownership of their characters' visual style.[35] For instance, the tattoos on the back of Rhino's neck and those on Mo's neck and hand were decided after Loach consulted with the actors as to what type of tattoo that they thought their characters might have.[36] The make-up deployed, then, draws on the actors' lived experiences, decentralising decision-making,

---

[34] Information from interview with author. Indicative of the filmmakers' approach, on the first day of shooting, producer Rebecca O'Brien, in consultation with casting director Kahleen Crawford and Loach, suggested that my on-set presence during the courtroom scene could be best facilitated if I was dressed as a reporter. When I arrived, sporting a rather bland, grey suit, Fraser approved and I spent my first day on set in the courtroom press gallery with notepad and pen in hand, acting the part of a journalist observing the court's activities.

[35] Interview with author. Brotherston adds that if an actor prefers to have make-up that augments their natural look, then that is permitted provided it requires no or little maintenance during the day.

[36] Information from interview with Brotherston.

and further developing this sense of the film's aesthetics being attached to pre-existing entities.

Camera position

Discussing his approach toward cinematography, Loach highlights the importance of camera placement by posing two questions: 'Where does the camera stand so that you can draw the best out of what everyone is doing? Where do you put the camera and what do you try to cover within the shot?'[37] The reference to camera placement in the first instance I take to refer to how the cinematic apparatus impacts on cast and crew activity during filming. I deal with this process in detail in Chapter 4; here, it is worth noting the importance that Loach's method places on minimising the presence of the cinematic apparatus on set. The importance attached to performance ensures that, where possible, anything deemed to interfere with it, be that crew members or equipment, is concealed from the actors as much as is practical. While we might conjure a picture of a film set as one replete with monitors and technological paraphernalia, a Loach set is pared down with the cinematic apparatus and film personnel kept to the bare essentials. Loach's camera (predominantly a solitary one) is normally positioned on a tripod, at the eye level of Loach and the cinematographer, and is placed as far as is practical from the actors with long lenses used to shoot the action.[38] During my fieldwork, aside from when the camera was moving, there were two instances when the camera was not placed at approximately eye level: when the gang are sitting down after pitching their tent in a field overlooking the distillery, and when potential bidders arrive at the distillery. These, however, stand out as exceptional.

This filmmaking method evidently impacts on the quote's second aspect, that is, what is covered 'within the shot', which maps onto what will be directly projected on-screen.

As indicated above, Loach's early film form was characterised by self-reflexivity, reaching its height in *The End of Arthur's Marriage* (BBC, 1965) in which Loach appears as a film director marshalling a camera crew on loca-

[37] Quoted in *Distilling* The Angels' Share (McArdle, 2012),
[38] The only occasions when I observed two cameras being used were for filming the potential buyers arriving at the auction and during the filming of the auction itself. In interview Robbie Ryan states, 'Camera almost always on a tripod. When necessary hand-held. If it's in a car he'll happily go hand-held. If he's in a tight space, he'll go hand-held.'

Figure 2.3 Filming the gang in a field overlooking the distillery. One of the few occasions when a stationary camera is placed below the standing eye-level of Loach and Ryan

Figure 2.4 The camera is placed on a platform to enable a better view of potential bidders arriving at the distillery

tion. As his form became more self-effacing, the cinematography became more observational. Loach points to the influence of Chris Menges, who worked as camera assistant on *Poor Cow* and cinematographer on *Kes*, in developing this approach. Prior to shooting *Kes*, Menges had worked as assistant to Miroslav Ondříček, a prominent cinematographer of the Czech New Wave whose films included *Lásky jedné plavovlásky/A Blonde in Love*

(Forman, 1965) and *Hoří, má panenko/The Firemen's Ball* (Forman, 1967). Loach states that Menges' experiences with Ondříček influenced his own approach:

> Chris was very taken with the lighting which was very sympathetic but naturalistic, not studio lighting, and with the kind of lenses they would use, there was a simplicity to it. We thought that what happened in front of the camera was more important than the camerawork, so in order to get the best out of what was happening in front of it we had to find a very simple way of shooting. That led to using certain lenses and camera positions; it became about observation rather than chasing. *Kes* was the first film that we worked in that way, and that set the pattern for later work.[39]

This quote further highlights the connection between how a scene is shot and how it is seen by the viewer; however, the shift that is identified from 'chasing' to 'observation' is crucial in understanding the films' cinematographic style. Since working with Menges on *Kes*, Loach has worked with several cinematographers, most regularly Barry Ackroyd and Menges himself. Robbie Ryan first worked with Loach on *The Angels' Share* and has worked on all Loach's subsequent fictional features. However, although I have identified different aesthetic approaches across the films, the audience, at least from around *Kes* onwards, is routinely placed in the position of an observer, watching the action unfold at a distance, regardless of the cinematographer employed. Jacob Leigh (2002: 60–1) provides a useful summary of the approach:

> The most common strategy that he and Menges use is to have the camera follow the action. From a distance, with a long focal lens, usually about seventy millimetres, the camera seems to discover its subject and frame it in a medium close shot. The use of a long lens for close shots and long shots, panning and re-focusing between framings, flattens space and minimises perspective; there is often a shallow depth-of-field in Loach's films, with only one plane in focus. This aspect of his photographic style remains generally consistent in his career.

Although Leigh's analysis deals only with the period up to 2001, the films released subsequently also employ a similar approach.[40] The camera is normally positioned as an observer to the action, also positioning the viewer as an observer on the edge of the space, and is shot in a manner which does

---

[39] Menges was Ondříček's assistant on *If...* (Anderson, UK, 1966).
[40] Robbie Ryan in interview states, 'Ken's very much into longer lenses, he likes to shoot from a distance, he likes the idea of a compressed image, he doesn't shoot wider than a 50mm lens if he can help it.'

not call attention to itself or to the spectator's subjective positioning, but steers the spectator towards concentrating on character and narrative.[41]

In 'The Work of Art in the Age of Mechanical Production', Walter Benjamin suggests that (2007: 228)

> the film actor lacks the opportunity of the stage actor to adjust to the audience during his performance, since he does not present his performance to the audience in person. This permits the audience to take the position of a critic, without experiencing any personal contact with the actor. The audience's identification with the actor is really an identification with the camera. Consequently the audience takes the position of the camera.

Benjamin's observations resonate with Loach's cinematic approach. Here, the cinematographic approach invites character identification, through an identification with the apparatus, but as it is presented at a distance, both in terms of physical distance from the camera and in the absence of tight shots and close-ups, it also enables a space for reflection. For Benjamin, the spectator is placed in the position of the camera: for Loach, the camera is placed in the position of the spectator. If the viewer moves with the action, they often move as if on the characters' shoulder: for instance, as Leonie's uncle and his associates chase Robbie down a flight of hospital stairs, the camera/audience is positioned as if they are trying to keep up with the action.[42] The viewer is positioned close enough to witness the action at first hand; however, they are also positioned such that they observe the action from outwith the characters' space.[43] One factor which highlights this is the relative lack of quite clear point-of-view shots, or more accurately, point-of-view shots from the films' characters, particularly when they are in close proximity to each other.[44] In *The Angels' Share*, there is a point-of-view shot

---

[41] Loach himself has stated that is his approach is to, as he puts it (Fuller 1998: 51) 'shoot it like you're a sympathetic observer'.

[42] Other examples beyond *The Angels' Share* might be as the revolutionary militia advance on a fascist outpost in *Land and Freedom*.

[43] Discussing *Days of Hope*, Caughie (2000: 110–11) advances the terms 'documentary gaze' (camera as observer) and 'dramatic look' (conventional point of view, reverse cutting, eyeline match etc) to distinguish the different methods employed by Loach. Caughie (2000: 112) critiques Loach's approach, suggesting that in *Days of Hope* 'the class which, in Marxist terms, is meant to be the subject of history, appears as the object of the gaze', championing instead, what he regards as a more modernist form of television drama. Caughie's analysis, though, does not move beyond the text itself, an approach that I critique in Chapter 6.

[44] One could cite the social workers looking through Maggie and Jorge's letterbox in *Ladybird Ladybird* or Liza Jane (Katie Proctor) in *Sorry We Missed You* as she surveys

when Robbie siphons whisky from a barrel; however, character point-of-view shots are less common precisely because the camera predominantly positions the viewer as observer of, rather than participant in, the action.[45]

This notion of looking at a distance becomes apparent as the viewer is often positioned as observing the action through a door or window from an adjacent room. This connects with Loach's desire to minimise the apparatus's presence; the effect bleeds into the aesthetic, as evidenced in the scenes shot in Leonie's aunt's flat and in Harry's flat in which the action is evidently shot from outside the room.[46] This is, however, not conventional frame within a frame photography which calls attention to itself, as exemplified by the iconoclastic, visually striking concluding sequence in *The Searchers* (Ford, 1956) or, perhaps closer to Glasgow, when Jamie looks through a window to a golden field of dreams in *Ratcatcher* (Ramsay, 1999). On the contrary, the frames in Loach's work function to reinforce the sense that the viewer is voyeuristically observing the action. André Bazin notes (1967: 92) that it was Jean Cocteau who said that 'cinema is an event as seen through a keyhole'; for Loach, at least in several interior settings, the world is often seen through a door frame.

Camera movement

The aesthetic effect of Loach's approach to cinematography is that movement on-screen predominantly emerges from the camera following action within the frame rather than the camera itself moving. A small anecdote revealing something of the general approach emerged in interview with sound recordist, Ray Beckett, who notes that in the Loach films he had worked on, that is, every fictional feature since *Raining Stones*, he had never observed the camera being placed on tracks. The rationale appears to be that as the camera is routinely positioned from an observer's perspective, and humans do not routinely move on tracks, dollies or cranes, then why would the camera? Movement, then, often comes in following shots, pans and tilts, rather than tracking or crane shots. There are, of course, instances in which the camera itself moves, for instance, when Robbie is chased in

---

the damage done to a range of family portraits by her wayward brother, Seb (Rhys Stone), however, these stand out as notable exceptions.
[45] This can be contrasted with more conventional shot-reverse cutting.
[46] In addition, part of the whisky-tasting sequence is shot through an aperture in a wall, although this is not evident in the film itself.

the hospital described above, when the community paybackers travel in a van with Harry to the distillery, and when the gang hitch-hike through the Highlands. Here, though, the effect is still to position the camera as observer. For instance, when the camper van drives off in the concluding sequence, this is filmed either from inside the vehicle, establishing a direct human perspective, or, as it travels through the countryside, from a stationary perspective as if a roadside observer. This cinematographic approach further locates Loach within the realist tradition for as Dimitris Eleftheriotis notes (2010: 4), 'Historically, movement of/in the frame has been seen as a foundational aspect of the realist nature of film as a medium.' Rather than constructing a sense of movement by moving the camera, the movement is in the frame itself. As Eleftheriotis observes (41),

> camera movement that attracts attention to itself has the potential to hint towards (or even reveal) the presence of an enunciating apparatus and thus disturb the self-sufficiency, naturalness and transparency of the diegetic world. Overreliance on movement, which openly intervenes in the telling of the story and points towards the identification of the camera as the enunciator, represents a dangerous tightrope that puts in jeopardy the supremacy of narrative.

Loach's approach, then, does not highlight the camera–audience relationship, which tends only to emerge in active viewing. Rather, the cinematography is placed, as Eleftheriotis suggests, at the service of narrative.

The importance placed on narrative also emerges in interview with Robbie Ryan who conveys something of the relationship between the director and cinematographer when he discusses his own role:

> When we were filming when the kids were hitch-hiking in Loch Lomond there are some beautiful places to film there and we had a bit of time and I said, 'Ken do you want if we have any chance and I can maybe get a shot of a nice vista,' and he says 'Nah.' It doesn't help the story. Because he knew in his head where that was going to be.

It might be useful here to draw out a distinction between this approach and what David Forrest (2013: 38) describes as 'image-led narration' in British realist films directed by Andrea Arnold, Lynne Ramsay and Pawel Pawlikowski. Forrest argues (38) that 'what distinguishes Loach's *mise en scène* from that of the contemporary filmmakers is the codified organisation of the images into fixed and narrativized thematic discourses'. Without drawing a stark binary between image and story, in interview Ryan explicitly connects the cinematographic style strongly to narrative progression: 'There's no faff, there's no fluffiness, trying to embellish an image just to make it look nice. It's got to be storytelling. He wants to get it told with as little fuss as possible because that makes it more honest. It's honest filmmaking.'[47] Ryan's comments further highlight the discourses of truth and authenticity which emerge consistently from Loach's collaborators, but also Loach's preference for an unspectacular cinematographic style, one which foregrounds the character and the drama in the frame as the focus, not how the character and the drama are shot.

Lighting

The desire to minimise the apparatus's presence also has implications for lighting. Robbie Ryan states, 'He wants to try and keep it as real as possible without too much additional lighting to create a mood that wouldn't necessarily be there.' Mindful of the aesthetic considerations, Ryan adds, 'Obviously he wants to make it look nice, but he doesn't want to light it in a way that's not true.' One practical application of this approach is that in filming interiors, actors are often placed near a window so that natural light will illuminate their environment, and the existing light be supplemented with film lights only if essential. As Ryan notes, somewhat light-heartedly, 'Ken's got a lighting approach. You go around most of the locations and he'll find a window and he'll put the characters beside the window.' Several interior scenes in *The Angels' Share* illustrate this with the action positioned close to windows in the scenes in Harry's flat, the flat in the West End where Robbie and his family moves temporarily, Robbie's temporary accommodation, which is the scene of a whisky-tasting session, and the distillery visit discussed above. In most of these shots this results in naturalist, low-contrast lighting, although in the scene shot in Robbie's temporary accommodation, bright light cascades across the four characters, creating an image high in contrast.

Gaffer Andy Cole suggests that the restrictions placed on the lighting 'creates its own challenges' highlighting specific problems that emerge in shooting tight interiors with no lights in the space.[48] He also notes that this approach is not fetishised and, for example, that pulley lights were uti-

---

[47] A contrast here is how Ryan discusses his work with Andrea Arnold with whom he had previously worked on, including *Red Road* (2006), *Fish Tank* (2009) and *Wuthering Heights* (2011): in interview, he states, 'The two of us collaborate. She lets me be a bit free and whatever I feel like doing I do, and that's very liberating for me. I really enjoy that. That's quite a lot different to working with Ken as Ken will pick the shots.'

[48] Interview with author. Cole also notes that they had difficulties lighting the scene in Harry's flat, but these were resolved after time.

Figure 2.5 Albert prepares to fall backwards onto the train tracks

lised in the filming of the auction sequence. Cole explains that in this scene, once the auction had concluded, one of the pulley lamps was weighted so that the light is directed slightly more onto the front of the room (where the American bidder and the gang assemble) than would be the case if it was hanging down of its own accord. Similarly, when Albert falls back onto the tracks, the night-time setting demanded film lighting and a large lamp sits behind Albert's head (on the other side of the track) to illuminate the action.

Overall, additional lighting is kept to a minimum with the desire, concomitant with the overall aesthetic, to achieve a self-effacing realist lighting design. There are, however, moments when the lighting design frames characters in noticeably aesthetically pleasing lights, for instance in the courtroom sequence the characters being sentenced are framed in tight portraits against black backgrounds. While these images stand out somewhat, as with the whisky-tasting scene above, they remain within the realms of realist photography.

Although the cinematography and lighting combine to create a broadly invisible aesthetic, the relative detachment of the camera positioning, coupled with the extensive use of medium long shots rather than tighter close-ups, creates a space for critical reflection at the point of reception. In writing about this form of shooting in relation to documentary filmmaking Bill Nichols (2001: 111) says 'The filmmaker's retirement to the position of observer calls on the viewer to take a more active role in determining the significance of what is said and done.' Loach's method of filming, then, sits somewhere between an immersive cinematic practice and Brechtian estrangement, creating a certain space for a detached spectatorial response.

Snookered

To illustrate how these aspects are combined, I offer a short analysis of the snooker hall scene. I have selected this scene in part because I witnessed it being filmed, but also because it exemplifies the filmmakers' general approach.[49] In the scene, Robbie, Mo, Rhino and Albert are playing snooker when Clancy and his gang attack them, resulting in Robbie fleeing with his rivals in hot pursuit. The scene takes place after 39 minutes, lasts for 70 seconds, and comprises nine separate shots as follows:

1. Mid shot of Robbie wearing a grey hooded top as he strikes the white cue ball. The viewer is positioned close to the action, slightly above Robbie's body, which is level with the height of the snooker table, suggesting that the camera is positioned at eye height looking down. Off-screen, Mo says, 'Yeah,' signifying that Robbie's shot has been successful, and the camera tilts up slightly to meet the level of Robbie's eyes as he rises from the table before it pans, first to the right, then to the left, to follow him as he moves around the table. When he stops to prepare his next shot, the camera continues panning left and, as we hear the (off-screen) sound of the balls being struck once more, the camera comes to rest on a mid shot of Rhino who is sporting a short-sleeved grey t-shirt. Framed against a dark, black-brown background, his figure stands although it is initially blurred before it is brought into tighter focus. With the camera positioned at eye level, Rhino says, 'look at that' in an exasperated manner and slams his snooker chalk down onto the table frame. As he does so, the camera follows his movements in a downward tilt before panning back to the right and stopping as we see that the white ball has nestled behind the yellow, snookering Rhino and making evident the rationale for his exasperation.
2. Long shot of Albert, Rhino, Robbie and Mo at a snooker table in the background with two vacant snooker tables and the edge of a third in the foreground. Noticeably the balls are in a different position from how they ended in the previous shot. Albert is wearing a grey-hooded sweat top; Mo, double denim and a blue hoodie. Mo, positioned on the left of the frame, holds a snooker cue, as do Rhino and Robbie who are on the right. Positioned between them, Albert attempts, and fails, to pot a long red. The presence of the tables indicates that, although this set-up is shot from the same side of the room as the

---

[49] I also return to this scene in Chapter 5 when discussing how actors influence the words spoken in the film.

previous shot, it is further from the action, and to the right, thereby offering a slightly different, more distanced perspective, and creating a greater sense of the space. In contrast to how the camera follows the action in shot 1, here the image is fixed.
3. The image is also fixed in the third shot, a long shot of a door as a young man, almost in silhouette, opens it briefly, peers in and leaves. Off-screen dialogue from the ongoing snooker game, sounds of balls being struck and sections of two snooker tables on the left of the frame signifies that this is an entrance to the snooker hall. Noticeably, it is not a reverse shot from the direction of the previous camera set-up, so it is not the gang's perspective. Rather, it appears to have been shot in a line with the camera position from shot 1 but in a different direction, suggesting the position of an onlooker to the action.
4. Mid shot which focuses initially on Robbie from the waist up as he takes another shot, bringing the viewer much closer to the action. The camera seems again to be at eye level and it tilts slightly down and moves to the left as Robbie lowers his body to lie across the baize and take his shot. Initially Robbie is framed between the blurred figures of Albert and Rhino, somewhat obscuring the action in its totality. As he takes his shot, the left side of Albert's body, appearing out-of-focus, enters the frame on the left, moves out, and then re-enters. Given the tight framing, it is harder to discern the exact direction from where the viewer is observing the action although they seem to be in the same position as in shot 1. A sense of the viewer looking over, or to the side of, Albert's shoulder is created. As the shot nears its conclusion, the off-screen sound of a door opening is heard.
5. Long shot of Clancy and his gang as they enter through the door, giving the same perspective as shot 3. Initially, the camera is still before it pans left, following the assailants as they move between the snooker tables, advancing towards the gang, and Clancy says, 'Good shot,' and then, 'Yous three . . .' as the shot concludes.
6. Mid shot of Robbie from the same general position as shots 1 and 4 as Clancy continues his address from the previous scene, '. . . get tae fuck. I want a word with Robbie's. The camera pans left and tilts down to follow Robbie's hand as he picks up a snooker ball. As he gathers the ball in his hand and moves rightwards towards Clancy, the camera tilts back up to Robbie's eye level and pans slightly to the right catching him in a profile shot against the black background.
7. Long shot of Clancy and his gang. As they advance closer towards Robbie, the camera pans to the left to follow their movement before Rhino enters screen left, wielding a snooker cue to fend off their threatening advances. This shot creates the same viewing position as shots 1 and 3.
8. Mid shot of Rhino waving the cue furiously to fend off Clancy et al. The action is shot as if from off-screen left; however, here it is positioned more akin to the position in shot 2, to the gang's left.
9. Mid shot from behind Rhino, but still from off-screen left, as he fends off the attackers and through a haze of out-of-focus bodies the camera follows Robbie as he moves across the right of the frame and escapes through an emergency exit. The camera movement here is jagged

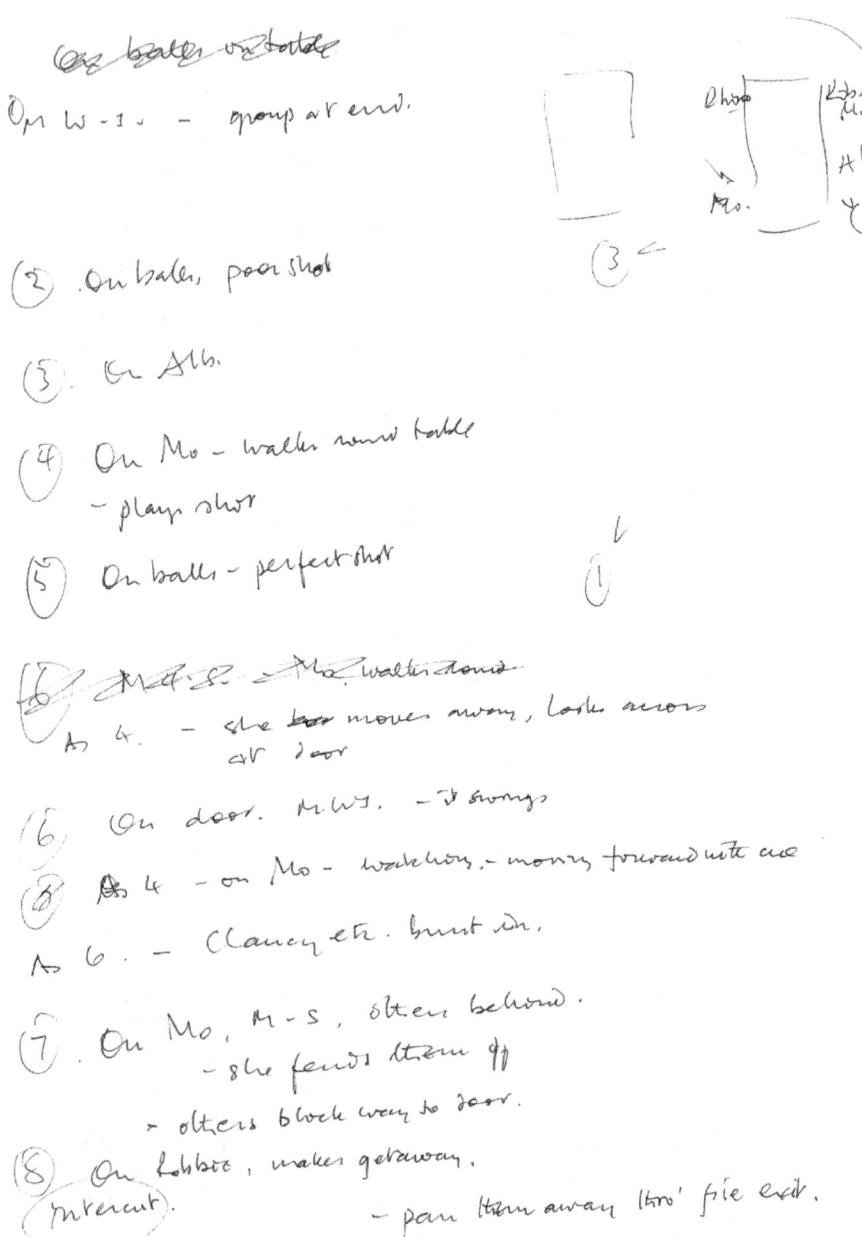

On balls outside

① M.W.S. — group at end.

② On balls, poor shot

③ On Alb.

④ On Mo — walks round table
— plays shot

⑤ On balls — perfect shot

⑥ M.S. Mo walks down
As 4. — she moves away, looks across
at door

⑥ On door. M.W.S. — it swings

⑧ As 4 — on Mo — watching, — moves forward with cue
As 6. — Clancy etc. burst in.

⑦ On Mo, M-S, others behind.
— she fends them off
— others block way to door.

⑧ On Robbie, makes getaway.
(intercut).
— pan them away thro' fire exit.

Figure 2.6 Notes on filming the snooker hall scene from Loach's shooting script

and rapid, connoting a sense of the chaos and fear of the fight scene itself. As Robbie departs, non-diegetic militaristic drumming begins.

There is an economy of action in these nine shots, which establishes the locale, the sense of camaraderie between the lead characters, and creates suspense, before moving onto the confrontation and Robbie's departure. The camera is repeatedly positioned such that it helps create the impression that the viewer is observing this action at close proximity. Eight of the shots are from the left of the snooker table on which Robbie and his friends play, with the final shot from the left and behind. As more of the space is revealed, we see that their table is one of six and is positioned in the room's top right corner, diagonally opposite the main entrance. As the sequence progresses, the framing is tighter and camera movement becomes faster, particularly in the final two shots, which convey the action's frenetic pace in a disorienting manner. The four central characters' costume further highlights the film's blue-grey palette, at least in the urban settings. The snooker table's green baize stands out in contrast, but parallels the vast green Highland landscapes the group encounter when they leave Glasgow. In terms of the aesthetics of the characters' faces, they are often shot against a black background, recalling the courtroom scenes, and connecting their snooker hall activity with their criminal past. As this short description makes evident, there is a recognisable aesthetic quality to the sequence, however, it is not designed to call attention to itself.

Editing

The participant observation element of this study was based primarily on attending the shoot, however, I also spent a short time with Loach and his long-term editor, Jonathan Morris, in the edit suite. When I visited, film cans, rolls of film stock and a Steenbeck editing machine signified that *The Angels' Share* would be cut by hand.

On utilising this approach, Loach comments:

> We use a mechanical process as opposed to sitting at a computer and it appears slower but actually because you have fewer choices you consider the choices more precisely. It's like film stock, because film stock is expensive you try not to waste it by takes where you just shoot and shoot and shoot which gives you far more work in the cutting room but we cut on film partly because of the indulgence of me but also it's a mechanical process so you can see the sequence developing and I find it much easier to have a sense of the rhythm of the piece than something which is hidden inside a computer and which you can race backwards

Figure 2.7 Editor Jonathan Morris at work on *The Angels' Share* auction scene

and forwards over. I think people tend to not cut in such a linear way. If you cut on film, you just build it up scene by scene. You do have a sense of the ongoing rhythm and what is necessary and what isn't necessary. But I guess in the end it's what you grow up with.[50]

During my visit, Morris outlined that they had already assembled an initial 138-minute cut and then created a 118-minute cut which had been screened to O'Brien, Laverty and story editor, Roger Smith. They were tasked now with taking on board their comments and trimming further with the ideal, if unrealisable, target of 90 minutes.[51] 'By the time I'm through, hopefully we'll have lost about half an hour,' Morris comments. In highlighting the centrality of narrative, he notes that they were 'trying to lose things where it drags', but adds, 'we can't sacrifice the sense of the story. We're trying to make it shorter without losing any essence.'

The snooker hall sequence outlined above illustrates something of the general method as continuity editing is utilised to create the illusion of continuous action. The duration of the sequence is 70 seconds, equating to an average shot length (ASL) of around 8 seconds, which is significantly less than some of the slower, more contemplatively shot films such as *The Gamekeeper* and *Days of Hope*.[52] Indeed, when I ask Morris if he feels that

[50] Interview with the author. All subsequent quotes from Morris in this chapter are taken from this interview. Loach has, however, utilised digital editing in more recent films.
[51] The final film is 97 minutes long.
[52] Caughie (2000: 115) notes that the opening 5 minutes of *Up the Junction* have an ASL of 7.8 seconds.

the ASL has been constant since he first worked with Loach on the documentary *The Red and the Blue: Impressions of Two Political Conferences – Autumn 1982,* he replies, 'No . . . we've moved on a bit; I think we cut faster than we used to.'[53] There does appear to be a continuity break between the first and second shots: although Rhino is preparing to take the shot, it is Albert that does so, and the balls are in a different position from the end of the previous shot. Indeed, at the end of shot 1 we hear Robbie comment (off-screen), 'You've left him a long red,' when in the next shot his opponent is snookered. While this could be a jump forward in time, there is nothing which registers the shift. This is not, however, an instance of discontinuous editing; rather, I suggest, a calculation that the discontinuity is so minimal as to remain unnoticed and is only evident after repeated close viewings. As such, it is an instance in which an element of real-time continuity editing is sacrificed in the interest of narrative progression.

If the editing in the snooker hall sequence is generally self-effacing, there are other moments in which it is clearly visible. For instance, when the gang head to the Highlands several scenes are edited together to collapse the journey's timescale: the gang hitching a lift on a bus full of nuns, interactions with French tourists and shots of the Scottish countryside as we hear the first use of The Proclaimers' '500 Miles'. This instance of American Montage, a classical convention of US cinema exemplified by the breakfast-table sequence in *Citizen Kane* (Welles, 1941) or the eponymous boxer's training sequences in *Rocky* (Avildsen, 1976), indicates the conventionality rather than radicality of this editing technique. In interview, Morris relays an instructive anecdote about the editing process of *Sweet Sixteen*:

> Sometimes you want to be a bit flashy in the editing. There's a scene where Pinball drives into a health centre through a plate glass window and the first edit was quite sexy. There were three cameras and I got him hitting the wall three times and I was waiting for Ken to make a comment about the fact that this is not the way it happens and that we are bound by our social realism. He quite liked it, I thought, but gradually as we're doing the film and whittling away, by the time we've finished it hits the wall once.

Morris suggests that in developing their work 'we have a duty as social realists, if you like, to not break the spell'.[54] As such, the filmmakers seek

---

[53] Interview with author.
[54] There is recourse to post-production digital editing; for instance, Morris notes in interview, 'On *The Wind That Shakes the Barley,* the footage of the train coming in had the reflection of a crew member which was removed in digital post-production.' There

to create self-effacing editing style concomitant with the film's overall self-effacing visual aesthetic.

Soundtrack

Most scholarship on Loach's work focuses on visual style, and thematic concerns with the films' sonic qualities are relatively neglected. In part, this is in keeping with film studies' prioritisation of the medium's visual dimension, but also because the discipline gravitates towards analysis of more expressive and experimental forms: an expressionist soundtrack will likely generate more critical attention than a realist soundtrack, paralleling the industry's broad thinking on sound design. Ray Beckett received an Academy Award for his work on *The Hurt Locker* (Bigelow, 2008), the soundtrack of which is laden with expressive explosions in keeping with the work of a US bomb-disposal unit.[55] He has not received awards for the construction of a social realist sound design, one which seeks to minimise its own presence, nor is he likely to.

For the purposes of this analysis, I use the term soundtrack to comprise three aspects of film sound: 1) dialogue, location sound and sound effects, 2) musical score, and 3), non-diegetic pop songs. In keeping with the construction of a visual style which occludes its construction, a realist sound design also works to mask its constructed nature, indeed the very word 'design' might appear somewhat incongruous. Beckett states that in completing his work, there is a constant guard against what he terms 'a discontinuity which will take the audience out of the film'.[56] Beckett stresses the importance of the ideology of documentary to the work: 'We're both documentary people. That's the other thing about Ken, he's really a documentary maker rather than a feature filmmaker and his films are like extended documentaries.' As with many of Loach's other collaborators, Beckett discusses the work in realist discourse: 'You're recording reality rather

---

is always the possibility that film will inadvertently break the spell and, notably, the reflection of the camera team in the pub window when Robbie and Thaddeus meet to exchange the whisky is evident in *The Angels' Share*.

[55] Barry Ackroyd, who has shot numerous Loach films and is credited as 'second camera', alongside Alastair Rae, on *The Angels' Share*, was *The Hurt Locker*'s director of photography. Ackroyd was behind the camera for the railway re-shoot and Rae for the Balblair filming.

[56] Interview with author. All subsequent quotes from Beckett in this chapter are from this interview.

than imposing on it.' The film's credits include post-production activity; my study, however, did not involve observation of post-production and, consequently, my observations are limited here. Perhaps something of the approach is indicated when Beckett suggests, 'Ken won't do post-synch. It's completely against his principles to get an actor three months later to emote in the same way as they did on screen.'

Loach's long-term collaborator, composer George Fenton, describes the development of a Loach score in terms of '"hair shirt" simplicity'.[57] While expressive film music often steers the viewer, or listener, towards a specific position, Fenton suggests that this process is minimised when he works with Loach: 'Ken doesn't want any shorthand, so it can mean writing in a counter-intuitive way. He does want the music to make one feel the moment more, but not in a way that bypasses anything that's on the screen right then.'[58] Speaking of how music interacts with editing, Johnathan Morris suggests, 'It has to emerge. It very rarely thrashes in. It generally emerges from the sound so that you may not be totally aware of it coming in but all of a sudden it's there.' The snooker hall scene is exceptional as here the drums kick in to provoke a sense of excitement. In a rare analysis of the use of music in Loach's work, Sofía López Hernández (2017) suggests that the music in *The Angels' Share* is used to manipulate emotion, albeit that it is often understated.[59] She identifies thirty-one blocks of music in the film lasting 34 minutes, or just over one third of the running time, suggesting that this is a relatively minimal amount for a film, contrasting it with the music in *Groundhog Day* (Ramis, 1993) also written by Fenton, which features for 54 per cent of the film's running time. López Hernández argues that the relative lack of orchestral or symphonic music is indicative of Loach's 'intimate and realistic' style overall. She notes, however, that strings often accompany Robbie when he appears on-screen and when the film is in more contemplative mode, for instance when he is in discussion with Leonie or when he toasts his son's birth with Harry, thereby steering the audience towards a specific emotional engagement. This observation

---

[57] Quoted in Daniel Schweiger (2016) 'Interview with George Fenton', *Film Music Magazine*, 11 January 2016, https://filmmusicinstitute.com/interview-with-george-fenton/ (last accessed 2 February 2022). In addition to scoring numerous Loach films, Fenton has worked extensively in film and television. For a full list see https://georgefenton.com/film/ (last accessed 4 July 2020).

[58] Ibid.

[59] In contrast, in a rare moment of criticism of the music in Loach's work, R. J. Cardullo (2016: 208) suggests that in *Riff-Raff*, 'Stewart Copeland's jaunty piano music ... comes close to animating the action instead of simply accompanying it.'

supports John Hill's (2011: 118) view that this approach 'may also be related to the "melodramatic" (and subsequently comic) strains in Loach's work that seek to solicit strong emotional reactions to the social and psychological predicaments of the films' characters'. There are other scenes, often associated with movement when the gang are on-screen, in which electronic music alongside drums, guitars and percussion function to energise the film, and operate as sonic corollaries of the gear shifts taking place in the narrative.

There is, of course, nothing realistic about non-diegetic music in cinema; cinematic convention ensures that it does not disrupt the viewing experience. The use of music evidently from outwith the film's fictional cosmos, what is referred to in the industry as 'needledrop', can, on the other hand, create a disrupting or distancing effect, even if it remains within cinematic conventions. The two uses of The Proclaimers '500 Miles', the first when the gang depart for the Highlands, the second when Robbie, Leonie and Luke drive off in the camper van are more clearly linked to narrative development. As indicated in the previous chapter, the song's words connect with the themes of love and work which permeate the film's narrative, but they also connect with the film's overall energy. With '500 Miles', however, there is something more in keeping with the non-naturalist use of music in the early Loach outputs such as *Up the Junction*, in which sound and image sit dialectically, or at least dialogically, rather than being stitched seamlessly into the narrative. Hill (2011: 21) suggests that in Loach's early work the use of song is deployed in a Brechtian manner, not simply additional to the drama but also to comment on it politically or socially. The use of the Proclaimers' anthemic tune in *The Angels' Share* fulfils several functions, energising the film, supplementing the narrative, but also creating a form of creative disjunction supplementing and developing the already existing space for critical reflection.

Conclusion

Analysis of Loach's output across his career indicates that there is no singular, simple Loach aesthetic, that the films from *Kes* onwards gently stretch the boundaries of social realism and that elements of the film form developed in his formative years remain, even as the films have developed a more conventional narrative form. Chambers (2014) describes Loach as a 'formal opportunist', although perhaps this might be more sympathetically articulated as 'formal pragmatist' or 'formal pluralist', and he might be considered as a filmmaker attuned to adapting to the specific demands of the screenplay on which he works. Close analysis of *The Angels' Share* production process indicates an unresolved tension between the filmmakers' desire for the authenticity of the real and the authenticity of the cinematic experience. This is best exemplified by prominent crew members' repeated references to discourses of the real in a manner which recall's Bazin's observation (1967: 16) that photography was 'an hallucination that is also a fact'. If there is consistency across the films in the post-*Kes* period, then it relates to a continuous political focus on the oppressed, as outlined in the previous chapter, and the development of a shooting style that sympathetically observes their experiences: a world in action, from a working-class perspective.

3

Team Loach

> ... the cinema is quite simply becoming a means of expression, just as all the arts have been before it, and in particular painting and the novel. After having been successfully a fairground attraction, an amusement analogous to boulevard theatre, or a means of preserving the images of an era, it is gradually becoming a language. By language, I mean a form in which and by which an artist can express his thoughts, however abstract they may be, or translate his obsessions exactly as he does in the new contemporary essay or novel. That is why I would like to call this new age of cinema the age of *caméra-stylo*.
>
> Alexander Astruc[1]

> In the art film world, we all know the film by the director, in Hollywood by the producer or the star, and it's all horseshit.
>
> Tony Garnett[2]

When *The Angels' Share* was being shot in Tain, in the county of Ross-shire in the Highlands, I spent one week on location and on a few occasions joined the younger-in-spirit and more agile cast and crew members who spent downtime playing football on a grassy park near to their digs. I recalled the experience when listening to Loach's speech on receiving the Cannes Film Festival Palme d'Or for *I, Daniel Blake*: 'The first thought is for all the people who helped you make it. If you were a football team winning the championship, everybody would get a medal but in films, the director has to go up. Obviously, it is for the whole team.'[3] In foregrounding filmmaking's collaborative nature and comparing its production to a working-class team sport, Loach's observations contrast sharply with the

---

[1] Quoted in Caughie (1981: 9).
[2] Interview with author. Subsequent quotes from Garnett in this chapter are also from this interview unless otherwise stated.
[3] Quoted in Macnab (2016).

auteurist discourses which dominate popular film culture, and which continue to haunt film scholarship. In this chapter, I explore this contrast and seek to illuminate understanding of tendencies (8) the importance of teams and leaders on- and off-screen, and (9) control of production, of the Certain Tendencies in Loach's Cinema laid out in the Introduction. I do this through analysis of four imbricated areas: debates on authorship in film and television scholarship; the functioning of leadership and teams in the production of *The Angels' Share* and Loach's wider body of work; how Sixteen Films present this production context publicly; and how leadership and teams are represented in the films themselves.[4]

Theories of authorship

Film studies' critical orthodoxy initially tended to conceptualise cinema as a vehicle for the director's personal expression in a framework inherited from Enlightenment thought, a perspective encapsulated by Alexander Astruc above. The inclusion of Roland Barthes' 1967 essay 'La mort de l'auteur'/'The Death of the Author' in John Caughie's influential edited collection, *Theories of Authorship* (1981), was indicative of a structuralist/post-structuralist impulse to consign the auteur to the grave. Returning to these debates in 2007, however, Caughie notes that the grave to which the auteur had been consigned was largely empty (2007: 408). For Caughie, a recognition of how specific groups championed seemingly representative auteurs was evident, alongside the emergence of a more tempered and nuanced director-centred criticism, which had replaced those on offer in auteurism's pioneering days. Other work has highlighted auteurism's ongoing appeal; for instance, Steve Neale (1981), Tim Corrigan (1990) and Catherine Grant (2000, 2008) have illustrated how auteurist discourses feature heavily in the marketing and consumption of cinema. Notably, moreover, film scholars continue to conduct and publish auteurist-based research, exemplified by the titles of a range of monographs on specific filmmakers, from Elizabeth Ezra's *Georges Méliès: The Birth of the Auteur*, to work on more contemporary filmmakers in Brian Michael Goss' *Global*

---

[4] Sixteen Films is a private limited company, incorporated on 10 June 1997. Prior to utilising its current title, it traded under two previous names, Sixteen Films (Joe) Ltd between 18 April 2002 and 3 December 2002, and Parallax (Joe) Limited between 10 June 1997 and 18 April 2002. Loach and O'Brien are the two shareholders. https://beta.companieshouse.gov.uk/company/03386848 (last accessed 20 February 2022).

Auteurs: Politics in the Films of Almodóvar, von Trier, and Winterbottom. There is a trend, however, to recognise the director's role beyond the personal expression of conventional auteurist discourse. In *Authoring Hal Ashby: The Myth of the New Hollywood Auteur*, for example, Aaron Hunter points to Ashby's collaborative working practices, arguing that this was more widespread in the New Hollywood Cinema than is commonly understood, and in *Another Steven Soderbergh Experience: Authorship and Contemporary Hollywood*, Mark Gallagher highlights more recent collaborative processes and complex working practices in Hollywood production which complicate traditional auteurist discourse.

Critical approaches which seek to highlight filmmaking's collaborative nature, that there is no singular creative source, and that our thinking, and actions, are always already entangled with those with whom we interact is, I contend, closer to the conditions of most film production. In Powdermaker's anthropological study of Hollywood in the 1940s she comments,

> Since the making of movies is a highly collaborative enterprise, in which no one works alone, a study of the relations between the people who share the understanding is essential. The writer's situation cannot be understood unless his relationship with the producer is known; and the actor's problems are unintelligible without a knowledge of his relationship with directors; all these are interrelated with front-office executives, agents, publicity writers, and many others. (Powdermaker 1951: 29)

My own thinking is broadly in line with Powdermaker's position as expressed here, yet I am cognisant of the apparent contradiction in writing a book which focuses on one filmmaker, particularly one on whom 'auteur' status has been afforded. John Hill highlights that films directed by Loach are exhibited and distributed in an auteurist context (2011: 5), and the international film festival circuit on which Loach has had significant success is governed predominantly on auteurist lines.[5] 'Ken Loach' is also deployed as brand in the DVD box sets' titles, *The Ken Loach Collection* (Sixteen Films, 2007) and *Ken Loach at the BBC* (Sixteen Films/BFI/BBC, 2011). Loach himself rejects the *auteur* label, repeatedly highlighting cinema's collaborative nature, but also stressing the centrality of the writer in both film and television.[6]

Although Loach has garnered significant success in cinema, it was his early television work with which he first achieved both critical acclaim and

---

[5] For a fuller account of Loach's record at Cannes see Chapter 6.

[6] Interview with the author. See Chapter 5 for more on the role of the writer.

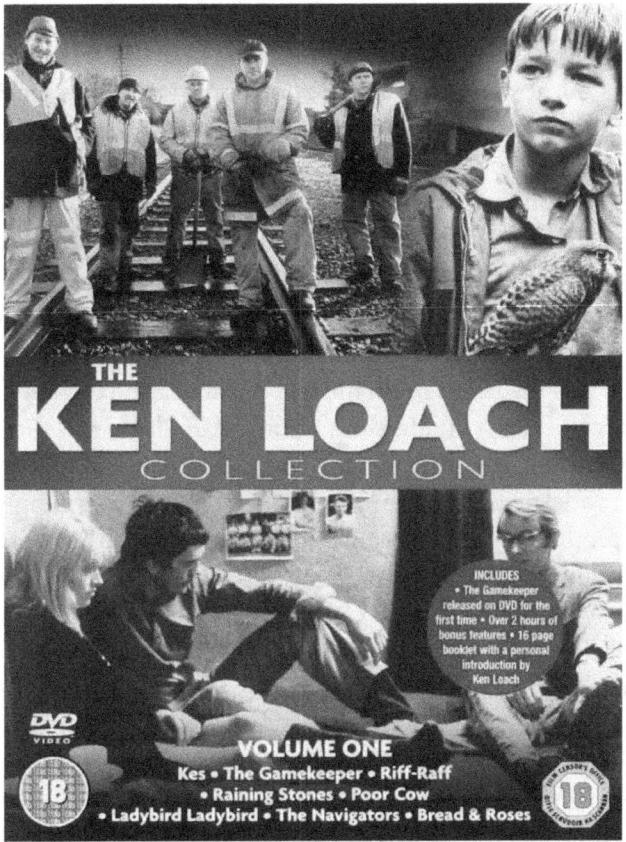

Figure 3.1 *The Ken Loach Collection* (Volume One) DVD cover

public recognition. Andy Willis notes that numerous major figures identified with British television drama's so-called 'Golden Age' were writers (2009: 300). Consequently, in contrast to film studies' focus on the director, the discourse around authorship in British television often centred on the writer. The subject of Willis's article is Jim Allen, who was influential in developing Loach's political outlook, and factoring the longer-term impact of Allen's Trotskyism into Loach's work disrupts *auteurist* discourses.[7] As I outlined in Chapter 1, Trotskyist thinking, particularly its focus on leadership, is evident in several projects on which they collaborated but also on projects which Loach developed without Allen, most explicitly, the television documentaries *A Question of Leadership* (ATV, 1981) and *Questions of Leadership* (Channel 4, 1983). John Caughie notes that in traditional French film criticism, the term *auteur* was utilised to refer to the

---

[7] For more on Allen see Paul Madden (1981).

scriptwriter or to the 'artist who created the film' (1981: 9). Writing more recently, Richard Corliss contends that the writer should be credited with *auteur* status because, as he puts it, 'Auteur criticism is essentially theme criticism; and themes – as expressed through plot, characterisation, and dialogue – belong primarily to the writer' (2008: 143).

Critics have pointed to differences in thematic concerns and formal qualities when analysing Loach's work with different writers. For instance, Dave Forrest (2019: 155) argues that in *Kes* (1969), *The Price of Coal* (1977), *The Gamekeeper* (1980) and *Looks and Smiles* (1981), 'Loach's familiar interest in class politics was reimagined with a pointedly lyrical, poetic voice' which was the result of 'an intense collaboration between Loach and [writer] Barry Hines'.[8] In addition, although *Fatherland* (1986), scripted by Trevor Griffiths, is politically and thematically consistent with Loach's output, its modernist, monochrome dreamscapes are strikingly dissimilar to the predominantly social realist aesthetic of the other work. In more recent films with Paul Laverty, who has scripted every full fictional feature bar *The Navigators* (2000) since *Carla's Song* (1996), there are times when socialist politics are evident, exemplified by the prominence given to the ideas of the Scottish Marxist, James Connolly, in *The Wind That Shakes the Barley* (2006); however, the Lessons of Defeat trope evident in the Allen scripts is less prominent. Laverty's screenplays, moreover, contain more experimental features than those scripted by Allen, exemplified by *Looking for Eric*'s fantasy sequences or *The Angels' Share*'s caperish, playful tone. It would be unwise to exaggerate the differences here, however, fuller examination of the involvement of the other writers with whom Loach has worked would tease out further thematic and formal differences.

In addition to the writers' influence, the long-term influence of other early Loach collaborators is evident. Formative is the relationship established with producer Tony Garnett who played a central role in most of the early work, from *Cathy Come Home* to *Black Jack* (1979), which were often identified as Loach–Garnett productions. In addition, the pair helped establish Kestrel Films which co-produced *Kes*. In interview, Garnett indicates something of the nature of their working relationship when he states that there are 'three things to making a film – What? How and Who?' and

[8] In their book-length study on Barry Hines, David Forrest and Sue Vice lament the marginalisation of the writer's work arguing that 'some of the fullest analyses of Hines's work take place at a remove, and without much mention of the writer himself' (2017: 10). They also argue for a greater recognition of Hines' role in the film, noting that, as with many of the writers that Loach works with, Hines was involved in casting, filming and editing and that 'his role in these works transcend that simply of writer' (10).

on the division of labour between the pair comments, 'I decided what we were gonna do. His job was the "How" question. We both sorted the "Who" question together.'[9] Garnett explicitly rejects auteurism when he states,

> It's a misunderstanding of what filmmaking is. A film is not like a novel with an author. A film is a result of complex social activity where a number of people who have precise skills are brought together in the hope that they can become a creative whole and a film will result. It is a journalistic conviction and, to their shame, a critical conviction.

Perhaps somewhat ironically, in his book-length study on Garnett, Stephen Lacey (2012: 5) suggests that the producer's work is characterised by an 'authorial signature', one which is 'intimately connected to a realist politics and aesthetics', thereby illustrating how film and television can be narrativised around producer-as-auteur discourses. Indeed, Powdermaker (1951: 100) suggests that Hollywood executives and producers had 'the greatest power to stamp the movies with their personal daydreams and fantasies'. Further to this, in Thomas Schatz's research on Hollywood (1988: 5–6), he highlights that directors such as John Ford, Howard Hawks, Frank Capra and Alfred Hitchcock, who had 'an unusual degree of authority and a certain style', earned this due to their status as producers rather than directors.[10] Schatz also suggests that commercial success was the basis for this authority. It was not, however, the producer's potential commercial power which accounts for Garnett's influence, but a recognition of the producer's creative role within British public sector broadcasting of the period.[11] As outlined in the previous chapter, Loach also cites the significant influence of cinematographer Chris Menges on his work.[12] The long-term influence of Allen, Garnett and Menges, then, problematises the director-as-auteur discourse whilst also highlighting that auteurism itself can accommodate different roles in the production process.

More recent scholarship on auteurism in television studies has focused on the producer, the writer, and the showrunner; the notion of negotiated, collective or multiple authorship has also been championed by a range of scholars (Gaut 1997; Mayer, Banks and Caldwell 2009; Hunter

---

[9] Interview with author.
[10] In their lengthy study of Hollywood, David Bordwell, Janet Staiger and Kristin Thompson (1985) also downplay the director's significance in the studio system.
[11] See Stephen Lacey (2012), particularly chapter one, 'From actor to producer: into the driving seat', pp. 11–33.
[12] For an account of the cinematographer as auteur see Philip Cowan (2012).

2016; Sellors 2007, 2010; Caldwell 2008). Whilst this research advances thinking about the complexities of production across both film and television, the notion of auteurism remains an ever-present barrier rather than a boon to understanding cinema. That film studies emerged in the arts and humanities helped foster an enlightenment focus on individual creativity, however, it has been at the expense of other perspectives. The word auteur is derived from the Latin word *auctorem*, which we might understand as founder, master or leader, and Loach's comments about football and teams outlined above are worth factoring in here. Like cinema, football is a collaborative project with leading roles played by specific individuals: we could trade club owners, managers, trainers and players for producers, directors, writers and actors (or players). There is a recognition, however, that at its heart, it is a team game. A cursory reading of the popular literature on football, including ex-Manchester United Football Club manager Alex Ferguson's *Leading* and ex-A. C. Milan and Real Madrid manager Carlo Ancelotti's *Quiet Leadership: Winning Hearts, Minds and Matches*, illustrates that this discourse foregrounds football's collaborative nature.[13] Individuals and leaders are important, but the focus is on teams, or more precisely, on the dialectical relationship between individuals and teams, a focus that remains underexplored in the scholarly understanding of film. My contention here is that film (and television) scholars could learn from how football, and indeed other team sports, are discussed and understood.

Team Loach

In partially rectifying this trend, in this part of the chapter I explore how teams and leadership function in the production of and the discourse surrounding Loach's more recent work. It is important first, however, to highlight some historical background pertaining to production.

For almost sixty years, Loach has created work in numerous production contexts, often negotiating the demands of corporations and institutions, and of the marketplace. Pierre Bourdieu's work on fields of cultural production highlights that 'The literary or artistic field is a field of forces, but

---

[13] In an echo of the slogans of the Paris 1968 student movement, Ferguson suggests that in football leadership the task 'was to make everyone understand that the impossible was possible' (2015: 239). In offering a 'leader as visionary' position it would be possible to contrast football's leader/manager dichotomy with cinema's *auteur/metteur en scène* division with the latter, for Bazin, a director, lacking a 'truly personal style' (quoted in Caughie 1981: 23).

it is also a field of struggles tending to transform or conserve this field of forces' (1993: 30). Bourdieu's concept allows us to better understand the structural factors, or field of forces, influencing the work Loach and his collaborators have created whilst negotiating this field of struggles. Although Loach has achieved considerable success, it has not been an unproblematic process. As outlined in the Introduction, in television, cuts have been required of work created for the BBC: the *Save the Children Fund Film* was consigned to a BFI vault for fifty years, documentaries have had delayed broadcasts, and Loach's cinematic output has also not been constant; rather, in keeping with the British film industry's fragile nature, there have been significant fallow periods.[14] As they moved into film production in the late 1960s, Loach and Garnett helped establish Kestrel Films which, as Jacob Leigh puts it (2002: 59), 'afforded Loach artistic freedom, albeit one related to the economic, social and political constraints of the British film and television industry'. In addition to *Kes*, Kestrel Films was credited as a production company on *After a Lifetime* (1971), *Save the Children Fund Film* (1971), *Family Life* (1971), *Black Jack* (1979) and *Looks and Smiles* (1981).[15]

Paradoxically, money from television, initially with the development of Channel 4 in the 1980s, enabled Loach to move back into film production following his difficult period making television documentaries. It is notable that production was never on a solid footing: for instance, files in the BFI Ken Loach archive indicate the perilous state of the financing of *Fatherland*.[16] Since the release of *Hidden Agenda* (1990), however, Loach's output has been increasingly regular. Initially this was through the cooperative production company, Parallax Pictures, which produced the films from *Riff-Raff* (1991) to *The Navigators* (2000). John Hill (2011: 158), however, suggests that 'it was only when he developed a relationship with [producers] Sally Hibbin and Rebecca O'Brien in the 1990s that his career

---

[14] Loach's credits as producer in several of the television documentaries should also be noted here.

[15] Kestrel Films also produced several other films, often associated with Garnett. A list is available at https://www.bfi.org.uk/films-tv-people/4ce2b9440ebcf (last accessed 28 October 2021). In addition, Kestrel II is listed as one of the production companies on *Fatherland*.

[16] Letter from executive producer Irving Teitelbaum to Ken Loach, 2 June 1986: 'The position there is very serious. It appears that we have to pay out £1,316.00 for the period up to 31st December, 1983 . . . I only hope that there will be enough money in the Fatherland Account to pay this, but I do have real anxieties', BFI Ken Loach archive, KCL-19-7-2.

managed to regain full momentum'. Loach and O'Brien subsequently established Sixteen Films which has produced the films from *Sweet Sixteen* (2002) to the present, enabling him significantly greater control over all aspects of production and increasingly put production on a sure financial footing.

As Loach's career developed it created possibilities to operate on a transnational plane and Huw Jones (2016: 369) highlights that Loach's prolific output since the 1990s is connected to successful co-productions. Jones also notes that earlier co-productions, including *Black Jack* and *Fatherland*, involved significant interference from their co-producing partners (2016: 374–5). To add to Jones's study, research at the BFI Ken Loach archive reveals that Loach faced direct interventions from the German co-producers of *Fatherland* who attempted to force changes to the film's final version.[17] Jones outlines that Loach had more successful experiences with Tornasol (Spain) and Road Movies (Germany), which were involved on a finance-only basis on several films from the mid 1990s to the mid 2000s. It was during this period that Sixteen Films made a significant step forward via collaborations with the French company, Why Not Productions, and European sales company, Wild Bunch, which have both acted as co-producers on the films since *Looking for Eric*.[18]

In turn, Sixteen Films has acted as co-producer on *Les Bien-aimés/The Beloved* (Honoré, France, UK, Czech Republic, 2011), which was led by Why Not, thereby developing the connection between the companies, and also worked as co-producing partners on significant films, most notably *You Were Never Really Here* (Ramsay, 2017). Eimhear McMahon suggests, 'The way that they work allows us to very simply finance our films, and reduce the amount of paperwork.'[19] In short, with Sixteen Films operating on a transnational basis, Loach has developed a solid production base

---

[17] Letter from Irving Teitelbaum to Fritz (presumably co-producer, Fritz Buttenstedt), undated: 'we must comment on your interference with the performers on the day of shooting itself. It is unprecedented in our own experience for a producer to ask actors not to say a particular line, as I believe you did to Genulf Pannach. Fortunately he had the determination to stick to the script', BFI Ken Loach archive, KCL-19-7-3v.

[18] It is perhaps no coincidence that it is a French-based company with which Loach has developed such a relationship. His work has long been more celebrated in France than in the UK, a point noted by Lucy Mazdon in the introduction to *Je t'aimé moi non plus: Franco-British cinematic relations* in which she notes that in the discussion of the success of British filmmakers in France, Loach is, as she puts it, an 'oft-cited example'. (Mazdon and Wheatley, 2010: 9)

[19] Interview with author.

Figure 3.2 Eric Cantona casts a glance at his footballing self in *Looking for Eric*

for his cinematic output, one which is unparalleled in his career. As the company has moved onto a more stable financial basis, this has prevented interference from co-producers over content and acted as a positive factor in terms of exhibition.[20] The process towards a more stable, and successful, production background illustrates tendency (9) in my analysis of Loach's method. Here, increased control of production, albeit one which relies on state funding and investment from public sector broadcasters and private film companies, has enabled greater creative freedom. This is the production context in which Loach has achieved consistent cinematic output, which includes ten full-length fictional features and two documentaries in a period spanning approximately two decades, and significant success as signified by a host of international awards, not least two Palmes d'Or for *The Wind That Shakes the Barley* and *I, Daniel Blake*.

Lamenting the scholarly attention paid to production in film studies, Steve Presence and Andrew Spicer suggest, 'Production companies are not only invisible to the general public, they are also, it appears, invisible to media scholars who continue to be preoccupied with individual writers and directors such as Paul Abbott or Shane Meadows without an understanding of these companies' production cultures to their creativity' (2016: 26). In developing insights into specific production conditions, production

---

[20] In contrast to the censorship problems Loach encountered with his documentary work in the 1980s, *The Spirit of '45* received widespread cinematic distribution, emblematic of Sixteen Films' international success and Loach's status as a commercially viable filmmaker.

studies have challenged film studies' once-dominant, and never quite abandoned, auteurist tendency, creating a more precise understanding of how film and television comes into existence. Presence and Spicer (2016: 6) note that Edgar Schein, a prominent scholar on organisational culture, suggests that analysing organisations involves comprehending three fields, 'artefacts, espoused beliefs and underlying assumptions'. For the purposes of this study, I take artefacts to be Sixteen Films' website and promotional material, espoused beliefs to be the production narratives surrounding their work, and underlying assumptions to be the manner (often unspoken) in which the company operates during the production process. In relation to artefacts, the importance of the team to the production process is evident in various aspects of Sixteen Films' public profile. The company's website profiles five individuals on its 'Team' page: Loach and O'Brien, but also Emma Lawson ('manages diaries, expectations, and swears like a trooper'), Habib Rahman (accountant) and Jack Thomas-O'Brien (Sixteen Films' head of development).[21] Loach and O'Brien are positioned at the top of the page, presenting something of a hierarchy, however, space afforded to each of the individuals is similar, pointing towards the espoused beliefs or the discourse of collaboration that the company promotes. For instance, when 'Sixteen Films & Friends (AKA Team Loach)' received The Special Jury Prize at the 2013 British Independent Film Awards, O'Brien furthered this discourse of collaboration: 'There are so many people behind the camera on Ken's films and so often they go unrecognised. And Ken would be the first person to acknowledge that.'[22] She continues by stressing the importance of teams: 'I think that there's something to be said for the sort of films that we've been able to make because we've worked with a team.'[23]

---

[21] http://www.sixteenfilms.co.uk/team (last accessed 29 October 2021). In a previous version of this chapter, I wrote, 'The company's website lists eight individuals in a "Team Album". In addition to Laverty, Loach and O'Brien, these are Camilla Bray, producer of two Sixteen Films productions not directed by Ken Loach, *Summer* (Glenaan, 2008) and *Oranges and Sunshine* (Jim Loach, 2009), accountant, Habib Rahman, Jack Thomas-O'Brien, whose credits include assistant producer on *Spirit of '45*, Eimhear McMahon, who has fulfilled various production roles since 2007, and Ann Cattrall, Loach's PA.' This was based on analysis of the website on 24 December 2016, conducted for research which was published as (2017) 'Team Loach and Sixteen Films: Authorship, Collaboration, Leadership (and Football)', in Ewa Mazierska and Lars Kristensen (eds) *Contemporary Cinema and Ideology: Neoliberal Capitalism and Its Alternatives in Filmmaking*, New York and London: Routledge.

[22] This interview is available to view at http://www.youtube.com/watch?v=TZ3Q8gmhuH0 (last accessed 31 October 2021).

[23] Ibid.

O'Brien, who co-produced *Hidden Agenda* and has produced all of Loach's films since *The Flickering Flame: A Story of Contemporary Morality* (BBC, 1996), has been central in ensuring the run of films since the mid 1990s, in terms of quantity of product, but also critical and commercial success, and argues that 'casting the crew is as crucial as casting the actors'.[24] Notably, the company works regularly with many of the same production crew. As indicated previously, an almost ever-present part of the 'team' in recent years has been Paul Laverty, and, signifying the central creative position which the company places on the writer, in marketing materials, something approaching equal billing is allocated to Laverty and Loach.[25]

In relation to cinematography, although since the late 1960s Loach worked primarily with Chris Menges and Barry Ackroyd, Robbie Ryan has shot *The Angels' Share*, *Jimmy's Hall*, *I, Daniel Blake* and *Sorry We Missed You*. George Fenton has provided the music for all feature-length films since *Ladybird Ladybird* (1994). Jonathan Morris has edited every feature-length film since *Fatherland*. Ray Beckett, sound mixer/recordist, has worked on every film since *Raining Stones*. Designer Martin Johnson worked on *Days of Hope*, then *Black Jack* and all major productions until *Ae Fond Kiss . . . .* Following Johnson's death in 2003, Fergus Clegg, who had previously worked as art director on the seven films between *Raining Stones* and *Ae Fond Kiss . . .*, was assigned the role of production designer and has worked in that capacity on the features since, from *The Wind That Shakes the Barley* to *Sorry We Missed You*. Joss Barratt worked as stills photographer on all fictional features from *Carla's Song* to *Sorry We Missed You* bar *My Name is Joe* and *Bread and Roses* and Kahleen Crawford has been casting director on every film since *Ae Fond Kiss . . . .* This list is not exhaustive, but it illustrates that there is a team of regular production crew behind the camera, as well as in the production office.[26] Moreover, the existence of the team of individuals who regularly return to work together contributes to a shared, and often unarticulated, understanding of their creative practice, or, following Schein, the underlying assumptions about their working methodologies. One instance which illustrates the nature of this unspoken ethos is that the gaffer on *The Angels' Share*, Andy Cole, comments on how he picks up

[24] Interview with author.
[25] This is evident, for instance, on *The Angels' Share* DVD cover which reads 'DIRECTED BY KEN LOACH AND WRITTEN BY PAUL LAVERTY'. Although Loach is listed first, both names are presented in the same font size, which is unusual in film marketing as it tends to focus on the director (in the absence of a famous star or writer).
[26] Loach does not use the same actors on a regular basis. See Chapter 4 for more on performance.

the aesthetic approach that is desired: 'You look around you and you feel what they want,' he comments. 'I learned on the recce with Ken that he really didn't want to distract his actors.' When asked if Loach gave specific instructions, he replies, 'No, I felt it. He never said it outright. He said it in indirect ways. You just gauge it, and you pick it up as you go along.'[27]

Of course, working with the same team members is dependent on having the institutional status to support it. Loach, in interview in 1982, stated of his earlier years at the BBC: 'You can't maintain working relationships with people who work outside the BBC, which I think is very damaging.'[28] It is having the reins to the company which creates the opportunity for Team Loach to be developed on its own terms. While my focus in this chapter has been on the more recent films, in 1980 Garnett had already identified this process at work: 'We see films as a social activity, a collaborative art. Films aren't novels, they're a collective creation. Our editors work very closely with us, and we have established a core working crew over the last decade and a half.'[29] Having increased control of production enables the team dynamic to come into being in this specific manner. Paul Dave (2006: 71) suggests that the deployment of the term 'team' works to 'abolish the division of labour between "worker" and "boss" with a new collective – the team'. While there is merit in Dave's critique of neoliberal managerialism, the inclusion of 'Loach' in 'Team Loach' appears to accurately describe the relation between the leadership and the collective in the making of Sixteen Films' output.

During my participant observation and interviews, it became apparent that there was a strong team ethos on set, one which is established from the top, that is, primarily from Loach and O'Brien. As Garnett's comments indicate, this is a long-standing method to the work. In interview, he also suggests that in their formative productions they sought to provide a safe and welcoming environment for actors to operate in, and to

> create an atmosphere on the set of love, of acceptance. An assumption that they are good. So that they can relax. That we believe in them so they start to believe in themselves. The atmosphere must be quiet, affectionate. And when they are offered that, they relax. So they can just be.

The driver here may well have been performance (which I discuss further in Chapter 4), however, this also appears to be the approach taken with the crew. This 'atmosphere' maps onto the underlying assumptions

---

[27] Interview with the author.
[28] Quoted in Petley (1982: 9).
[29] Quoted in Quart (1980: 28).

described above and is characterised by respect for each other's work, a sense that everyone is working to create something greater than their own specific contribution, and that the team combined is working on a project of importance and value, aesthetically and politically. In addition, there was an expectation that the outcome would have significant profile and a healthy shelf life. Notably, not all of Loach's collaborators voiced support for Loach's politics, rather, it was support for the film and the opportunity to be involved in its production that were the dominant drivers. James Burns (1978: 19) suggests that successful leaders build relationships with their collaborators (he deploys the term followers) based on developing a shared sense of wants and needs. This process emerges during interview as Loach's collaborators often express the view that, although they were working to create a shared project, their own specific contribution was valued, thereby meeting individual and collective needs. What also emerged from my observations is that although there is a discourse of collectivism and collaboration, reflecting a togetherness, intercorporeality or even solidarity, Loach has a hands-on individual leadership role across all aspects of the production, as is evidenced by the comments from crew members on locations, casting and set design in the previous chapter. A more unusual example of Loach's direct interventionist approach emerges in interview when Jas Brown, one of the drivers, recounts a story that when scouting for locations on previous Scottish-based films, Loach would at any moment ask him to stop the minibus so that he could dart up a tenement close (common Glaswegian usage for stairwell) and survey its usefulness as a possible location, thereby earning Loach the nickname 'Head of Closes'.

My observations from the cutting room, albeit brief, also reinforced the idea that Loach is attendant throughout the entire process, sitting by, or slightly behind, Morris as they discuss the choices to be made, building the story frame by frame. In interview with Loach he states, 'Jonathan's opinions count – in every shot. It's a cliché to say that it's a collective but it clearly is.'[30] This is echoed by Morris: 'We're working on the cut together so his cut is my cut and my cut is his cut.'[31] Moreover, it also emerged through interview that Loach has a strong and specific idea of what he wants from other team members. For instance, cinematographer Robbie Ryan rather modestly downplays his own role to suggest that the director almost always knows what set-up to use when positioning the camera. Ryan adds, 'He's very adept at knowing what is needed. He's kind of got a cameraman's mind.

[30] Interview with author.
[31] Interview with author.

All I'm helping do is realise that vision.'[32] Ryan's comments are typical of the comments I received from the crew who speak with a remarkable level of respect for Loach as a filmmaker, as an employer, but also as an individual. For instance, Jonathan Morris states, 'This is the plum job that we all want – to work with Ken.'[33] When asked to expand on why this is the case, he points to Loach's personal qualities and offers, 'First and foremost it's him.'[34] Locations manager Michael Higson confirms that one of the attractions of working with Loach is that 'you get a chance to have an input', highlighting the balance between individual and collective contributions.[35] Responding to a similar question, production designer Fergus Clegg suggests, 'It's always been very collaborative,' contrasting his experience of working with Loach to most other productions on which he had worked: 'A lot of films end up in very compartmentalised groups vying for attention or power.'[36] Clegg adds that it is rare for such a team to be developed in film and comments: 'People wouldn't come back if they didn't enjoy it. If I get a sniff of a job, two years in advance, working with Ken then I will make sure that that window is clear.' First assistant director David Gilchrist expresses a similar sentiment when he states that on the occasions when O'Brien has advised him that a job is forthcoming, 'I've knocked back other work and made myself unemployed to make myself available to take that job,' and adds, 'If I was asked back, I would always do what I can to make myself available.'[37] Interviewing Why Not's Pascal Caucheteux on his desire to collaborate with Sixteen Films and Loach, he casts his response in auteurist terms, and points to their shared interest in cinema.[38] An example of what Mette Hjort might term 'auteurist transnationalism' (2010), Caucheteux stresses that the factor motivating his desire to work with Loach – who he described as pro-Palestinian, and with Claude Lanzmann (most wellknown for *Shoah*, 1985) who he described as pro-Israeli – was Loach and Lanzmann's status as 'Masters', not their politics. He also emphasises, however, aspects of Loach's character – humility and honesty – and their shared love of football, pointing to Why Not's involvement with *Looking for Eric* as the starting point for their relationship.[39] Notably, several of Loach's collab-

---

[32] Interview with author.
[33] Interview with author.
[34] Ibid.
[35] Interview with author.
[36] Interview with author.
[37] Interview with author.
[38] Interview with author.
[39] Why Not do have an involvement in Sixteen Films' production process. For instance,

orators discuss the director in auteurist terms: for instance, Rona Munro, who scripted *Ladybird Ladybird*, states,

> I did know that he's an auteur in the sense that it is one vision, it's not a collective film process. It operates as a collective because everyone's given equal status, but you're working as a collective to make a Ken Loach film, and I think that's fair enough because he's brilliant.[40]

As such, there is an ongoing tension between Loach's rejection of the auteur label, the development of team discourse, and Loach's leadership role in making the work.

As I indicated in the Introduction, I am aware of the dangers of simply replicating dominant production narratives from material sourced in interview and cognisant of the fact that many of the interviewees are talking about someone who employs them on a regular basis. Nevertheless, Anthony Hayward appears to corroborate the regard in which Loach is viewed by his collaborators when he noted that in his interviews for *Which Side Are You On? Ken Loach and His Films*, Loach's collaborators 'talked of him [Loach] in such hallowed tones that I often wondered whether I was writing about a saint' (2004: 2).[41] In his work on leadership, Max Weber argues that there are three sources of personal authority – traditional, legal-rational and charismatic. Of the latter, Weber suggests that it relates to 'an extraordinary quality of a person, regardless of whether this quality is actual, alleged or presumed' (1948: 295). Repeatedly in interview, Loach's collaborators said that they regarded him as having extraordinary qualities as a filmmaker, but also as an individual. These qualities were critical in ensuring the interviewees' continuing involvement with Sixteen Films. So, although I am arguing for a rejection of the term 'auteur', I am not arguing for the rejection of recognising the contribution of prominent individuals to the filmmaking process: Loach's qualities as an individual, as a filmmaker, and as a leader, are pivotal to the success of Team Loach.

It is worthwhile contrasting my research findings with Powdermaker's, who suggests that while there is a general recognition in Hollywood that-

---

their staff visited *The Angels' Share* set in Glasgow and attended a screening of the rough cut in London. According to Caucheteux, however, their involvement is light-touch: although they can comment on draft scripts and rough cuts, he states in interview, 'We are not going to give Ken Loach a lesson in filmmaking.'

[40] Quoted in John Tulloch (1999).
[41] This trend is also evident in the BBC Radio 4's *Kaleidoscope Feature: Carla's Song*, which was based on Mike Gonzalez's observations of the making of the film. Transmitted 7 September 1996.

filmmaking is a collaborative enterprise, individuals and groups jostle constantly for domination. She argues, 'The overt verbal behavior in all these relationships is that of love and friendship. Warm words of endearment and great cordiality set the tone. But underneath is hostility amounting frequently to hatred, and, even more important, a lack of respect for each other's work' (1951: 29). This position is also endorsed in Schatz's study of Hollywood when he notes that 'studio filmmaking was less a process of collaboration than of negotiation and struggle – occasionally approaching armed conflict' (1988: 12). Powdermaker suggests that Hollywood is marked by 'a striking and complete lack of mutual respect as well as trust. The *esprit de corps* of the industry is exceedingly low' (1951: 295–6). Although I did witness the occasional minor conflict between individuals, which is perhaps inevitable in any workplace, the *esprit de corps* on *The Angels' Share* set was high, and the crew in particular seemed to have a strong sense of respect for their collaborating partners.

Peter Gallagher, line producer on *The Angels' Share* and also *The Navigators*, *Sweet Sixteen* and *Ae Fond Kiss . . .*, comments on the Monday morning production meetings which take place during filming: 'Normally on a film you would have one production meeting at the beginning of the film and it's not run by the director, it's run by the assistant director and the producer, and the director is there to input as it were, not really to run it. Whereas with Ken, the production meetings are run by Ken, chaired by him and the discussion is steered by him.'[42] He laughs and adds, 'But he does it always in a way which never leads you to suspect that he's controlling things.'[43] The nature of the Team Loach power dynamics are also developed in interview when Joss Barratt affectionately describes Loach as the leader of a 'collective autocracy'. He then adds, 'It's not meant in a negative way, it's meant in an analytical, sociological way.'[44] When I put this to Loach he rejected the phrase, suggesting that it contains 'the whiff of the jackboot'; but he also states,

> You can't do it without leadership otherwise it would just disintegrate. The unit's got to work with a common voice and that's what the director has got to find. It's got to be a voice that everybody feels is their own,

---

[42] Interview with author.
[43] Ibid.
[44] Interview with author. Barratt also adds, 'Ken has a very intensely specific way of being ferocious with the outcome but very humane as a person.' When I ask Ryan about the notion of Loach as autocrat, he laughs uproariously and then says, 'I would agree with that. As autocrats go, he's a nice one. You don't meet many people like Ken, he's a true gentleman.'

but equally it's got to be unified so that the trick really is to try and get both.⁴⁵

Loach's thinking here chimes with the comments from Munro above, however, in casting leadership not in terms of vision, as Munro does, but as a form of polyphonic unification, Loach's response, and his directorial approach in general, brings to mind legendary football manager Bill Shankly's words when discussing the success of Glasgow Celtic Football Club manager Jock Stein:

> If he's got useful players, and he trains them the right way and he gets them all to do what they can do well. The little things that they can do, and he merges them all together, it's a form of socialism you know, without the politics, of course.⁴⁶

In highlighting Stein's leadership qualities, Shankly's comments suggest that politics is always embedded in the mode of production, and in this instance finds expression in the concept of teams, but teams which are led. Loach previously flagged the power dynamic on set as follows: 'I can't use the word democracy really because what I do is quite manipulative in the end – it has to be. Only one or two people are looking through the lens and so only one or two people can make the judgements about what needs to happen' (Fuller 1998: 114). There is a parallel, then, with the mode of production of Loach's work, and the recurring theme of leadership in the films, as outlined above, however, this is also the case in relation to teams.

Teams in the films

Given Sixteen Films' 'artefacts, espoused beliefs and underlying assumptions', it is appropriate that football teams and supporters feature regularly in Loach's output, including *The Golden Vision* (BBC, 1968), *Kes*, *My Name is Joe* (1998), *Tickets* (2005), *Ae Fond Kiss . . .*, *It's a Free World . . .*, *Looking for Eric* and *Sorry We Missed You*.

This is indicative of a wider interest in teams: although several films in Loach's *oeuvre* centre on individual characters, as is indicated often by the titles – *Cathy Come Home*, *Carla's Song*, *My Name is Joe* – the importance

---

[45] Interview with the author.
[46] This quote is available to view in archive footage at https://www.youtube.com/watch?v=XnsQw5gG3Nk (last accessed 3 January 2021).

Figure 3.3 The celebrated football scene from *Kes*, replete with on-screen scores

of the collective recurs regularly. For instance, we have the criminal gang in *A Tap on the Shoulder* (BBC, 1965) and the drug-dealing, pizza-delivery gang in *Sweet Sixteen*. Indicative of their increased marginalisation and emasculation, trade unions have featured significantly less in Loach's work since the 1980s, however, we still have groups of workers suffering the effects of weakened trade union organisation in *Riff-Raff* (1991), *Bread and Roses* (2000), *The Navigators*, *It's a Free World . . .* and *Sorry We Missed You*, with revolutionary militias featuring in *Land and Freedom*. Collectivism is not fetishised: in contrast to the groups of organised trade unionists who assemble to discuss their working conditions in *The Big Flame* and *The Rank and File*, *The Navigators* reveals how discourses on teams have been co-opted under neoliberal capitalism. In one scene, a group of rail workers is called to a meeting, but not to discuss union organisation; rather, management have assembled them to watch a company promotional video during which the managing director states, 'There are no limits to what this team can achieve together.' That *The Navigators* concludes with the death of one of their number both critiques the privatisation of the railways that forms the film's background and the neoliberal appropriation of discourses on collaboration and collectivism.

There is also a strong sense of leadership in *The Angels' Share* team. Although Albert, Mo and Rhino have their separate talents, Robbie is the undisputed team leader: in addition to his nascent 'nose' for whisky, the whisky heist is his idea, he develops the plan to conduct it but keeps it secret from the others, he steals the whisky, negotiates the deal with Thaddeus, and also makes executive decisions about dividing the spoils by giving one of the remaining two bottles to Harry. Robbie controls all aspects of the operation, and while each of the gang receive £25,000, ensuring an equal division of the money, there is no equal division of decision-making. In the conclusion, moreover, it is Robbie who departs with his happy family, his future seemingly secure, while the others head to a local hostelry in pursuit of inebriation.

Overall, then, teams are represented as forces for progressive change and spaces for social and political action, embedding alternative approaches to how we might live in the future in the collective solidarities of the present. In *Looking for Eric*, postal worker Eric (Steve Evets) asks his namesake, Eric Cantona, what was the 'sweetest moment' of his footballing career, perhaps expecting to hear of one of the French international's numerous celebrated goals for Manchester United. 'It was a pass,' Cantona responds, before the film cuts to archive footage of him sending an exquisite, clipped ball to Denis Irwin who then scores against Spurs. 'What if he had missed?' asks the postal worker. When Cantona replies, 'You have to trust your teammates, always. If not, we are lost,' it furthers this team discourse, highlights the dialectical interaction between individual talent and teamwork, and the importance of remembering and recognising the contribution of both.

Conclusion

The term 'Team Loach' clearly flags that filmmaking is a collaborative enterprise whilst simultaneously reinforcing Loach's centrality in the production process. Although auteurist discourses can be cognisant of filmmaking's collaborative nature, clearly one of its downsides has been a tendency to erase the labour and artistic input of other film production workers. What I have attempted to do here is illustrate the contribution of several creative individuals, but more importantly their status as part of a creative team, in the production of Loach's more recent output. Reflecting on film studies' engagement with auteurism, John Caughie writes,

> The work of theory is still contestatory, moving forward dialectically, rather like Walter Benjamin's Angel of History, continually looking backwards to pick up any fragments which may have been lost in the rubble of earlier encounters. The questions of art and authorship, creativity and imagination, may still prove an irritant in our attempts to come to terms with our complex engagements with cinema. (2007: 421)

In striving to come to terms with the work of Ken Loach and Sixteen Films, we can add leadership, collaboration, and football to the mix. I realise that there may appear to be an apparent contradiction between arguing that the auteur figure is a hindrance in understanding film and television, whilst, simultaneously, arguing for an engagement with the contribution of specific creative individuals in the production process, nevertheless, to develop a fuller understanding of the processes by which film and television comes into existence, it seems vital.

4
Performance

> For an actor to be effective on the screen it is not enough for him to be understandable. He has to be truthful.
> Andrei Tarkovsky (2003: 155)

> When Rebecca phoned me up and said about the part, I said, 'I'm not an actor,' and she said, 'That's the point. Ken likes you just to be yourself.'
> Charles MacLean (Rory McAllister)[1]

One wet morning, sometime early in 2005, a small bus winds its way through the quiet country lanes of West Cork. Inside, twenty or thirty men regaled in green and brown military attire are belting out anthemic Irish Republican songs as the grassy-green landscape glides slowly by. The men are en route to film the ambush of a group of British soldiers during the Irish War of Independence and seem to be relishing this opportunity to get into character. I am with them, although not in costume, gathering material for an on-location newspaper feature on the film they are preparing for, *The Wind That Shakes the Barley*. When I ask the red-headed man sitting next to me, William Ruane, what he expects from the day, he responds that he anticipates a confrontation but is uncertain of detail.[2] His contract is soon to expire, he says, and, as such, is braced for his character's death, but he hopes for a stay of execution, for his character and for his contract. This encounter highlights something of the ongoing tension between the true and the false, the authentic and the artificial, the real and the constructed, that is embodied in the relationship between actor and character as they enter and assemble the fictional cosmos in Loach's cinema.

---

[1] Interview with author.
[2] Ruane plays Rhino in *The Angels' Share*.

As outlined in Chapter 2, Loach often discusses his work in discourses of truth and authenticity, discourses which are also brought to bear on performance. In press coverage of *The Angels' Share*, for example, Loach uses the term 'emotional truth' to describe Paul Brannigan's performance as Robbie.[3] His collaborators often do likewise: for instance, in identifying Loach's directorial strengths, Tony Garnett comments, 'Ken just gets truthful moments better than anyone I've ever come across.'[4] Phillip B. Zarrilli (1995: 9) highlights the prevalence of discourses of truth in performance and articulates the rationale behind it when he notes,

> The use of 'believe' or its commonplace synonym 'be honest' by many acting teachers and directors stems from the predominant viewpoint implicit in realistic acting that a character must conform to everyday social reality as constructed from the spectator's point of view. The audience needs to be convinced that the character is behaving as s/he would in 'ordinary life' within the 'given circumstances' of the scene.

Such discourses may well be applicable to realist aesthetics, which are predicated on constructing characters whose actions are as believable as the fictional worlds they inhabit. That Andrei Tarkovsky in this chapter's epigraph discusses his surrealist-tinged, experimental cinematic practice, with its religious undertones and visually arresting cinematography, in similar terms indicates its purchase beyond realism. As Philip Auslander observes (2002: 60), 'Theorists as diverse as Stanislavsky, Brecht and Grotowski all implicitly designate the actor's self as the logos of performance; all assume that the actor's self precedes and grounds her performance and that it is the presence of this self in performance that provides the audience with access to human truths.' As cinema increasingly circulates in hyper-mediated landscapes in which actors' lives generate more column inches than critical responses to the films themselves, the concept of an unmediated truth is difficult to conjure. Even to discuss an actor's performance highlights its fictivity; however, rather than focusing solely on pre-existing truth in performance, we might factor in Gilles Deleuze's (1985: 147) observa-

---

[3] Quoted in Catherine Shoard (2012) '*The Angels' Share*'s Paul Brannigan: "I've been slashed, stabbed and shot at"', *The Guardian*, 31 May 2012, https://www.theguardian.com/film/2012/may/31/the-angels-share-paul-brannigan (last accessed 15 February 2021). This is indicative of the press response, which also draws on similar forms of discourse. For example, a *Boston Herald* review describes Brannigan as a 'natural', https://www.bostonherald.com/2013/04/26/take-drink-from-angels-share/ (last accessed 3 November 2021).
[4] Interview with author. All subsequent quotes from Garnett in this chapter are taken from this interview.

tion that the artist (or actor) is *'creator of truth*, because truth is not to be achieved, formed or reproduced; it has to be created'. Rather than develop a false binary between the true and the false in performance, then, the two co-exist in a constantly evolving and unresolvable tension, one which has been ever-present in Loach's work.

Whilst studying law at Oxford University, Loach acted in and directed student theatre productions and, following graduation, had several minor acting roles in professional theatre before starting at the BBC. In 1968, he drew on this background to lay out his thoughts on acting in an A5 BBC notebook, which is now housed at the BFI Ken Loach archive. Here, he suggests that 'Traditional theatrical' acting was characterised by a 'long period of rehearsal, then presentation' and 'Traditional cinema' by 'short rehearsal, mainly concerned with marks on studio floor'.[5] He argues that television acting 'combines worst of both: the action is robbed of spontaneity by detailed repetition, then hammered lifeless by actors looking for marks'.[6] He then advances his own approach: 'Aim in Realistic play is to make it appear that something is happening for first time,' and cites 'springing surprises on actors', and 'treating actors as inventive people rather (than professional robots)' as appropriate methods for creating moments of 'genuine exchange'.[7] He turns his attention to locations and suggests that this is 'impossible in T.V. studios' and concludes by stating that he sees it as his 'Duty to present issues of modern society with clarity & truth – as far as one can.'[8]

These brief words summarise Loach's early approach and he has subsequently developed a unique method of working with actors: casting both professional and non-professionals, often those who share character similarities with those they will play on-screen; location shooting; linear shooting; minimal use of rehearsals; restricting actors' access to the script and minimising the presence of the cinematic apparatus on set. These methods have resulted in numerous celebrated performances from first-time actors, including David Bradley (*Kes*), Chrissie Rock (*Ladybird Ladybird*), Martin Compston (*Sweet Sixteen*) and Paul Brannigan (*The Angels' Share*).[9] The performances from first-time actors have garnered great critical and public attention, correlating with Jennifer Beth Spiegel's

[5] BFI Ken Loach archive, KCL 4/8/2.
[6] Ibid.
[7] Ibid.
[8] Ibid.
[9] For her performance, Rock received Best Actor Award at the Berlinale. Actors in *The Angels' Share* also achieved recognition with Siobhan Reilly and Paul Brannigan both

(2020: 122) observation that the 'performance of the amateur is presumed pure, untainted by the disciplinary training and career aspirations of the professional'. Throughout his career, however, Loach, has also cast numerous established actors in prominent roles, including Terence Stamp (*Poor Cow*), Frances McDormand (*Hidden Agenda*), Adrien Brody (*Bread and Roses*), Robert Carlyle (*Carla's Song*), Peter Mullan (*My Name is Joe*) and Cillian Murphy (*The Wind That Shakes the Barley*).[10]

In this chapter, I offer some insights into how these performances are created in *The Angels' Share*, integrating observations from casting sessions and the shoot with interviews with Loach, Laverty, casting director Kahleen Crawford, Tony Garnett, line producer Peter Gallagher, and several actors, and from research at the BFI Ken Loach archive. This material is used to illuminate tendencies (10) realist casting, (11) pared-down set, and (12) linear shooting and withholding script of Certain Tendencies in Loach's Cinema, demonstrating how the filmmakers and actors operate as creators of truths, and falsehoods.

Casting

In the documentary *Casting By* (Donahue, 2012), Martin Scorsese suggests that 'More than 90 per cent of directing the picture is the right casting'. This figure has previously been apocryphally attributed to numerous directors from John Ford to Elia Kazan, however, even allowing for some exaggeration from these master storytellers, there is a disparity between how filmmakers view casting's importance and the quantity of scholarly literature on the topic. This absence correlates with the lack of access to this aspect of film production, with film scholars relying mainly on materials released by film publicists and in filmmakers' and actors' publicity interviews; observing the process in action and conducting on-set interviews enables a fuller understanding to emerge.[11]

---

nominated for the 2012 British Academy of Film and Television Association Scotland Award for Best Actor, which Brannigan won.

[10] Notably, Mullan received the Best Actor Award at Cannes. In interview on the set of *The Wind That Shakes the Barley*, O'Brien advised me that they were initially reluctant to cast Murphy because his film-star good looks made him stand out from the rest of the cast and threatened to disrupt the perceived authentic image of early-twentieth-century rural life in Cork that they sought to depict. She added, though, that his skills as an actor were evident in workshops and this eventually outweighed their fears.

[11] For a discussion of what she describes as 'casting with a conscience' and further ques-

In interview, Crawford outlines the unique nature of Loach's casting methods. Firstly, she notes that whereas on regular film productions a star actor's potential to raise finance can influence casting decisions, the relatively successful position that Sixteen Films has secured frees them from this pressure. Consequently, there is 'total freedom to pick the right person for the job regardless of who they are, what they've done, if they're famous, or not.'[12] She adds, 'You don't have executive producers involving themselves in casting decisions. Ken and I can pretty much do what Ken and I, and Rebecca and Paul, want, because Rebecca and Paul are very much involved in the big parts and then we do everything else.' The second difference she identifies is the amount of time spent on the process, noting that Sixteen Films contracted her from November 2010 to June 2011, a period considerably longer than what would be normal for a comparable project, thereby ensuring greater time to discover new people beyond existing or established contacts.[13] Thirdly, there is no restriction on resources and budget, in terms of travel and ancillary expenses incurred in searching for new potential actors. Finally, she notes that working with a high proportion of first-time actors involves greater levels of pastoral care than might normally be case: 'You get much more involved with actors on Ken's films. I'm the first face they see and something of a comfort blanket.'

In casting *The Angels' Share*, Crawford notes that the process begins with the writer. Whilst researching the conditions and problems his characters might face, Laverty encounters individuals whose lives mirror the screenplay's characters and passes a list of any potential actors to Crawford.[14]

tions of casting and authenticity in *The Wire* (HBO, 2002–8), see Lisa Kelly, 'Casting *The Wire*: Complicating Notions of Performance, Authenticity, and "Otherness"', *darkmatter: in the ruins of imperial culture*, 29 May 2009, http://www.darkmatter101.org/site/2009/05/29/casting-the-wire-complicating-notions-of-performance-authenticity-and-otherness/ (last accessed 18 December 2021).

[12] Interview with author. Subsequent quotes from Crawford in this chapter are also from this interview. In contrast, John Hill notes (2011: 203) that Loach struggled to raise the finance for *Land and Freedom* because he was 'reluctant to go down the "American star" route'.

[13] The June date coincided with the conclusion of principal photography and Crawford was on location through much of the shoot. As a point of comparison, in interview Crawford states that the time allocated for casting the three-hour television series, *Young James Herriot* (BBC, 2010–11) was three to four weeks and that even three to four months would be a long time for her to be contracted to work on a film.

[14] Crawford has worked on all Loach fictional features since *Ae Fond Kiss* . . . . She states in interview that on her initial films, Loach initially sat in with all casting sessions, but

The list also contains individuals from organisations encountered during research, which Crawford then contacts to pursue potential cast members, a process related to the desire to cast actors with similar socio-economic backgrounds to their character.[15] Bertolt Brecht suggests that effective actors must have a progressive political outlook:

> Without opinions and objectives one can represent nothing at all. Without knowledge one can show nothing; how could one know what would be worth knowing? Unless the actor is satisfied to be a parrot or a monkey he must master our period's knowledge of human social life by himself joining in the war of the classes. (1978: 196)

Loach, however, often casts actors committed to their character's world view, rather than his own political positions. For instance, whilst interviewing Cillian Murphy on the set of *The Wind That Shakes the Barley*, Murphy expressed to me an affinity with his character's Irish Republican politics. McDonald (2000: 30) suggests that in narrative cinema the believability of performance is predicated on the extent to which actors become their characters and that 'reading a performance involves bringing together of actor and character'. American method acting is famously, if falsely, understood to involve actors living the role in preparation for the performance, thereby partially collapsing the actor/character division. By casting actors who share their characters' backgrounds, Loach ensures that the actors will be unavoidably living both something of their own and of their character's experience as they prepare. There is something in Loach's approach to casting, then, which echoes Stanislavski's assertion (2008) that the actor cannot remove himself from his own body and simply replace it. Actors, in this sense, always embody themselves in performance and Loach's method involves the actor drawing on, even if inadvertently, both private and socio-political experience as they perform 'versions of themselves' in fictional situations. This is not a fetishised approach, however, and experienced actors have been cast in roles beyond their own experience, for instance, Ray Winstone as the abusive father figure in *Ladybird Ladybird* and David Hayman as the gangland leader in *My Name is Joe*.

---

he now normally sees a selection of Crawford's choosing. Echoing the Team Loach group dynamics outlined in Chapter 4, in interview Crawford speaks about Loach in terms approaching the status of a father figure and also states that when O'Brien calls with dates for the next production, 'You just do that, no questions asked. You just clear your diary.'

[15] Information from author's interview with Crawford.

In interview before the main roles in *The Angels' Share* had been cast, Laverty comments on one young man he had recommended to Crawford, suggesting he is typical of the people he encounters during his research:

> Like Paul Brannigan, for example, a little fella we met in research who'd been to prison, who'd lived an absolutely chaotic life and then had started working with street gangs. He was a fantastic kid and you think 'let's give him a chance' and we were at a casting session with him yesterday. He was absolutely marvellous. Never acted in his life before, but he'd lived these experiences. Who knows what will come of it? But there's a whole list of suggestions like that.[16]

Laverty first encountered Brannigan while conducting research at Strathclyde Police's Violence Reduction Unit, where, at the time, the latter was coaching local young people in football.[17] Brannigan's own life mirrors his character's: born in Glasgow's East End, his parents were habitual drug users, he had attempted suicide as a teenager, been involved in gangland feuding, served an extensive prison sentence for violent crimes, had recently fathered a child, and was attempting to go straight.[18] It is not, however, simply a task of finding people with similar backgrounds to the characters, they must also be able to act. In interview, Loach states that in casting the lead role the task is to find an individual with the capacity to, as he puts it, 'carry the film'.[19] As such, potential actors' skills are tested in extensive workshops with experienced actors, and from this process, Brannigan emerged as the favoured candidate and was cast in the lead role.[20]

In investing significant resources and time to find the appropriate people, Crawford arranges extensive interviews with actors. She notes, 'Ken and I would hold days where I would bring in thirty actors. We would ... chat to them about where they're from, what their families do, how they got into acting.' Of Loach's approach to casting she says, 'He puts faith in people's characters more than their experience. He doesn't read their CVs because he's not interested, it's just that he's more interested in their

---

[16] Interview with author.
[17] Information from interview with Laverty.
[18] Information from interview with Brannigan.
[19] Interview with author.
[20] In interview, Crawford adds that they organise group sessions with all potential actors to ensure that there is a dynamic between them, and suggests that, as she puts it, 'It's about combinations.' As an example, she notes that, although John Henshaw was provisionally cast to play Harry, he went through group rehearsals to test the dynamic with the group of youngsters.

characters.' In casting *The Angels' Share*, Sixteen Films also advertised on a local recruitment website for the parts of Mo and Leonie, and I attended an afternoon of meetings during which Loach interviewed some of the 900 respondents which Crawford had shortlisted.[21] During the interviews, Loach asks several questions to the thirty or so interviewees who attended; notably, none are about previous acting experience. Three questions recur, paraphrased roughly as: 'Where do you live?', 'Are you working at present?' and, less frequently, 'What do you think about your boss?' The answers to these questions geographically situate the respondent, establish their class position, and their attitude to it, whilst also allowing for an assessment of the applicants' general presence, diction, confidence and manner. Loach concludes by asking the attendees for permission to take their photograph, a task which Crawford undertakes, and he concludes the interview positively by stating that they may be in touch. In the end, the two women cast both had some acting experience: Jasmine Riggins (Mo) had undertaken drama workshops and Siobhan Reilly (Leonie) trained at Royal Scottish Academy of Music and Drama (now the Royal Conservatoire of Scotland) and had also acted professionally. In both instances, however, this was their first major role.[22]

The two other gang members, Gary Maitland (Albert) and William Ruane (Rhino), had previously appeared in both *Sweet Sixteen* and *Tickets*; while Ruane subsequently developed a successful acting career, Maitland was working as a cleaning operative in advance of the shoot. Indicative of the fact that Loach does indeed use experienced actors, two established British film and television actors, both of whom have appeared in previous Loach films, Roger Allam (*The Wind That Shakes the Barley*) and John Henshaw (*Looking for Eric*), were also cast, as whisky entrepreneur Thaddeus and avuncular community payback officer Harry.[23] Allam and Henshaw pro-

---

[21] Information from interview with Crawford.

[22] This episode illustrates the mediated nature of the process in that the making of *The Angels' Share* itself became a media event. Uncharacteristically for a Loach production, some information about the script was released with the BBC: 'The film is about a troublemaker given one last chance to stay out of jail . . . A kind-hearted community service officer gets him on the straight and narrow and helps him carve out a new future for himself.' http://www.bbc.co.uk/news/uk-scotland-glasgow-west-12861014 (last accessed 27 February 2018). So, although Brannigan does not bring a conventional intertextual background to the role, he does bring an intertextual background connected to his real-life off-screen persona. As such, the production narrative surrounding him is grounded in discourses of truth and authenticity yet wrapped in glitz and glamour.

[23] The actors have widely different acting backgrounds: Allam is an established film and

vide a point of contrast with two other film debutants: Charles MacLean, who plays whisky-tasting expert Rory McAllister, and Bruce Addison, who plays the auctioneer; the latter two both perform these roles in their daily lives off-screen.[24] There is also, it emerges, room for improvisation in casting: in interview, Crawford advises that Loach bumped into Scott Dymond, who had previously appeared in *Sweet Sixteen*, on a Glasgow street during pre-production. Crawford states that as Loach wanted Dymond involved, a gang member, Willy, was added to the cast and he appears in the cemetery and initial distillery sequences. Crawford notes that in casting Dymond 'the part was bigger in the film than in the script and we changed the character of Willy because we wanted to cast Scott'.[25] For instance, when the group visit the distillery in the film, Robbie removes a cigarette from Willy, although in the script (72) it is simply 'YOUTH 1' who has the cigarette.[26] In addition to the prominent roles, established Scottish actors are cast in several smaller parts, for example, Gilbert Martin (Matt), Vincent Friell (Procurator Fiscal) and Barrie Hunter (Police Inspector), demonstrating further that the match between character and actor is not fetishised and tends to be concentrated on the main characters. As these accounts make evident, although the lead role is played by a first-time actor, the cast overall have varied levels of experience and the majority have in fact appeared on film before.

The approach to finding people who have similarities with their characters also extends to 'extras' or 'supporting artists' and Crawford notes that their preference is to find people who fulfil similar roles in life, rather than using an agency. As she notes, 'When you find people locally, they just fit into the world.' Therefore, several supporting artists who appear in the film are doing their standard jobs. The advantage of this approach is evident when observing filming of the initial distillery tour. On the relevant call

---

stage actor, a regular performer at the Royal Shakespeare Company, and the recipient of two Olivier Awards for Best Actor, whereas Henshaw worked as a bin man until he was forty before becoming an actor. Laverty's screenplay (2012: 173) provides an appendix devoted to Thaddeus which states, 'He knows Arab princes by their first name, and, of course, can get tickets for a Chelsea game at the drop of a hat for the latest baron from Kyrgyzstan. But he is not a snob. He enjoys and is attracted to characters.'

[24] Indicative of the process's holistic nature, MacLean also provided a day's training in whisky tasting for Allam and Henshaw. In interview, he suggests, 'I suppose it helps them to get into the part rather than being sprung into being a whisky enthusiast.'

[25] I discuss how the script is amended further during production in Chapter 5.

[26] Dymond also features in a scene in which he is arrested following an excursion to the top of a statue of the Duke of Wellington, although this scene is not in the final film.

sheets, the list of attendees for the day includes Bung Flogger (Andrew) and Fermentation Room Worker (Craig), with an added note: 'Working at the distillery so he'll be on set from 0900.'[27] During filming, it becomes evident that 'flogging the bung', or opening the cask with a wooden mallet, is a skilled task, therefore, casting someone with this experience saves time and expense, and authenticates the performance. This was also the case in filming the Caledonian Hotel sequence, in which waiting staff were on hand to discuss what would happen in certain situations, for instance in the laying out of tables, in effect functioning as advisers.[28] The approach to casting, then, both actors and supporting artists, returns us to the notion of Loach's realist practice as connecting to pre-existing things, discussed in Chapter 3: in this instance, it often involves working with individuals, trained or untrained, whose life mirrors their character, although as the examples above demonstrate, this is never absolute.

Linear shooting

It is a common sense of commercial filmmaking that scenes should be shot in an order that minimises the movement of equipment and people, and, therefore, minimises expenditure on time and money. Conventional thinking suggests that actors, who are, lest we forget, tasked with the art of pretending, should be able to act in any given scene regardless of where in the shooting schedule that scene occurs. Loach does not employ this approach. Rather, he aims to film in an order that correlate the actors' experiences with the characters' experiences as the narrative progresses.[29] On occasion, this can involve considerable additional work and expense. For instance, flashback scenes which take place in Nicaragua involving the titular figure in *Carla's Song*, were filmed in that country at the start of

---

[27] Call Sheet 13, Thursday 26 May 2011. As a small aside, to locate a suitable candidate for the part of Leonie and Robbie's son, Luke, Call Sheet 05 states: 'Anyone know anyone having a wean in the next 72 hours, please let Kahleen or Michael know.'

[28] It does not always work, however, and although a group of nuns had agreed initially to appear in the scene in which the gang hitch a lift on a bus, the nuns withdrew at the last minute, leaving a significant gap in terms of personnel, and, given how the production often utilises the costume of the actors involved, also for the costume designer. Information from interview with Carole Fraser.

[29] In interview, the four young actors advised me that they were contracted for the full shoot, so they knew that they, and consequently their characters, were in for the duration of the filming.

production so that the actor (Oyanka Cabezas) could draw on these experiences whilst filming the Glasgow scenes. The cast and crew then returned to Nicaragua for a second time to film subsequent scenes there, ensuring that filming followed the character's development through the narrative.[30]

Loach outlined his line of thinking on this process during an interview on *The South Bank Show* in 1993:

> There are really two sorts of acting. There's theatre acting and there is film acting, I think, which can be something different, where somebody can be taken through a story and experience the story and put themselves in that position and respond as they would respond. So that you're really experiencing that person in that story. And I guess that's what we've tried to do, over the years. I mean that's developed into a way of working ... So that, in a way ... when we make the film, they'll obviously be going through the experience of the character as written, but in a sense it may be, in part, a sort of documentary about them as well.' (quoted in Leigh 2002: 17)

As is evidenced by the draft shooting schedule (see Appendix III), *The Angels' Share* production also follows the characters' journeys. An indicator of how this works in practice is that the flashbacks (Rhino on the statue, Robbie's violent attack and Albert's descent onto the train tracks) are filmed before the opening courtroom scene is filmed, even though they appear after this scene has started. The filming of the opening scenes (Sheriff Court) through to the closing scenes (Robbie and family departing in camper van), are then shot in narrative order. This progression, however, is not always implemented for practical reasons which arise during filming. In one instance, for example, Scott Kyle (Clancy) pulled a muscle during the post-snooker hall chase scene and the filming of this scene was rescheduled.[31] There are other pick-ups and reshoots in which scenes are shot out of sequence, for instance, the courtroom scene and Albert's railway fall were reshot in October 2011, four months after principal photography was completed.[32] The shoot's trajectory, however, is planned to follow

---

[30] See Laverty (1997).

[31] Information from interview with continuity coordinator Susanna Lenton. Lenton also notes that given the gap between the original filming of this scene and its rescheduled filming, the filmmakers viewed rushes assembled on a DVD as a continuity aide, something which they would not normally use.

[32] A rare occasion when this when did not occur was in the filming of Harry and the gang arriving and leaving the whisky-tasting session in Edinburgh. There is no real emotional involvement required of the actors in these scenes and they were filmed slightly out of sequence, that is: scene 26 part 1, EXT. PRINCES STREET TO CALEDONIAN HOTEL; 25, INT. WAVERLEY / EXT. PRINCES STREET; 27,

the trajectory of the characters' unfolding experiences, which is connected to Loach's method in restricting the actors' knowledge of their characters' futures.[33]

Withholding the script

Loach keeps the script largely secret from the actors, normally releasing sections the day before filming a specific scene or sequence. The rationale here is that as the shoot develops, actors experience events as their character would, or as close to it as is practical. This has been a long-standing approach and Tony Garnett indicates something of the thinking when he states: 'Why should the actor be burdened by knowledge which in real life they wouldn't have? The actor should know no more than the character they are playing.' The importance of this is emphasised in the daily call sheets distributed to crew (not cast) members, which come with the following message, in bold type and block capitals for emphasis:

> **PLEASE DO NO LEAVE CALL SHEETS, SCHEDULES OR SCRIPTS ANYWHERE THE CAST MIGHT SEE THEM, THANKS.**

Rather than being tasked with learning the full script in advance and rehearsing specific scenes, the actors are given a general sense of what might occur on the day and may also be tasked with learning some specific lines. As Jasmine Riggins (Mo) outlines,

> Every day we're turning up and we don't really know what we're going to do. But sometimes we get a few lines to learn. He always tells you you don't need to know it word by word. I think he just likes to feel as if it is actually happening to you. Like what you would say if you were really in that situation. You're no' under pressure, you're no' worrying. Like, we don't know what's happening next week. So, we're no' worrying about nothing. 'How am I going to say that? How am I going to say this?' Just

---

EXT. PRINCES STREET. (Call Sheet 19, Friday 3 June 2011). The sequence inside the Caledonian Hotel (scene 26, part 2), was filmed in the two days preceding (Call Sheet 17, Wednesday 1 June 2011 and Call Sheet 18, Thursday 2 June 2011).

[33] Loach suggests that the shooting of one scene functions as a rehearsal for the next day's filming (Fuller 1998: 97). There is on occasion some time set aside for rehearsal, however, these are primarily for talking through the logistics rather than perfecting performance. For instance, in filming the scene in which Albert falls onto the train tracks, the actors, Gary Maitland and Ford Kiernan, were both called for a two-hour rehearsal in advance of filming (Call Sheet Number: reshoot 1, Thursday 13 October 2011).

THE ANGELS' SHARE

Callsheet Number: 04 **Monday 25th April 2011**

Sixteen Scotland Limited. Production Office: 5th Floor, Trongate 103, Glasgow 5HD. Tel: ▓▓▓▓▓▓▓ Fax: ▓▓▓▓▓▓▓

Director: Ken Loach. Producer: Rebecca O'Brien. Writer: Paul Laverty

Locations: Robbie (▓▓▓▓▓) Line Producer: Peter (▓▓▓▓▓) 2nd AD: Michael (▓▓▓▓▓), Unit phone: Stephen (▓▓▓▓▓)

Location:	1. Glasgow Sheriff Court, 1 Carlton Place, Glasgow G5 9DA	**Crew Call: 0800**
Base:	1. Glasgow Sheriff Court, 1 Carlton Place, Glasgow G5 9DA	**Breakfast from 0700 - 0900**
		Lunch: 1300 - 1400
Sunrise/Sunset: 0549/2041		**EARLY CALL LX: 0600**
Weather: Showery morning, dry, sunny afternoon. Max 13C		**EARLY CALL CAMERA: 0730**

PLEASE DO NOT LEAVE CALLSHEETS, SCHEDULES OR SCRIPTS ANYWHERE THE CAST MIGHT SEE THEM. THANKS.

Loc.	Sc. No	Set/ Description		D/N	Pages	Cast
1	2	INT. COURT		D1	4 7/8	1,2,3,4,6,7,10,13,14,29,35, 41,47,50,51,52,59
1	4	EXT. COURT		D1	1	1,2,3,4,6,7,10,13,14,29,35, 41,47,50,51,52,59
				Page total	5 7/8	

Id. No	Cast	Character	P/up	M/Up Costume		On Set
29	Nick Farr	Tongs Ted's Defence Lawyer 1	0700	From 0715		0800
35	Stewart Preston	Sheriff	0700	From 0715		0800
41	Vincent Friell	Fiscal	0700	From 0715		0800
47	Eric Robertson	Sheriff Clerk	0700	From 0715		0800
50	Charles Jamieson	Matthew's Defence Lawyer	0640	From 0715		0800
51	Kirstin Murray	Robbie's Defence Lawyer	0700	From 0715		0800
59	Ted Davitt	Tongs Ted	O/T	From 0715		0800
2	Jasmin Riggins	Mo	0700	From 0715		0830
3	William Ruane	Rhino	0650	From 0715		0830
4	Gary Maitland	Albert	0650	From 0715		0830
7	Elizabeth McGovern	Susan	0640	From 0715		0830
13	Lorne MacFadyen	Matthew	0700	From 0715		0830
1	Paul Brannigan	Robbie	0705	From 0745		0900
6	Siobhan Reilly	Leonie	0700	From 0745		0900
10	Neil Leiper	Sniper	0700	From 0745		0900
14	Scott Kyle	Clancy	O/T	From 0745		0900
52	Lee Fanning	Sniper's pal	0715	From 0745		0900

Sc. No	Others		P/up	M/Up Costume	Rehearse	On Set
2	2 x COURT OFFICERS (real) - Mandy Davies		O/T	From 0730		0815
2	1 x CLERK'S ASSISTANT (real) - Natalie Ducie		O/T	From 0730		0815
2	3 x Reliance Security (real) - David, Ian, Margaret		O/T	From 0730		0815
2	2 x Lawyers (real) - Jim, Erica		O/T	From 0730		0815
2	2 x Lawyers (Kirsty, Mark,)		O/T	From 0730		0830
2	2 x Policemen (Brian, Derek)		O/T	From 0730		0830
2	1 x Agency press (David Archibald)		O/T	From 0730		0830
2	3 x FEATURED ACCUSED (Jack, James, Thomas)		O/T	From 0830		0900
2	6 x other accused		O/T	From 0830		0900
2	7 x Public gallery		O/T	From 0830		0900
2	13 x remaining public gallery		0830	From 0900		0930
4	2 x Different policemen		O/T	From 1530		1600
4	11 x different visitors etc.		O/T	From 1530		1600
4	2 x different lawyers		O/T	From 1530		1600

ART DEPT / PROPS:	As per script and Fergus Clegg's instructions. To include: A small forest worth of files, papers, reports and other legal paraphernalia.
CAMERA:	As per Robbie Ryan's instructions. 2nd camera and crew. Operator Alastair Rae, clapper loader Grant McPhee. Early call LX: 0730
ELECTRICAL:	As per Andy Cole's instructions. Early call LX: 0600
SOUND:	As per Ray Beckett's instructions.
ADVISERS:	Drew Crombie (Acting head of estates and administration, Sheriff Court) and Jim Clarke, criminal lawyer on set as advisers. On set: 0800 Jim also playing a background lawyer. Practical DVD player c/o Sheriff Court.
PRODUCTION:	DVD of Rhino and Albert flashbacks on set for 0800. DVD apparatus c/o Sheriff Court.
STILLS:	As per Joss Barratt's instructions.
MAKE UP:	As per Karen Brotherston's instructions.
COSTUME:	As per Carole Fraser's instructions. 'Bump' padding for Leonie.
LOCATIONS:	As per Michael Higson's instructions.

Figure 4.1 Crew call sheets make it clear that anything which might reveal aspects of the plot should be kept from the actors

act instantly. It's just whatever comes into your head. It's just a natural reaction basically.[34]

Riggins adds that if there were any lines that she thought were inappropriate to her character, she would raise this with Loach and that he would advise her to 'put it into your own words'.[35] She also notes that Loach often has a quiet word with the actors just before shooting, perhaps to do something differently, to provoke, as she puts it 'a natural reaction' from other cast members. Garnett suggests that actors can often hide emotionally behind props, and behind specific lines in the screenplay:

> They can know their lines, but they are hiding emotionally. And Ken, quite rightly won't have that. So, he'll do a take and then if it's between two people then he'll go to one of them and whisper to do something different. So that everybody is on their toes; everybody is responding in the moment. It's a little trick so that they're not repeating it like actors.

Ruane also confirms these general processes when he notes, 'We get tomorrow's script today. Obviously, you here whispers about what's going to happen, but you don't know really.'[36] He also compares this experience with other film and television experiences he has undertaken since first working with Loach: 'It's weird coming back and doing it this way. It's not difficult by any means. It's not as demanding this way. These roles aren't really challenging in a way. You just do it.'[37] Both Riggins and Ruane stress how comfortable they feel about this work, and that the approach is often about capturing a natural response, albeit one constructed under very unnatural circumstances.

James Naremore (1990: 44) suggests that naturalist filmmakers are struck by William Gillette's concept of 'the illusion of the first time', and, as such 'they also encourage a good deal of improvisation, trying to create situations where the actors will be forced to fumble along, or where one player will do something unexpected, forcing the others to react spontaneously'. This corelates with Loach's intentions of 'springing surprises on actors', when actors only discover what will happen once the camera is turn-

---

[34] Interview with author. Subsequent quotes from Riggins in this chapter are from this interview.
[35] There is some crossover here with how the actors influence the words spoken in the film, a process I return to in Chapter 5.
[36] Interview with author. Subsequent quotes from Ruane in this chapter are from this interview.
[37] Ruane worked mainly on Scottish television drama between *Sweet Sixteen* and *The Angels' Share*.

Figure 4.2 Mo appears genuinely shocked as Albert smashes the whisky-filled Irn Bru bottles

ing over. This often involves bleak moments, for instance, Blanca's death in *Land and Freedom*.[38] There is nothing quite so dramatic in *The Angels' Share*; however, the method is employed when the gang return to Glasgow with their liquid swag in four Irn Bru bottles. Observing this scene being filmed, it emerges that only Maitland (Albert) is aware that two bottles will be smashed during an exchange they have after the police depart the scene. In Loach's annotated script (86), a handwritten note reads, 'Don't show rest of scene', a reminder that the other actors are to be kept in the dark about this action. The prop bottles are made with a glass substitute, which is evident in a further note which reinforces the point: 'Keep sugarglass bottles hidden!' As continuity coordinator Susanna Lenton notes, 'We had to keep that a secret from all the other actors so that you could get on camera their first, horrified reaction when that happened. So that was all set-up and that worked, really well.'[39] In the film, the moment is presented in a wide shot: Albert says 'cheers' and in clinking bottles with Mo, smashes them both and the element of surprise is captured most dramatically on Mo's face.

Naremore suggests (1990: 40), 'The camera's mobility and tight framing of faces, its ability to "give" the focus of the screen to any player at any moment, also means that films tend to favour *reactions*.' This scene, however, is indicative of how Loach refuses to frame shocks and reactions in

---

[38] See David Archibald (2012).
[39] Lenton notes that although they hoped to capture this reaction on the first take, they shot an additional five takes.

close-up, preferring wider compositions which create an overall sense of the situation, and correlates with the idea that the viewer is observing the action at distance. Another instance of 'springing surprises' is when Dougie (James Casey) drinks a beaker containing the liquid remains of the gang's domestic whisky-tasting session. Here, unaware that the props team has switched the contents, the actors assume Dougie was unknowingly drinking their saliva/whisky cocktail, and disgust at his indecorous behaviour is writ large on their faces in the finished film.[40] As with other aspects of Loach's method, withholding the script is not fetishised, indeed he states that this is a policy he has utilised 'perhaps sometimes more rigorously than others' (Fuller 1998: 46). For instance, in interview, Roger Allam suggests that he was aware of the story's broad outlines prior to accepting the role: 'I saw a substantial portion of the script,' although he adds, 'I didn't see all of my bits.'[41] MacLean, moreover, had read the full script as he advised on the whisky logistics 'to make sure they'd got the descriptions right'. Withholding the script reinforces the process in which the actors go through an experience approximate to that of their character, although these examples are also a reminder that Loach's method is flexible, tending to involve guidelines rather than tramlines.

What is a Loach set like?

Hannah Arendt suggests (1958: 177), 'To act, in its most general sense, means to take an initiative, to begin (as the Greek word *archein*, "to begin," "to lead", and eventually "to rule", indicates), to set something into motion (which is the original meaning of the Latin *agere*).' In this sense, Loach is the most prominent actor on the set. Filmmaking consists of long hours and ten hours on set was not exceptional when I attended; however, aside from during lunch, I never once saw Loach sit down. Although there are often extended breaks between filming which enable actors to rest, and, conversely, some crew members can relax during filming itself, Loach appears always to be working. Usually dressed in a blue denim shirt, often buttoned up to the neck, casual blue trousers, brown shoes, a blue or brown jacket, or when outside, a weatherproof coat, and sometimes a cap, he moves around commanding the operation in a polite and restrained manner, bringing to

---

[40] Information from author's interview with Campbell Mitchell.
[41] Interview with author. Subsequent quotes from Allam in this chapter are taken from this interview.

mind the Russian theatre director Vsevolod Meyerhold's assertion, 'In art it is always a question of arrangement of the material.'[42] Loach oversees the arrangement of actors and props directly, looking through the viewfinder regularly as he discusses set-ups and compositions with cinematographer Robbie Ryan. On the occasions when Laverty and O'Brien are present, he regularly discusses filming logistics with them directly, and he continuously fields questions and queries from various cast and crew members. In advancing the shoot itself, he discusses all next steps with first assistant director David Gilchrist, who is a calm yet commanding presence on set.

During the first day filming of the courtroom scenes (25 April 2011), Loach suffered a serious fall, and filming was suspended.[43] When it recommenced after a three-week long break, he wore the signs of injury: he still moved around, whispering a word into an actor's ear here and there, but his movement appeared restricted. Initially, he attempted to deploy his son, Jim Loach, to carry last-minute instructions to the actors but stopped when he realised that he often did not know the precise nature of the note until he was en route.[44]

In the egalitarian spirit of Team Loach, cast and crew share the same facilities; there are no special spaces reserved for more established actors and during breaks everyone queues for food at the catering van positioned nearby and all are welcome to partake of the far-from-expensive tea, coffee and biscuits that are on hand. At lunch, which Loach takes in the same space as the cast and crew, he humorously, but with more serious undertones, suggests that overindulging might lead to post-lunch energy levels dipping. As such, there is an ordinariness about the set, which seems far removed from the image one might construct of a Hollywood film set equipped with trailers for celebrities with personal assistants constantly on call. Commenting on the crew's presence on set, Gilchrist states, 'When you come to work with Ken it's a much quieter atmosphere and less intrusive. It's almost as if we're not there,' which is concomitant with a desire to minimise the presence of the cinematic apparatus.[45]

---

[42] Quoted in McAuley (2010: 126).
[43] See Appendix II for a production schedule.
[44] Information from interview with O'Brien.
[45] Interview with author.

The apparatus

Writing on technology's impact on film performance, Sean Aita notes (2014: 258), 'Film acting does not grow organically from the performer's psyche in isolation, but is affected, sometimes quite radically, by technical, dramaturgical, scenographic and environmental considerations imposed on the performer by the media through which the performance takes place' (2014: 258). Cognisant of the on-set apparatus's potential influence, a Loach set is pared down and relatively free of technological paraphernalia. As I outlined in Chapter 2, the camera is generally placed on a tripod at around Loach's eye level and long lenses employed so that the camera can be placed at distance from the action.[46] There are no calls for 'action', no snap of the clapperboard at the start of each scene; rather, Loach will say something casual like, 'on you go then', or 'in you come'. The actors are not expected to hit specific marks and can move freely, with the camera following their action. When filming interiors, actors are often placed near a window so that natural light illuminates their environment thereby reducing the need for film lights. Line producer Peter Gallagher recounts an instructive tale from the making of *My Name is Joe*, which was also shot in Glasgow:

> There were a few things on *Joe* that I got caught out with, which surprised me. For instance, the lighting equipment came from Germany and was as small-key as we could make it, but these black trucks arrived with huge purple writing across the side of them advertising this lighting company; it was like some kind of porn movie lettering, and I was taken aside by Rebecca and advised that Ken had seen the trucks and was not happy with the lettering and the statement of the film. It was almost like too much of 'the circus coming to town'. So, we had to cover up the lettering with black gaffer tape so that they then become undercover trucks as it were.[47]

Tuck away

Gallagher's comments highlight that the task of minimising the cinematic apparatus is not simply on the set itself but in the surrounding area, indeed, anything which creates the atmosphere of a conventional film set

---

[46] One consequence here is the relative shallow depth of field in the films. As noted in Chapter 2, the only occasions when I observed two cameras being used were for filming the potential buyers arriving at the auction and at the auction itself.

[47] Interview with author.

Figure 4.3 Boom operator Pete Murphy hiding in plain sight on the set of *The Angels' Share*

is pushed as much as possible. Noticeably, just as filming is about to commence, Loach quietly says, 'tuck away' and crew members whose presence is deemed unessential at that moment, perhaps the props, make-up and costume staff, secrete themselves out of the actors' sight. Those remaining, mainly Loach, the cinematographer, focus-puller and camera assistant, continuity coordinator, first assistant director, and on occasion the producer and writer, bunch behind or close to the camera, minimising their physical presence from the actors' view. Ray Beckett and his portable sound desk are positioned out of the actors' line of vision, often in an adjacent room.[48] The boom operator, Pete Murphy, must be closer to the actors to record their voices and there is something incongruous about his presence as he stands, boom pole and microphone aloft, hiding in plain sight as the presence of all others is minimised.

Those remaining within the actors' vision tend to look away from the action, and even Loach tends to not look towards the actors as filming commences, either casting his eyes towards the ground, listening intently as he does, or looking into the small monitor attached to the camera. Only when the action is fully in flow might he visually survey the performers. As Campbell Mitchell, standby props, suggests, every scene is shot with the

[48] In interview, Ray Beckett comments, 'With Ken you learn to mic everybody all the time because there will always be the asides which may or may not be used in that take or may not happen again. Because then it becomes organic.'

level of unobtrusiveness that many film directors create only when shooting a sex scene.[49] When a scene is completed Loach will announce 'okay, end board it there', and the camera assistant will 'clap' the clapperboard so that image and sound can be synchronised in post-production.[50] By minimising the apparatus's presence, Loach's directorial approach strives to maintain some form of liveness; not the liveness of the theatre performance, which is clearly staged, but a liveness which is predicated on a form of suspension of disbelief, not on the part of the audience, but on the part of the actor.

Since cinema's formative years, filmmakers have understood that awareness of the apparatus influences how people respond.[51] James Naremore (1990: 38) suggests that during the period

> The first step in facilitating the change toward psychological realism was to shorten the distance between actors and camera. Prior to 1909, scenes were usually played up to a line drawn perpendicular to the lens axis at a distance of twelve feet, with the camera set at eye level; soon afterward, a 'nine-foot line' came into vogue, so that the standard group shot framed the upper three-quarters of the actors' bodies, with the camera at chest height.

Naremore posits that this enabled the camera to adopt the position of a participant of the action, rather than an audience member observing at distance. As Loach uses long lenses, however, it enables the camera to be placed considerably beyond any imaginary nine-foot line, whilst delivering footage which places the spectator seemingly near the action, as if it was a close observer's perspective.

Walter Benjamin asserts (2007: 228) that technology facilitated a shift in acting from theatre to cinema which, through the process of reproduction, effectively removes the performer's on-stage aura. Benjamin also suggests that the actor in cinema, unlike the stage actor, cannot adjust their

---

[49] Interview with author.

[50] The use of 'endboarding' has consequences for the editing process in terms of increasing the work involved. As Paul Clegg, first assistant editor, notes: 'If it's front boards [the conventional approach] it's just a matter of syncing it up at the front; but when it's end boards you physically have to wind through until you get to the end board, mark up the picture then find the sound, then wind it back to the front yet again and put a little sync mark so that we can number it. We do what we call rubber numbering. Each plate is individually numbered. They then have to go back and sync it at the front as if it was front boarded.'

[51] In interview, Garnett cites Stanislavski's 'Circle of Attention' in relation to the absence of any extraneous presence on set as an influence. For more on the Russian director and his approach to acting, see Konstantin Stanislavski (2008).

performance to the audience. In both instances, Benjamin conjures the notion of the actor as an agent fully conscious of the audience, either in person in the present, or beyond the camera in some indeterminate future. Yet, as I have indicated, Loach's actors are encouraged as much as possible to act as if there is no audience, either in the present, or in the future, as they play out an imagined reality. Despite the seeming incongruity of this process, the numerous accolades bestowed on actors in Loach's work is testament to how something of this imagined reality is successfully, and repeatedly, conjured.

Brannigan and MacLean

Brannigan and MacLean are both non-professional actors with no previous film experience and yet they present decidedly different types of performances.[52] It is a commonplace of popular thinking to recognise that humans play out their interactions with the world through a series of continuous and conscious performances: we are all, in a sense, always performing.[53] There are notable differences, however, in performing our private lives, performing our public and professional lives, and performing for film. If Brannigan remains largely understated and within the confines of the real, MacLean is consciously ostentatious and the borderline between the performance of MacLean playing MacLean and MacLean playing Rory McAllister is indiscernible. There is, in fact, something self-reflexive about MacLean's performance, at both a textual and an extra-textual level, as the actor appears only in scenes in which his character is himself performing before an audience, extemporising rhapsodically about the qualities of amber nectar in an ebullient showman's style. Brannigan, conversely, is tasked with acting out experiences which utilise a range of emotions – anger (when he is attacked repeatedly), remorse (when he is confronted by the boy he attacked), and love (for Leonie and his son) – in a way that masks the performance.[54] In one sense, Brannigan, his presence

---

[52] Cynthia Baron and Sharon Marie Carnicke (2008: 18) point to the desire in the popular press to propagate 'the myth of the born performer whose natural talents and genuine feelings are first captured by the camera and then presented on screen'. This helps explains how Brannigan and MacLean were narrativised in the popular press, as the media fetishises the unprofessional actor as a signifier of authenticity and in Brannigan's case produced a familiar rags-to-riches production narrative.

[53] See, for instance, Erving Goffman (1959).

[54] In interview, make-up designer Karen Brotherston notes that on a conventional set the

characterised by a sense of stillness, slight frame, piercing blue eyes, and a recognisable facial scar, is required to do more acting than MacLean, but the audience is never encouraged to see it as acting. Discussing his working relationship with Loach, Brannigan says,

> He always asks me, 'Are you fine with your lines?' And I tell him aye. I'll maybe suggest something to him that I think should be said differently. He will always let me speak, say my bit and nine times out of ten he'll allow me to go with it but he'll guide me on it and he'll say to me, 'Right, do it. Don't make it an argument. Make it that you're just making a point.' He'll tell you certain places to staun' and at what times to lift your heid.[55]

In discussing Loach's last-minute interventions, Brannigan adds, 'Sometimes he'll come up just before a scene and give you a reminder about what's happened in order that you can get the emotions back in,' indicating further Loach's directorial strategy in constantly recreating the fictional cosmos that the actors are expected to inhabit in the moment.[56]

In contrast to Brannigan who appears in most scenes, MacLean appears only in the Caledonian Hotel whisky tasting and at the Balblair auction. There is considerable pleasure in observing MacLean's exuberant and showy performance, clad as he is in his tweed and 'The Keepers of the Quaich' tartan, and sporting a larger-than-life moustache, as he waxes lyrical about the wonders of whisky.[57] There is a paradox here in that MacLean's entire performance takes him, in a sense, beyond the parameters of the real, and yet it is this 'beyond the real', which is the criteria of the real in this instance. There is nothing invisible about MacLean's performance, indeed, in one sense, his task is to make his performance visible. Discussing the great French actor Benôit-Constant Coquelin, Sharon Marie Carnicke (2012: 189–90) suggests that the actor had a first self, which is the player, and a second self, which is their instrument and suggests that 'actors

---

first assistant director would call 'Final Checks' and costume and make-up crew would conduct a last-minute appraisal of their work before filming commences; on a Loach set, as there are no final checks, they only intervene if they deem it to be essential. As such, the scar deployed on Robbie's face was, by necessity, 'low-maintenance'.

[55] Interview with author. Subsequent quotes from Brannigan in this chapter are taken from this interview.

[56] Throughout the filming, Brannigan and other gang members commented continually on their good fortune, speculated about what the finished film would look like, and whether they would attend Cannes as if it was an otherworldly adventure. Brannigan received considerable attention because of his new-found fame and appeared subsequently in several film and television projects, most notably *Under the Skin* (Glazer, 2013) and the Scottish soap opera, *River City* (BBC, 2002–present).

[57] Information provided from interview with MacLean.

do indeed play themselves, but in the same way as musicians play their instruments'. From the perspective of watching this process on set, both Brannigan and MacLean are being asked to play versions of themselves, but as outlined, Brannigan is asked to venture into new territory more than MacLean.[58]

Loach, then, draws on their life experience in terms of the social conditions of the actors he casts, and in MacLean's case their established performative skills, to minimise the amount of acting that is being done, and is seen to be being done. The term 'amount of acting' is taken from Michael Kirby's celebrated essay 'Acting and non-acting' in which he makes a distinction between acting and public speaking:

> Public speaking, whether it is extemporaneous or makes use of a script, may involve emotion, but it does not necessarily involve acting. Yet some speakers, while retaining their own characters and remaining sincere, seem to be acting. At what point does acting appear? At the point at which the emotions are 'pushed' for the sake of the spectators. This does not mean that the speakers are false or do not believe what they are saying. It merely means that they are selecting and projecting an element of character – i.e. emotion – to the audience. (2005: 43)

There is some slippage between Kirby's use of acting, public speaking and performance. Kirby suggests (43) that 'If the performer does something to simulate, represent, impersonate and so forth, he or she is acting' and adds that acting 'can be said to exist in the smallest and simplest action that involves pretense'. Yet, because MacLean clearly performs in real life, or at least when he is performing the role of professional whisky connoisseur, the line between acting and performing is indivisible. Moreover, his acting/performing is marked by spectacular excess, an excess that induces a sense of pleasure that exceeds the limits of what we might expect of a social realist cinematic practice. When MacLean appears on-screen, the performance is not invisible in the sense that we can observe this excess in his costume and hear it in his florid pronouncements; however, this only works within the confines of a realist aesthetic if we believe that the excess is in the character rather than the actor.[59]

---

[58] Carnicke (2012: 198) offers an analysis of John Wayne's acting in *The Searchers* (Ford, 1956), suggesting that through study of his very detailed and conscious gestures and movements, it is possible to discern 'the star from the actor, the actor from the character and naturalism from natural behaviour'. Given the lack of performances against which to judge MacLean's behaviour, however, this distinction is discernible from my on-set observations.

[59] MacLean has an occasional presence in the Scottish media discussing whisky.

Off-screen, MacLean is as large a figure as he is on-screen. When I asked MacLean what his preparation for the scene had consisted of, he responds, 'Nothing at all' before letting out a large laugh. Of his own intervention, he says, 'It's not scripted at all. You are given guidelines and suggestions covering these sorts of things and then Ken would remind me of the points he wanted to get over for each bit but the rest I just ad-libbed. I do these tastings quite a lot so it's not as if I'm coming from nowhere. Blathering on about whisky – I can talk for Scotland about whisky.' MacLean also outlines some insights on his own experience as a public speaker:

> It's a funny experience. It's almost as if you are watching – you try not to – but you are aware of every gesture and to some extent aware of how you are talking and this and the next thing. And if you get too aware of it then you forget what you are talking about. But you are kind of detached from what you're doing.

To circle back to Trotsky, this notion of detachment was also developed in his own reflections on public speaking at mass rallies in the Petrograd Circus in the aftermath of the Russian Revolution (1930: 295):

> At times it seemed as if I felt, with my lips, the stern inquisitiveness of this crowd that had become merged into a single whole. Then all the arguments and words thought out in advance would break and recede under the imperative pressure of sympathy, and other words, other arguments, utterly unexpected by the orator but needed by these people, would emerge in full array from my subconsciousness. On such occasions I felt as if I were listening to the speaker from the outside, trying to keep pace with his ideas, afraid that, like a somnambulist, he might fall off the edge of the roof at the sound of my conscious reasoning.

MacLean's notion of being detached from his own performance points towards some form of critical distance in his work. There is, however, several ways in which distance is created in Loach performance as his work has changed over time. We know that Robbie is a fictional construct not least because of the extensive media narratives surrounding the actor who will play him. But this extratextuality has a dual effect: instead of seeing the star, which takes the viewer out of the film and into the real, the viewer sees the real and takes the viewer out of the film. The process is also evident in the scene in which the mother of the young man, Anthony (Roderick Cowie) who Robbie has badly beaten confronts him during a restoration of justice scene. It is an extremely raw moment in which Alison McGinnes delivers her lines with passion and intensity but also with a rough-around-the-edges ferocity that stands out somewhat. It is not 'bad' acting, but the performance is almost too real. It is like the red car or the policeman's armour discussed in Chapter 2: a moment where the excess of the real bursts through and takes the viewer out of the fictional cosmos. It functions like a reverse Brechtian moment: not a moment of estrangement which highlights the film's artifice, revealing it as a construct, but a moment which highlights that the fiction of the film is grounded, at least in part, in the actors' real experiences.[60] It is, rather weirdly, a social realism that calls attention to itself.

Loach's method has not always been favoured by actors who can regard it as a slight on their profession. In interview, Roger Allam states:

> When I first heard about it, I instinctively didn't like it. My whole working life has hopefully been about building up experience and getting better and being able to do one of the fundamental things of acting, I suppose, which is through repetition, when you have to repeat things, making it look and sound and feel as if it's not a repetition. And it's a craft and it's a job so I felt somewhat resistant to it.[61]

Allam also highlights the diversity of acting required across film, theatre and television and suggests that some of the non-professional actors cast in the film 'would be at a loss in a Molière play, for instance'. Allam contrasts the speed of filming in conventional Hollywood films to the rapid way that Loach works, suggesting that the whisky-tasting scene might take a week to film in Hollywood and that this, as he puts it, keeps things fresh, particularly for people who aren't actors: 'That kind of freshness and liveliness – Ken uses the phrase "catching things on the fly" – all of those things come together and when it works it's terrific.' Notably, Allam draws attention to MacLean's background, commenting that this enables him to deliver a performance which is 'absolutely genuine', further illustrating the discourses of the real in which cast and crew discuss their work.

Caledonian Hotel

In filming the whisky-tasting scene in Edinburgh's Caledonian Hotel, in several set-ups the camera is placed at the opposite end of the room from

---

[60] This process is also at work in other films, for instance, with Anne-Marie Kennedy's powerfully raw performance as the young female heroin user, Sabine, in *My Name is Joe*.

[61] Interview with author. All other quotes from Allam in this chapter are taken from this interview. Allam also related an instance from *The Wind That Shakes the Barley* when a first-time actor was unable to perform the task requested of them because they didn't have the necessary craft and skill which he believed it required. I am unaware of any instances when this situation arose whilst making *The Angels' Share*.

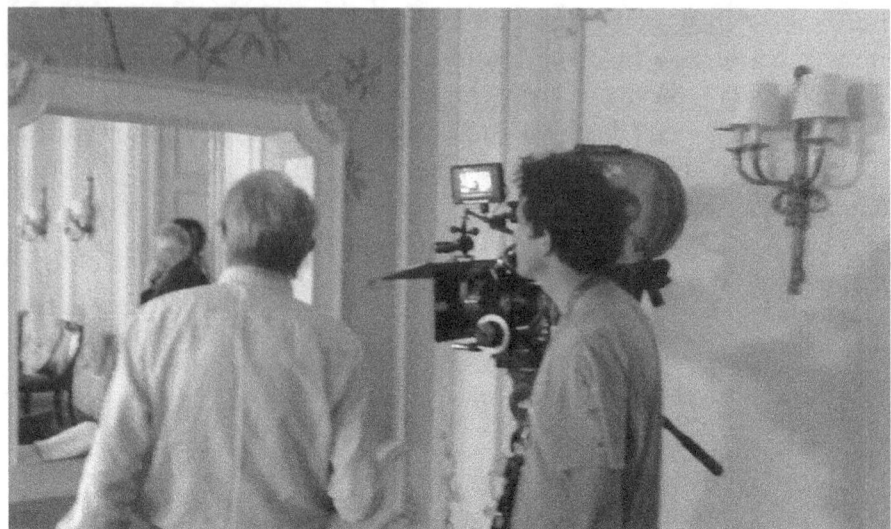

Figure 4.4 Loach and Ryan discuss the logistics of filming through a hole in the wall

the action being shot. Indeed, when Rory and the others are tasting the whisky, the action was shot, in part, through an aperture in a wall, some distance from the action, partially keeping the camera and crew from the actors' view, illustrating the desire to minimise its presence.

What was also notable about observing the filming of this scene was how Loach directs the supporting artists with as much attention as he gives to the actors. Rather than using a first or second assistant director as intermediary, he personally supervises their blocking on set, positioning them initially next to friends, to encourage them to feel comfortable and to interact with ease. He then addresses them directly: 'What you've come to is a tasting which is hosted by the Master of the Quaich,' before adding, 'I don't know if you've been to these things before, I haven't, but I think that you taste about six whiskies and Rory comments on them.' Loach then outlines plans for the day: 'It will take us most of the day. We'll run through six or seven different positions, two or three times in each position . . . so I ask for your forbearance in that.' He also advises that they will be drinking a lot of liquids, although not all the liquids will be whisky, in order 'to keep your palates sharp'. Then, with the assistance of Campbell Mitchell (standby props), Loach relays instructions on the order in which they will be consumed, ensuring that the last one matches the whisky that MacLean himself will consume. After looking through the camera to view the composition, he then makes minor amendments to the blocking, of chairs and of persons, altering slightly the seating arrangements. Once everything appears ready, he asks the crew, 'Are we okay to do one?' When he has had a positive response from the respective individuals, camera team, sound department, first AD and so on, he often has a quiet word in an ear of one the actors. We then hear, 'Okay', before Loach ushers all additional attendees to take up positions away from the actors' gaze, and instead of the 'action' one might expect to hear on a film set, he says, quietly, 'Here we go then. Turning over,' and invites the actors to begin with a 'When you're ready' or 'On you go'. If an additional take is required, he will say something like, 'Get ready to do one more.' During one take he says, 'Everyone should be out of Charlie's eye line, so everyone tuck well out of sight.' Once all was set, he continues, 'Okay, here we go. We're turning over. And off you go, Rory.' When the filming of each scene concludes, he will make an encouraging comment such as, 'Good. Okay, excellent,' and as the call is made to 'end board it there', the camera crew check the gate and Loach discusses next steps with cast and crew.

Discussing his approach to filming action, Loach states, 'If you break it down into separate shots it can get very bitty, so long takes are important,' and adds, 'if there's a dialogue scene the shot's as long as the scene is.' (Fuller 1998: 141). As the whisky-tasting scene is both dialogue-heavy and lengthy, the long takes, coupled with the heat from film lights, lead to

Figure 4.5 Loach and crew survey the set-up at the Caledonian Hotel

a certain amount of flagging, and Loach delivers something of a pep talk to raise the levels of energy and excitement before exploring who from among the assembled supporting artists might ask specific whisky-related questions ahead of the auction: 'What is it?' 'How much is it worth?' 'Which distillery?' Keeping with the desire for an improvisatory element, he suggests that the actors add more details and that 'the others can join in with questions'. Loach addresses the supporting artists like an understated but upbeat amateur football manager addressing the troops as he stokes their energies and enthusiasm as they enter extra time in a cup final. Cognisant of the need to keep up the momentum on set, he routinely adds, 'It's all going very well' and 'keep going', 'that's good', 'that's all good', before often adding, 'we'll just do one more' to laughter from the assembled throng as they begin to catch on that there may well be more than 'one more'. After the final take, he concludes the day by thanking everyone and asking the crowd to give a big hand to Charlie MacLean, deemed to be the star turn for the day. It is a strikingly collective experience, yet one in which Loach is integral to the smallest of details.

Balblair

The attention paid to small details helps to engender a sense of genuine drama during the filming of the auction sequence at Balblair. Here, utilising an existing whisky distillery as a location provided an authentic setting and it was supplemented with appropriate props. An example of the method employed to engender a sense of the real on set is that a handbook outlining the auction details is distributed to the attendees even though it does not appear in the film, nor was it designed to.

As production designer Fergus Clegg outlines, 'It will never be seen, but it's real and it just builds up a layer of reality.'[62] Clegg states that as the film is often shot on long lenses, he is cognisant that much of what he designs will never appear in the film: 'It's about facilitating a place for events to take place in ... to create an environment for the actors you have to create an environment that's often never seen, or only partially seen.'[63] This, then, is

---

[62] Interview with author. Subsequent quotes from Clegg in this chapter are from this interview.

[63] Clegg outlines a rare occasion when they could not locate a suitable extant location for filming the prison scene in *The Wind That Shakes the Barley*. In this instance, they built the set in the basement in an old town hall as the closest approximation to the real

Figure 4.6 A brochure outlining the details of the rare Malt Mill is distributed to the auction attendees even though it will never be seen on-screen

crucial in understanding the role of the production design: the task is not simply to prepare the set for what will appear on camera, rather, the task is to prepare a set in which the actors will feel as if they are in a real-life situation.

How advisers shaped this scene is also apparent in the contribution made by Bruce Addison, who plays the auctioneer. Sixteen Films contacted Addison to enlist his expertise in ensuring that the equipment supplied by the auctioneer he worked for, Bonhams, was 'as authentic as possible'.[64] After O'Brien viewed a showreel of him performing his auctioneering duties and then attended a live auction, he was offered the part.[65] In interview on set, he states that he then worked with Loach on the script in terms of establishing how the bids would come in, limits which they could not go beyond and so on. Addison was also tasked with advising specific details

---

thing; he adds, 'Although it was constructed, it had a sense of an old building. If you are going to build a set, build it in a building.'
[64] Interview with author.
[65] Information from interview with O'Brien.

to ensure that the set approximates to that of a real auction. He states, 'The phone bids are live. They have someone on the other side with a pre-agreed price that the person is going to bid up to. It feels right. It doesn't feel like make-believe. It feels like what you'd hope your dream sale would be.'[66] He adds to the discourse of authenticity running through cast and crew interviews when he states, 'It does make it a much more authentic feeling.'[67]

As with the Caledonian Hotel shoot, Loach directs the supporting artists with close attention.[68] Loach addresses them when they arrive at Balblair, in the room next to the distillery and in the distillery itself, mainly setting the scene for them. Supporting artists have been disparagingly described as 'props with as a pulse' yet one incident from the Balblair shoot exemplifies how their response is crucial to the authenticity of the situation, evident in their costume, look and response, but even when they are not appearing on camera. During the filming of Robbie offering to sell the whisky to Thaddeus in the distillery shop, Ray Beckett advises Loach that the supporting artists' presence is negatively impacting the sound recording. Rather than removing the supporting artists and only filming Robbie and Thaddeus, however, Loach suggests that the supporting artists are repositioned and are quieter. The driver here is to maintain their presence in the scene (if not in the shot) thereby conjuring a greater on-set reality aimed at strengthening the performance of the actors who will be in the shot, in this case, Brannigan and Allam.[69] As such, it highlights another example of how Loach views the importance of constructing a world approximate to the fictional world in which the actors are expected to perform.

Principles of performance: points of contrast

Correspondence between Loach and Trevor Griffiths, scriptwriter of *Fatherland*, is illuminating in clarifying Loach's approach towards per-

---

[66] Interview with author.
[67] Ibid.
[68] The extras are drawn mainly from the local community, however, Crawford had indicated in advance of the shoot that filming in the Highlands would generate problems of finding an ethnically diverse range of supporting artists from the local area: '[It's] going to be a struggle. We've got a lot of folk up there who are interested but he wants a good mix, Australians, Japanese, Chinese, and they're just not up there.' To guarantee the ethnic diversity that Loach had requested, actors were flown in from London.
[69] This is based on analysis of the finished film; it is possible that the supporting artists were filmed but that this was cut from the final version.

formance. I quote from this exchange in detail, as it crystallises much of Loach's thinking and indicates the diversity of approaches towards performance between the two figures. Griffiths writes,

> Most of the time . . . I'm in a total fug about your intentions and remain wholly unable to make out how you propose to direct the piece.
>
> Ken, let's stop fucking around and say what each of us feels this film needs. Out of respect as much as self-interest, I think we should agree in detail the production it demands before going further with it. We both care for it too much to watch it float down the tubes. For myself, I'd sooner see it not made at all than made wrongly.
>
> Like Country or Comedians or Occupations or any other of my plays, it's written to be <u>acted</u>, calls for performative skills to organize meaning within a dense, elliptical, imagistic text. Like all my other plays, it demands investigation and interrogation by the director and actors, who will otherwise not know what they are doing and simply wing it. It is impossible to 'tell' Fatherland to your actors on the day you shoot or whenever; they have to know it, above, below, and within, or we're doing something else, which may prove interesting but won't be the piece I wrote and want to see made.[70]

Outlining his experience in making the *Play for Today* episode *Country* (Eyre, BBC, 1981), Griffiths notes it was rehearsed for eight days and that several scenes were rehearsed on set before shooting started. He continues:

> All this you appear to reject, in favour of your own habituated process as a director, which you thereby implicitly prioritise over mine as a writer. <u>Acting</u> is for you a word of contempt, a basically false process, dead, unreal, unlifelike . . . For you, spontaneity, living in the moment, catching what happens in actual time among non-performing <u>people</u> briefed with a structure and a sense of who they are, constitute collectively the real stuff of drama.[71]

He concludes, 'My sense of how things are acknowledges a plurality of approaches; yours only yours, it seems.'[72]

Loach responds by stating that he will 'try to find people in the film who are most appropriate to the parts. They will, certainly, be mainly actors'.[73] He notes that actors played most of the main roles in *Days of Hope*, and stresses, 'My concern is first of all that what ends up in front of the camera . . . is as near as we can get to a genuine first-hand experience. The means

---

[70] Letter from Trevor Griffiths to Ken Loach, 30 January 1985: BFI Ken Loach archive, KCL-19-7-1-7. Emphasis in this quote and those which follow are in the original.
[71] Ibid.
[72] Ibid.
[73] Letter from Ken Loach to Trevor Griffiths, 1 February 1985: BFI Ken Loach archive, KCL-19-7-1-8. Emphasis in the original.

of trying to achieve this are many and varied . . . First of all, who is in the cast.'[74] Loach continues, 'Secondly, what they have to do,' and adds, 'far from putting my way of working above yours, I am prepared to use almost all methods.' He notes, acting 'for me is not "a word of 'contempt'" and adds that he has worked with actors for twenty-five years, but 'I've also worked with performers who were able to "act" as well as those actors who had extensive theatrical experience. All the generalisations [about my work] are wrong.'[75] He concludes by suggesting his approach is not that of the purist, but of the pluralist who will use whatever method works.[76] This exchange is useful in highlighting Loach's method in relation to casting and performance in general terms and corresponds with the observations from my fieldwork.

There are limited studies against which to compare Loach's methods, notably, however, John Cook's research into the making of *La Commune (Paris, 1871)* references Loach's methods as a point of contrast with those of Watkins. The two directors do share some similarities in relation to performance, for instance, Watkins makes considerable use of non-professional actors. Watkins, however, filmed on a set rather than locations, there is no full script, only an outline; Watkins is critical of Loach's use of surprises and the actors were involved in shaping the debates that ensued, which led to its planned 120-minute running time becoming 345 minutes (Cook 2010: 238); Watkins deploys an anachronistic television crew that reports on the action as it develops, thereby highlighting the apparatus, and he repeatedly instructed the actors (227), 'Don't forget to look into the camera', thereby ensuring that the on-set experience is also vastly different in terms of the construction of the performance. The comparison with Griffiths and Watkins serves to highlight the adage that if you spoke with ten filmmakers about their practice then you would encounter ten different ways of working.

What do film academics think that actors do?

There has been significant debate among film scholars over the extent to which acting is primarily created during filming, or during the editing process. As Paul McDonald (2000: 30) summarises: 'What is at stake in

---

[74] Ibid.
[75] Ibid.
[76] Ibid.

this conflict between the film actor and film technology is a debate about whether it is the actor or the film which is the primary source of meaning.' Cynthia Baron and Sharon Marie Carnicke (2008: 3) note, 'In the early years of cinema, film director Vsevolod Pudovkin, playwright Luigi Pirandello, and cultural theorist Rudolf Arnheim all argued that film actors should be seen as stage props and film performances as constricted by others.' Baron and Carnicke (49) suggest, moreover, that critics such as Christian Metz have neglected performance, focusing instead on how framing and editing constructs 'the act of looking itself'. In a lengthy summation of the actor's role, Baron and Carnicke bend the stick towards the centrality of performance (236):

> the unique demands of film production do not make training unnecessary but instead require actors to rely on training, experience, and more independent preparation than that required for stage performances. Compressed rehearsal time requires players to come to the set or location fully prepared, with a good understanding of their characters and a readiness to adjust that understanding to the director's vision as needed. Performers in leading roles must have their characters' physical and emotional journeys mapped out, so that even when scenes are shot out of sequence, they know how each scene fits into the story and their characters' development. Often required to portray moments of extreme emotion without rehearsal or without the presence of their screen partners, screen actors depend on the work they have done alone and in advance. They must also develop their ability to maintain concentration because the production process itself presents constant distractions. While stage acting requires physical awareness, acting in the cinema necessitates even greater awareness: movements must fit framing choices, and gestures must be modified to accommodate their magnification when projected. Because performance details are combined with a dense array of filmic elements, actors learn to home in on the essentials so that the audiences can locate the meaningful qualities in movement, gestures, and expressions. From the standpoint of actors, stage work and screen work involve differences in degree rather than kind. This insight implicitly informs the book's respect for actors' craft and their potential to contribute to films.

Perhaps this summation of the film actor's craft is accurate in many instances, however, as is evident by the detail above, this is almost the exact opposite of what actors are required to do in a film directed by Loach. Baron and Carnicke argue (46) that 'the status of performance elements is best clarified by analysis of the aesthetic choices actually seen on screen'. Of course, conventional film criticism has always relied on textual analysis and there is no way to discern who made such choices by observing the completed film: critics, and viewers, experience performance at the point of reception, not production. What I have attempted here is to indicate some of the ways in which performances are developed on the Loach set and to suggest that production studies can be helpful in indicating the process at play. It highlights that this type of fieldwork can enable more detailed understanding of the role of the actor, director and production crew in relation to performance, whilst cautioning against the dangers of making generalisations based on limited studies. As such 'ethnografilmic analysis', the term that I employed in the Introduction, can create new knowledge of individual film production practices through which we can develop a more nuanced understanding of the general, one which is alive to the practices of specific filmmakers and actors working in specific production contexts.

5
Words: Between script and screen

> To me the writer is king. That's the creative element in the film.
>
> Ken Loach[1]
>
> There's sometimes I've said to him [Loach] and he's said, 'No, I need you to say that.' But nine times out of ten he'll let you dae your ain thing as long as you stick to the guideline of the script.
>
> Paul Brannigan[2]
>
> What matters who's speaking?
>
> Samuel Beckett[3]

Greenock, 2001. I am on the set of *Sweet Sixteen* interviewing Ken Loach, asking him why he is returning to Scotland to make his third feature film in the country in five years. He responds: 'If you go where the writer writes well, where he understands the idiom and where the language rings true, you tend to get the better work.'[4] Loach's response is indicative of the importance he places on the central role of the writer in the creative process. In contrast to the notion of cinema as individual personal expression, throughout this book I have highlighted the collectivity involved in making the films under discussion, whilst fully cognisant of Loach's leadership role within the process. In this chapter, I explore how examining the words spoken in *The Angels' Share* interrogates conventional understanding of who is speaking in cinema, and, invoking the sentiment in Beckett's words above, reflect on how it might matter. These concerns relate to Certain

---

[1] Quoted in Ken Loach in *Conversation with Cillian Murphy* (BBC Four, 2015).
[2] Interview with author.
[3] Samuel Beckett (1974).
[4] Quoted in Archibald (2002).

Tendencies in Loach's Cinema (13) follow the writer and (14) screenplay as blueprint, and I start by sketching Loach's involvement with various writers before detailing his long-standing partnership with Laverty. I then turn to *The Angels' Share*, examining how the script is shaped during production through analysis of draft and published versions of the screenplay, the final film, and deleted scenes contained in the DVD. I draw on my participant observation to analyse the filming of specific scenes – the snooker hall confrontation, sentencing in Glasgow Sheriff Court, and the Balblair distillery whisky shop exchange – and I also utilise information gleaned from interviews with Loach, Laverty, Tony Garnett and the lead actors, and correspondence between Loach and Trevor Griffiths. Finally, I examine the use of the word 'cunt' in the filmmaking process and the film itself to illustrate how both actors and outside agents can influence what audiences see and hear. In offering insights into how the film moves from initial script to the point of reception, I hope to further disturb conventional understandings of authorial contribution and control by exploring how the script is realised on set, and influenced by external forces.

Follow the writer

Loach has a writer credit on several of the early films: *A Misfortune* (BBC, 1973), adapted from several Chekov short stories, and *Black Jack*, an adaption of Leon Garfield's novel; and a co-writer credit on *Poor Cow* and *Kes*. Symptomatic of how Loach routinely downplays his own role, speaking of the latter he states (Fuller 1998: 42), 'The script was a collaboration, but I don't want to make anything of that. The film is so close to the book anyway.'[5] While the director figure is often discussed, particularly in auteurist discourse, in terms of their artistic vision, a writer is often praised for their ability to find an authentic voice, either emanating from their personal experience, or by displaying 'an ear for dialogue' in their characters' verbal expressions. Developing the idea that Loach's realism is a practice as much as an aesthetic, notably he often collaborates with writers deeply connected with the communities of which they write. For example, in the Yorkshire-set work made with Barry Hines a strong sense of place is developed through the films' dialogue, and the actors' delivery. This is a long-

---

[5] In interview, Garnett states a similar position: 'Ken and I shared a screenplay credit for *Kes*, but we really didn't deserve it.' Notably, Tony Garnett also places the writer at the top of the film hierarchy.

standing aspect of Loach's work evident, for example, in the early television work scripted by Londoner and former career criminal John O'Connor, *A Tap on the Shoulder* and *The Coming Out Party*, shot in Britain's capital, and *Navigators*, which deals with the effects of railway privatisation, written by former railway worker Rob Dawber and shot in his native Sheffield.[6] An interesting partial exception is the work developed with Nell Dunn and Jeremy Sandford: in contrast to the other writers' working-class backgrounds, the then young married couple rejected their upper-class backgrounds and moved to Battersby in South London to live and work. There, Sandford wrote *Cathy Come Home*, and Dunn developed her short story collection *Up the Junction* and the novel *Poor Cow*; all drew heavily on their encounters with local working-class women.[7]

It is well-established that Loach often works with first-time actors, however, he has also worked with several first-time writers, or writers making their screen debuts, including Dawber, Dunn, Hines, Sandford and Laverty. In the 1990s, Laverty returned from Nicaragua where he was working as a legal adviser, supporting those on the receiving end of atrocities committed by the right-wing, US-backed Contras, and contacted Loach about the possibility of writing a screenplay based on these experiences.[8] This resulted in *Carla's Song*, and bar *Navigators*, Laverty has written all of Loach's subsequent fictional films.[9] In addition to *Carla's Song* and *The Angels' Share*, as outlined in Chapter 1, *My Name is Joe* (1998), *Sweet Sixteen* (2002), *Ae Fond Kiss . . .* (2004) and *Tickets* (2005) were all filmed mostly in Scotland. Although Laverty has filmed scripts with Loach

---

[6] Loach penned an obituary for Dawber in which he writes, 'His first script, which I was lucky enough to be sent, was full of life, characters and stories. It was about the break-up of the railways into private companies and sub-contractors.' See 'Rob Dawber: Radical rail worker and writer who sued his bosses over fatal illness', *The Guardian*, 23 February 2001, https://www.theguardian.com/news/2001/feb/23/guardianobituaries (last accessed 23 August 2020).

[7] Dunn had a sole writing credit for *Up the Junction* and shared the writing credit with Loach on *Poor Cow*.

[8] For background see the introduction to the *Carla's Song* screenplay (Laverty 1997).

[9] With Icíar Bollaín as director, Laverty also scripted *El olivo/The Olive Tree* and *Yuli/Yuli: The Carlos Acostas Story* (2018), and has a co-writer credit on *Katmandú, un espejo en el cielo/Katmandu Lullaby* (2012). A useful contrast with Laverty's work with other directors is provided by analysis of the opening scene of *También la lluvia/Even the Rain*. Here, as a Spanish production crew arrive in Bolivia, a helicopter flies overhead carrying a gigantic cross, referencing a similar scene in *La Dolce Vita* (Fellini, Italy, 1960); however, this type of cinematic intertextuality would seem out of place in a film directed by Loach.

elsewhere in Britain, Newcastle (*I, Daniel Blake, Sorry We Missed You*), London (*It's a Free World . . .*), Liverpool (*Looking for Eric*) and the short *11'09"01 September 11* (segment *United Kingdom*) (2002), most of their UK projects have been Scottish-based.[10] John Hill (2011: 182–3) cites three factors underlying what he describes as Loach's 'Scottish Turn': his ongoing relationship with Laverty, access to Scottish public funding, and that working-class identity remains prominent in Scottish public and political discourse. Hill lists these in this order, without establishing a hierarchy. Christopher Meir (2016: 131), on the other hand, suggests that financial support from Creative Scotland was the 'determining factor' for shooting much of their work in Scotland.[11] Whilst securing public funding has been central to Sixteen Films' business model, that *The Angels' Share* was financed by Belgian and French co-producers and the British Film Institute, not Creative Scotland, lends weight to the idea that Loach's approach to follow the writer is the primary factor at work here, particularly given the trend outlined above. On the set of *Sweet Sixteen*, Laverty outlined what he saw as the advantages of working in Scotland: 'It's really nice to come back home again and write in your own dialect and your own rhythm. It's a territory which is much easier to me because you're closer to what is going on.'[12] A decade later, on the set of *The Angels' Share*, Laverty speaks in similar terms: 'It's home territory. After having done the Bolivian one [*También la Lluvia/Even the Rain*] and *Route Irish* in Liverpool, there's always a sense of ease about coming back to do one in the west of Scotland.'[13] That one of the few occasions when Loach has ventured beyond Europe was to film *Bread*

[10] Peter Gallagher states in interview that *It's a Free World* was due to be filmed in Scotland but was relocated to London in part due to casting concerns.

[11] In discussing *Ae Fond Kiss . . .*, Meir (2015: 134) suggests that as Loach had stated that the film's themes could resonate just as well in the north of England, and as Laverty had written scripts set in several other countries, then, as he puts it, 'Taking these two reasons out of the equation leaves only public support as a determining factor for setting the film in Scotland.' That *The Angels' Share* received BFI rather than Creative Scotland funding somewhat negates this position. Notably, however, two subsequent films (*I, Daniel Blake* and *Sorry We Missed You*) were shot in the north-east of England, with another, *The Old Oak*, also slated for production there.

[12] Quoted in Archibald (2002). Laverty was born in Calcutta but grew up mostly in Scotland and states, 'I consider myself from Glasgow' (Kevin Conroy Scott 2005: 268).

[13] Interview with author. All subsequent quotes from Laverty in this chapter are taken from this interview. It should be noted, however, that Laverty and Loach have not returned to Scotland to make a film since, with *Jimmy's Hall* set in Ireland and both *I, Daniel Blake* and *Sorry We Missed You* set in Newcastle.

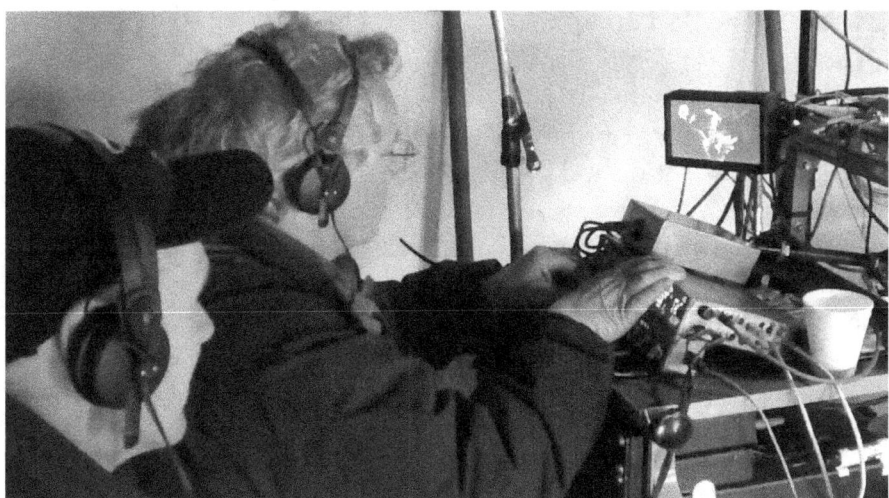

Figure 5.1 Paul Laverty and Ray Beckett monitoring the action at Balblair distillery

and Roses, which was based on Laverty's experiences observing campaigns to organise low-paid cleaners in Los Angeles when he lived there briefly in the 1990s, reinforces the idea that Loach travels to locales where the writer is comfortable or inspired by the material.

Commenting on the reasons for setting *The Old Oak*, which they hope to shoot in 2022, in the north-east of England, Laverty cites a 'rich working-class culture and vitality to the people'.[14] He adds that there is a variety in the area and that it is 'relatively compact', which 'makes a huge difference if you don't have to be commuting hours and hours every day'.[15] Notably, Laverty lives in Edinburgh, relatively close to the north-east of England, thereby making both research and filmmaking more practical and undoubtedly a factor in setting *I, Daniel Blake* and *Sorry We Missed You* in that part of Britain. Laverty has also stated that he spends extensive periods in the community researching the lives of those he writes about.[16] As such, the writers Loach has worked with are immersed in local working-class experience, adding a sense of geographical and political reality, and fitting more broadly into Loach's realist practice.

---

[14] Information in email to author dated 18 January 2022.
[15] Ibid.
[16] See Kevin Conroy Scott (2005) for an extended interview with Laverty about his approach to writing.

Screenplay as blueprint

John Thornton Caldwell (2008: 232) suggests that 'any screenplay or project developed in prime television or feature film today generates considerable attention and involvement at the earliest story sessions and producers' meetings by personnel from the firm's financing, marketing, co-production, distribution, merchandizing, and new media departments or divisions'. In the early years of Loach's career, working at the BBC and then with various producers as outlined in Chapter 3, Loach faced similar pressures. As director and co-owner of Sixteen Films, however, he can both select the writer he works with and be largely free of such interventions. The writers most identified as working with Loach are Allen, Hines and Laverty, however, some of the engagements with other writers are useful in illuminating Loach's practice. It is a commonplace of artistic production that the director and writer must be 'on the same page', so to speak. For instance, discussing *Ivanovo detstvo/Ivan's Childhood* (Tarkovsky, 1962), an adaptation of Vladimir Bogomolov's short story, Tarkovsky states (2003: 18), 'When a writer and a director have different aesthetic starting points, compromise is impossible. It will destroy the very conception of the film. The film will not happen.' In the previous chapter, I outlined some of the problems which arose when Loach collaborated with Trevor Griffiths on *Fatherland*. Correspondence between the two on their approaches towards writing are also instructive in illuminating stylistic and methodological difference.[17] In the correspondence, Griffiths lays out the importance of the actors being aware of and having fully rehearsed their lines.[18] By contrast, Loach states, 'Dialogue, it seems to me, is part of behaviour, and not something onto which behaviour is added. This does not imply lack of respect for the script, the opposite is the case.'[19] Contra Griffith's fixed position, Loach suggests that dialogue can, at least in part, emerge in the production process, in turn, enriching the script.

---

[17] For more on Griffiths, see John Tulloch's *Trevor Griffiths* (2011). Illustrating the divergent ways in which the screenplay is held by critics, in an extended analysis of the difference between the screenplay and the finished film, Romy Clark (1999: 117) is critical of Loach's approach on *Fatherland*: as he puts it, 'Loach goes beyond legitimate interpretation of the written screenplay text and ends up traducing it.'

[18] Letter from Trevor Griffiths to Ken Loach, 30 January 1985: BFI Ken Loach archive, KCL-19-7-1-7.

[19] Letter from Ken Loach to Trevor Griffiths, 1 February 1985: BFI Ken Loach archive, KCL-19-7-1-7.

While the difficulties in the Loach–Griffiths relationship ensured that *Fatherland* was both their first and last collaboration, Loach and Laverty have established a long-lasting, productive working relationship with Laverty involved in aspects of production well beyond the conventional writers' role. This is exemplified by his involvement in casting, discussed in the previous chapter, but also his involvement on set and in viewing rough cuts suggests an ongoing dialogical rather than strictly demarcated working relationship between director and writer. In discussing script development, Laverty outlines the process: 'We put it on paper, and we knock it back and forward. And then I'll go and do a whole first draft. And that's a very private part.' Following the first draft's completion, Loach and Laverty reconvene with script editor Roger Smith, who wrote Loach's television debut, *Catherine* (BBC, 1964), and who has worked repeatedly with Loach since. During this part of the process, Laverty states that the trio poses 'the toughest questions: Does the story work? Do these characters hold up? Does this story hold together?' Smith is not involved in the research and comes in as what Laverty describes as 'a total fresh eye' but also views an early cut, with Laverty and O'Brien.[20] Indicative of Smith's role, Laverty, on receiving the 2002 Cannes Film Festival Best Screenplay Award for *Sweet Sixteen*, stated, 'Every script I've ever come across needs a good Roger.'[21] Writing is understood primarily as a solitary experience, yet Smith's involvement further signifies the collaborative nature of the process in play here.[22]

The Angels' Share screenplay contains forty-seven scenes, all of which were shot in central Scotland, mostly Glasgow, and the Highlands.[23] There are some directorial notes: it opens with (Laverty 2012: 15), 'AGAINST BLACK: Sounds of solemn VOICES from inside the Sheriff Court,

---

[20] Information from author's interview with Laverty.
[21] Quoted in Laverty (2002: 3)
[22] Whilst television writing is more likely to be understood as often involving collective activity, film writing, I would suggest, particularly within the world of independent film production, is regarded as more of an individual act.
[23] Line manager Peter Gallagher suggests that most Loach films have around fifty scenes, which is considerably fewer than the industry average and speculates, 'It is almost as if the scripts are geared specifically to his way of working because they fit neatly into being shot in a sequential pattern in a five- or six-week period.' To add weight to this suggestion, the *Sweet Sixteen* published screenplay has 57 separate scenes. By way of contrast Stephen Fellows' quantitative analysis of 12,309 feature films scripts indicates that the average screenplay has 110 scenes. https://stephenfollows.com/what-the-average-screenplay-contains/#:~:text=The%20average%20script%20has%20110,the%20fewest%20(just%2098.5) (last accessed 14 August 2020).

Glasgow'; in the closing scene, as Leonie and Robbie drive off into the country (2012, 171), 'INSIDE: Robbie drives the VW'; and, following directions and dialogue, concludes, 'FROM OUTSIDE: The VW passes another glorious spot and disappears into the distance. FADE TO BLACK.' In contrast to Griffith's writing approach, Laverty's script is generally free of directorial guidance, in keeping with a more fluid approach to filming during the shoot itself. Although detailed in terms of narrative, content and structure, the script operates as a blueprint, or 'a means to and end' as Loach puts it, from which the final film will be developed.[24] Scholarly studies of screenplays have focused on published texts, whether in draft or final form; however, observing how the text is amended during filming allows a richer picture to emerge. In observing the filming of *The Angels' Share*, moreover, it is possible to discern the actors' role beyond performance itself, and how they contribute to shaping the words heard in the finished film.

The screenplay is evidently Laverty's work, and the structure and overall content of screenplay and film are the same. In the final film, however, there are several omissions, including the paring down of Robbie's feud with Clancy, and his borrowing of £500 from Harry to finance the Highlands expedition.[25] As I illustrate below, there are also several instances in which the dialogue differs, either cut completely, truncated, extended or amended. Loach suggests that there is a balance between the pre-existing plan and creating space for improvisation: 'You've got to have a plan and you've got to work that out as you go and make certain that what the actors are offering works within that framework. But on the other hand, the actors have got to feel that they are liberated to follow their instincts so that's a tightrope that you've got to tread.' As Brannigan notes at the top of this chapter, actors can utilise their own words, provided they stick to the narrative's general thrust. This is reinforced by observing Ruane during filming as he would continually use slightly different words in each take. He says,

> That is one of the good things – having freedom. On most things you need to stick to the script 90 per cent of the time, you maybe change a wee word here or there but you need to stick to it, whereas on this very rarely have I done the exact take twice. He'll also come up to you and

---

[24] Interview with author. All subsequent quotes from Loach in this chapter are from this interview.

[25] The flashback scene with Rhino, which was shot as if to replicate CCTV footage, is omitted from the final film. In the screenplay (23), Rhino describes one of the arresting officers as a 'big wanking beanpole'; during filming, the somewhat softer 'big baldy beanpole' was deployed. Notably on Loach's annotated shooting script (6, 84) 'wanking' is replaced by 'baldy' indicating his involvement in the process.

whisper something in your ear, 'Try this way, or try that way.' But he'll leave it up to you to put your wee bit in. The element of change and surprise is good.[26]

In interview, Garnett notes that this approach towards dialogue emerged in their working relationship's early years, when, as he puts it: 'We improvised a lot, but around a good tight screenplay.'[27] As such, this working method, has been finessed over decades to create moments of spontaneity within a fixed, yet fluid, structure.

As I indicated in the previous chapter, Loach keeps the script largely secret from the actors, normally releasing sections the day before shooting each sequence or scene. When Loach directs actors, he will say something like, 'Put it in your own words,' or 'Say what you'd say in that situation,' and a significant amount of the completed film's dialogue arises from the on-set collaborative process. This is evident in analysis of the scenes that I have selected, which reveals how Laverty's fictional characters are realised in and through the actors' embodied presence.

The actor's role in shaping the script

Casting actors who share similarities with their characters allows the filmmakers to draw on actors' specialist knowledge and, consequently, script changes are made which reflect information gleaned during pre-production and production. I detail several instances below; they are indicative of the general process.[28] In the first instance, Charles MacLean notes in interview that the 'Grand' was dropped from 'Grand Master of the Quaich' after he advised Loach that there was only one holder of such title.[29] A second instance emerged during filming of the courtroom sequence when a lawyer

---

[26] Interview with author.
[27] Interview with author.
[28] One apparent danger with improvisation is that in departing from the script, narrative slippage can occur. For instance, in the scene in the hospital when Robbie is attacked by Leonie's dad and uncles and Harry persuades Robbie not to go after them, the published script states, 'Are you going to let them win so easily? Eh? Never see your baby ... ever!' In the completed film, however, Harry says, 'Think of the baby ... think of Leonie. Do you want to see your boy grow up, eh?' At this point, however, Harry does not know that Leonie has given birth to a boy, or at least we have not witnessed him learning this. This is a rare slip; nevertheless, perhaps an additional factor in restricting the actors' knowledge of the character's looming actions.
[29] Information from interview with MacLean.

cast as a supporting artist advised Loach that when addressing the court, a lawyer might say that one crime was 'analogous' to another. Loach, seemingly eager to utilise this professionally approved dialogue, asks one actor playing a lawyer to incorporate 'analogous' into their lines. After a few takes, however, the actor appears uncomfortable pronouncing 'analogous' and Loach asks the actor to amend it to 'comparable'. This exchange, which is not in the completed film, highlights a moment of tension between the desire for authenticity at the levels of script and performance, resulting, in this instance, in the desire for authentic performance trumping the desire for authentic dialogue. In a third example, in the published screenplay (Laverty 2012: 19, 26), the miscreants are sentenced to 'community service' as an alternative to incarceration. After interventions from the on-set legal advisers this is corrected to 'community payback'. One final example is evident in filming of the auction sequence but only partially in the film itself. In preparing this scene, during the pre-shoot set-up, Loach goes over a few additional lines with Paul Birchard who plays the American whisky buyer. When he asks him where his character is from, he suggests 'Westport, Connecticut', to which Loach responds, 'Okay, that's good.' Seemingly happy with the detail provided, Loach encourages him to describe the kids as 'Scotch', which is in keeping with the script's comic tone, although Birchard does not take the bait, indicating that the actors have an element of ownership over their improvised interventions.

In the filming of this scene, a handful of professional journalists are invited on set to perform as journalists reporting on the auction's outcome.

Figure 5.2 Loach directs Paul Birchard as cast, crew and a group of journalists look on

Tasked with producing on-location reports which will be published to coincide with the film's release, this move, devised by Loach and O'Brien, is an ingenious utilisation of their presence. By incorporating them into the action, it saves on the expense and labour of sourcing suitable supporting artists to play journalists, ensures a more authentic response, prevents the journalists from being a distracting presence on set, and enables the journalists to gather material for copy, thereby increasing the likelihood that additional column inches will be added to their published reports. On set, the journalists gather around the whisky cask and the American buyer after the auction has concluded and formulate their own questions to be put to him. In Laverty's script, there are two instances of press dialogue in this scene. The first is as the media scramble to photograph the successful buyer of the whisky (147): 'PRESS [shouts] You must have one little taste Sir!' Secondly, after the buyer invites the gang to join him for the photo-opportunity (148): 'JOURNALIST You have to taste it! Tell us what it's like!' In contrast, in the final film the exchange is as follows:

> JOURNALIST 1: What's your name please, sir?
> AMERICAN BUYER: They call me Jim Vincent
> JOURNALIST 1: And where are you from?
> AMERICAN BUYER: Westport, Connecticut.
> JOURNALIST 2: And, and are you gonna have a drink?
> AMERICAN BUYER: I hope so.
> OFF-SCREEN VOICE: Yes, he is!

After the buyer has sampled the whisky and as the press pack take numerous photographs the exchange continues:

> JOURNALIST 2: How does it compare?
> AMERICAN BUYER: It's absolutely exquisite. It's really great. Really great.

This exchange illustrates how the scene's general thrust remains but is fleshed out through the actors' improvisations.

In a subsequent article written by one of the journalists who played a journalist in the film, Damian Whitworth outlines his experience:

> I expect there are few things more irritating to a director than an extra who tries to wangle his way into a speaking part, but I tentatively ask Loach if I should ask the man who he is. 'Yes,' Loach says doubtfully. 'Do it as you would do it.' I ask the American buyer his name and then push my luck with a second line: 'Where are you from?' The other reporters jump in with questions.[30]

---

[30] Damian Whitworth, 'Movie stardom in The Angel's [sic] Share? I'll drink to that', *The Times*, 22 May 2012, https://www.thetimes.co.uk/article/movie-stardom-in-the-an

Whitworth, perhaps somewhat disparagingly, perhaps tongue-in-cheek, adds, 'We do several takes and get no more direction from Loach. Is this how he made *Kes* and *The Wind That Shakes the Barley*? It feels like a school play being thrown together at the last minute by a very laid-back teacher.'[31] Whitworth's comments illustrate further the disparity between the expected razzamatazz of the film industry and Loach's method of creating an environment far removed from that experience. The paradox, of course, is that it is the apparent casual nature, the 'school play' atmosphere, which creates the relaxed environment in which celebrated performances have emerged.

These examples of how the words in the film come into being indicate Loach's eagerness to constantly listen to the voices around him; indeed, listening to the actors' voices is essential to the method. Jean-Luc Nancy draws a distinction between hearing and listening (2007: 7):

> If 'to hear' is to understand the sense (either in the so-called figurative sense, or in the so-called proper sense: to hear a siren, a bird, or a drum is already each time to understand at least the rough outline of a situation, a context if not a text), 'to listen' is to be straining towards a possible meaning, and consequently one that is not immediately accessible.

Perhaps what we can take from Nancy's thinking is that listening involves being open to the sounds of the world but also to the resonances which they create, that listening involves a move towards interpretation and, indeed, the construction of meaning. Loach's method lies in this resonance, one which finds its way into the completed film, which emerges in observing the filming of the snooker hall confrontation.

Snooker hall

There is no greater signifier of a seemingly misspent youth than images of time spent in a snooker hall. As Robbie, Mo, Albert and Rhino pass time hanging out and potting balls, the scene reinforces the film's working-class focus and, as Clancy and his gang appear, the connection between

---

gels-share-ill-drink-to-that-shhnz352gst (last accessed 14 March 2018). Although I could have analysed the Balblair shoot utilising only my own observations, I have included Whitworth's account as another source to corroborate the general processes at work.

[31] Ibid.

Figure 5.3 Loach discusses shooting the snooker scene with the actors

young, male working-class life and violence.[32] In observing the scene being prepared, how the actors' lived experience comes into play also emerges. This is first evident in the selection of weapons for fighting when, over the snooker table's green baize, Campbell Mitchell (standby props), lays out weapons, including a baseball bat, a chain and an assortment of knives. From these, the four assailants choose, their selections determined by their suitability for the forthcoming attack. Scott Kyle (Clancy) and Neil Leiper (Spider) also intervene to shape the scene's action and dialogue as they discuss how best to stage the confrontation.

Loach stands amidst the group, stunt coordinator Paul Heasman behind him ready to intervene, Mo next to him gingerly holding a cue that she is poised to wield to ward off the attackers. In trying to stitch the moment when the assailants will confront the gang together, Loach says, 'It just needs a line from Scott [Clancy)] about "are you just going to give us a couple of minutes". That's what will trigger it [the attack].' On hearing Loach's comments, Scott Kyle intervenes, 'Will I tell them to fuck off? See when I first come in, like that, "Good shot. Yous three, get tae fuck."' Loach quietly concurs, 'Yeah, yeah,' before Riggins (Mo) intervenes and says, 'That could bring me in,' and Kyle, leaning against the table, looking increasingly comfortable in

---

[32] The scene is similar in style to the one in *The Wednesday Play Just A Boys' Game* (BBC, 1979), which was directed by John Mackenzie but, in keeping with the tendency to identify writers with television drama, is more commonly associated with Peter MacDougall.

this space, suggests that then Mo could say, 'No, you get tae fuck.' Loach then adds, 'Yeah, I think that will do it.' Kyle, warming to the situation, continues, 'I think that's an important line. Rather than "Gie us a few minutes, it's a bit . . ."' before Neil Leiper (Spider), standing next to Kyle at the end of the table twirling a baseball bat interrupts, 'very formal'. To which Kyle repeats, 'very formal' and then Loach himself, adds, 'very formal. Okay.' Scott then adds, 'Yous three get tae fuck.' Loach turns to Riggins and says, 'Prompts the line from you,' then addressing Robbie says, 'That gives you the moment to get out.' Loach concurs quietly with Brannigan and says, 'Okay, we'll just do one more with that line.' I recount the words from this episode in detail as it exemplifies how the actors shape what is heard on-screen. As Clancy's 'get tae fuck' replaces Loach's initial suggestion of 'give us a few minutes', which Leiper describes as too 'formal', the actors' working-class, lived experience authenticates their dialogical exchanges.

In the screenplay, the first section of scene 22 reads as follows:

22 – SNOOKER HALL – DAY:

The white ball smacks powerfully against a new frame of red balls which scatter noisily around the table.

Robbie and Mo play snooker against Rhino and Albert. They are at the end table of the hall – one of around six, by the far end of the hall.

Albert takes ages to line up a shot as Rhino waits impatiently. Albert misses by a mile, as Rhino's face drops.

                      ALBERT
Light in here is shite by the way . . .

                      RHINO
Ah'd be better aff playin' wi Stevie Wonder . . .

Mo is terrific and pots a long ball. Robbie punches the air and there is a grin between them.

Mo catches the door swing open just a little and then close. Her face darkens. But it goes all quiet again.

As Robbie leans in to take a shot, the door opens a little more. Mo is wary and keeps her eye on it. A young lad enters and moves towards another table. She relaxes.

A shot now by Rhino.

Suddenly the door bursts open. Clancy, Sniper and three mates rush towards them screaming.

                      VOICES
Fucking get him!

> MO
> [screaming] Run Robbie... Run!
>
> Mo blocks the narrow space between the tables and bravely swings her cue wildly as she screams at them. Her frenzied antics delay them for a few minutes and gives Robbie a few seconds to run along the side of the hall. And crash through an emergency door. The alarm goes off. Robbie sprints down the stairs and they give chase.

As I outlined in Chapter 2, in the completed film the scene comprises nine shots which consists of the gang approaching the table, Rhino attempting to ward off the attackers with his cue and Robbie darting out of the emergency exit. As I have detailed, in preparing the scene, there is a sense that the actors and the director are thinking this through together and that the actors are given their head as contributors. Loach has stated (Fuller 1998: 47), 'When you get to the editing you often cut back to the script,' and Garnett also comments, 'If you do seven or eight takes, the one you choose in the cutting room is probably the one the writer wrote, or very close to it, because writers write better lines than actors make up.'[33] In this instance, the structure of the scene remains the same as the screenplay, however, there are significant amendments in terms of dialogue: Rhino's comments about Stevie Wonder are lost, and there is a significant exchange added when the assailants move towards Robbie and his friends and Clancy states, 'Good shot. Yous three, get tae fuck. I want a word with Robbie. Fuck off.' Robbie turns to address Clancy and replies, 'You want a word wi' me? Does it fucking take three of yiz, aye?' As we hear indiscernible threatening words from Clancy and his boys, Robbie continues, 'Fuck off ya fucking cunt.' In addition, as filming progressed, Loach deemed it increasingly implausible that Mo, short in both stature and snooker-cue wielding experience, could plausibly ward off the gang and Rhino is assigned the task. Therefore, the scene's format is as in the screenplay, but the specific dialogue and action, who pots what ball, who wields what weapon and so on, are all reformulated following an exchange between the participants. In this instance this involves the inclusion of an additional 'cunt'. Discussing realism and the screenplay, Jill Nelmes (2011: 218) suggests, 'Screenplay dialogue aims to convince the audience of its reality, to help "fix" the film text as a living, breathing world.' In an article on the completed screenplays of four films which draw on various forms of realist dialogue, she concludes (236) that 'it creates the illusion of being natural by using colloquial words yet its actual language construction is anything but; each word is

---

[33] Interview with author.

carefully chosen, more artifice than natural, a contrivance which aspires to be real but is not'. As I have illustrated in this chapter, however, as the actors shape the words spoken in the film, the situation is more complex in Loach's work than Nelmes' analysis might suggest with the distinction between illusion and reality somewhat blurred.

In discussing the tensions that arise with this method of working on this specific scene, Peter Gallagher comments,

> That was an interesting one because there was a collective discussion going on about how the scene should work and he [Loach] was obviously struggling because he was like, 'I need to let these people talk about it because they know what this fight would be like but I want to get this done and I want to get the mood and the energy going and the energy is going from it because we are discussing.' And he was struggling with that. After lunch he made a passing comment, 'I have to listen to them because they knew best what they are talking about.'

As Gallagher notes, this tension between allowing the actors space to develop dialogue which is authentic to the situation and Loach's desire to maintain the level of dynamism and energy required to keep the filming process alive and moving is a challenge Loach constantly negotiates throughout filming.

Bad language

The actors are not the only agents influencing the words spoken in the final film. The British Board of Film Classification (BBFC) initially allocated the film an '18' certificate with their report stating:

> The film contains multiple uses of strong language throughout and seven clear uses of very strong language. A single aggressive use of very strong language occurs when the central character is confronted by members of a gang in a pool hall. The use occurs amidst angry shouting as he attempts to stand up for himself. Other aggressive uses of very strong language that were originally present have been dubbed out. The other instances of non-aggressive very strong language tend to be used in a throwaway manner and often occur during remarks between friends.[34]

[34] The film was released in the UK cinemas with a '15' certificate. An uncut version was released as a Blu-ray disc; the sleeve draws on the whisky discourse: 'THE ORIGINAL 100% PROOF EDITION'. Detailed studies of these changes are available at 'Cutting Edge: Season 3: Episode 45: The Angels' Share', http://melonfarmers.co.uk/bbfc_cuts_angels_share.htm and 'The Angels' Share': https://www.movie-censorship.com/report.php?ID=637567 (last accessed 20 August 2020).

Given the negative commercial impact this classification would have, the filmmakers re-presented an edited version which the BBFC classified with a '15' certificate. As O'Brien notes, they removed 'all the non-aggressive "cunts" and we covered up the other "cunts" in order to secure a '15' release in the UK'.[35] In line with a similar controversy with *Sweet Sixteen*'s release, this became one of the film's talking points and received notable press coverage.[36]

In the BBFC report 'strong language' might be understood as the film's use of the word 'fuck' with 'very strong language' referring to 'cunt'; indeed, the report refers to the use of 'cunt' in the snooker hall scene. In noting that the word is often deployed in 'a throwaway manner' and 'between friends', it suggests that the word itself has meanings in this specific situation which are beyond what might be regarded as its most offensive. The diversity of its usage emerges when the gang are discussing stealing the whisky. Here, Albert says they are all 'friendly wee cunts up in the Highlands' somewhat playing off the mythology of friendly couthy Highlanders, and towards the conclusion Robbie says to Mo: 'ya wee cunt', almost as a term of endearment. Although several 'cunts' are added in improvisation, there are several instances of its use in the screenplay. For instance, in scene 29, Robbie, enquiring as to the whereabouts of Clancy, asks of Sniper, 'Where's that cunt living?' In addition, Harry nicknames one of the Sheriff Court accused, young University of Glasgow neurology student Matthew Bains, 'PC', after Rhino then Mo describe him as 'a posh cunt'.[37] Curtailing the 'cunts' effectively silences an aspect of working-class discourse, and therefore the BBFC operates as a censorial voice in the film. That the report censors language which, within the context of its immediate production, is associated with young, working-class

---

[35] Interview with author.
[36] The BBFC classified *Sweet Sixteen* '18' despite the filmmakers' protests. The BBFC published a case study of the film, which details some of their thinking: https://www.bbfc.co.uk/case-studies/sweet-sixteen (last accessed 27 August 2020).
[37] In the script the character is sentenced to twelve months in prison so it is unclear as to why he would be working on the community payback scheme. His character is edited out of the finished film. It is important to note here that these amendments, while perhaps deserving of only a small reference, are not incidental aspects of the production. Rather, they function as authenticating machines at various levels, their function geared towards the production of a film, which, at its heart, contains the most fundamental contradiction: an authentic fabrication.

Glaswegians, operates to erase, in part, the complexity of proletarian Scots discourse.[38]

Notably, much of the screenplay's dialogue is written in vernacular Scots.[39] For instance, in the sentencing sequence, the courtroom clerk asks Mo, 'Are you Maureen Stone?' to which she replies, 'Aye.' The stage directions then note 'the court officer beside whispers aggressively in her ear' and Mo then adds, 'Yes, yer Honourship!' In this scene, then, a pre-existing hierarchy of discourse is established in which proletarian Scots is deemed inferior, that which cannot be spoken, in the British state's courtrooms. Here, a fidelity to the local accent takes on a national dimension in that the voice of working-class Scotland, an urban demotic, which has Glasgow as its loudest voice, has been co-opted as part of a broader language struggle, spearheaded since the 1970s by writers such as James Kelman. Rather than viewing language as a neutral sign system, which humans utilise to communicate, it speaks in and through individuals and is not simply spoken by them; as such, language orders, rather than simply represents, the political world in which the work itself features. The use of particular words in *The Angels' Share*, then, moves the argument beyond questions of representation or authenticity; the controversy over the use of 'cunts' is not just whether this is an accurate depiction of how young working-class characters in Glasgow speak. Rather, as language produces the political, the use of 'cunt', and, indeed, its removal to facilitate a '15' version of the film, directly addresses questions concerning the nature of politics itself. In an article titled *The Problem of Speaking for Others* (1991/2: 7) Linda Alcoff suggests that the notion of 'privileged authors who speak on behalf of the oppressed is becoming increasingly criticized by members of those oppressed groups themselves'. This disturbs any popular sense that Loach is 'giving a voice to the voiceless', which is inherently problematic not simply because it raises who is deemed to be authorised to speak on behalf of the other, but also because speaking on behalf of the other can work to exclude the voice of the other itself – put simply, 'giving a voice to the voiceless' can silence the voiceless. These considerations, aside, Loach has never claimed to operate in such a manner. Moreover, if we regard

---

[38] I have concentrated on the class dimension to this controversy, however, there is also a national aspect at play here. Although Loach has said that the film could be set anywhere, this is the most 'Scottish' of the films, overflowing, as it is, with Irn Bru, whisky, The Proclaimers' music, and other stereotypical signifiers of Scotland.

[39] Notably, the film's Wikipedia page states that the languages of the film are English and Scots: https://en.wikipedia.org/wiki/The_Angels%27_Share (last accessed 14 January 2022).

Loach's work as an aesthetic and political intervention, then it effectively introduces working-class voices into and onto the political scene. Jacques Rancière contends that

> Political activity reconfigures the distribution of the perceptible. It introduces new objects and subjects onto the common stage. It makes visible what was invisible, it makes audible as speaking beings those who were previously heard only as noisy animals. (2011: 4)

This connection between coarse language and the animalistic way the working class have been described is an ongoing discussion in Scottish cultural life, perhaps best exemplified by the controversy surrounding James Kelman's success at being awarded the 1994 Booker Prize for *How Late It Was, How Late*. The novel was critiqued for its excessive use of 'bad language':

> It was all down to Sammy; every fucking last fucking thing man know what I mean know what I fucking mean it was down to him, Sammy, Sammy himself man that was who it was down to, him, nay other cunt, all this fucking crap man it was his and nay other cunt's, fucking his. (Kelman 1998: 322)[40]

Yet, Kelman responded to the critique of his language in overtly political terms:

> There is a literary tradition to which I hope my own work belongs, I see it as part of a much wider process – or movement – toward decolonization and self-determination: it is a tradition that assumes two things: 1) The validity of indigenous culture; and 2) The right to defend in the face of attack. It is a tradition premised on a rejection of the cultural values of imperial or colonial authority, offering a defence against cultural assimilation, in particular imposed assimilation.[41]

As such, Kelman ties the critique of his work to questions of class and national exploitation, rather than simply literary merit. In defence of Kelman's language, Willy Maley (1996: 107) writes,

> Swearing is the phatic communion of the factory, the barracks, the pub, the street. A sign of violent and impoverished masculinity, disenfranchised youth, socialist labour. 'Fuck' is both taboo and totem, it is both unspeakable and unduly fetishized. The focus on context has to include the nation. As well as a class context, and an urban context, there is a national context.[42]

---

[40] For more on this controversy see Maley (1996) and on Kelman more broadly see Scott Hames (2010).

[41] Kelman's acceptance speech is available at http://www.rastko.co.uk/kelman/ (last accessed 18 August 2020).

[42] There is, of course, an additional gendered factor at work here.

What we could add to Maley's defence of 'bad language' is the pleasure of transgressing the linguistic boundaries of bourgeois discourse. In rather straight-laced terms, Trotsky suggests (1973/1923: 52): 'Abusive language and swearing are a legacy of slavery, humiliation, and disrespect for human dignity – one's own and that of other people.' Loach, conversely, suggests that these are old words which we can enjoy.[43] As such, then, there is a quite complex process at work in *The Angels' Share* as it helps make visible, and audible, aspects of Scottish working-class existence and discourse which might otherwise be unseen and unheard. This highlights an additional set of political questions to those addressed in Chapter 1, and, indeed, in the extant Loach scholarship, indicating that the films are ripe for analyses on wider critical terrains.

Conclusion

In addition to highlighting how Loach 'follows the writer', this chapter sought to examine how Loach utilises the screenplay as a blueprint through observing the shooting process. Several points emerge from this. Firstly, that although the screenplay is completed and the parameters of the action demarcated, the completed film is both pared down and/or fleshed out through the production process by the deletion of scenes and the inclusion of additional words spoken during the film itself. Further, that during the production process, Loach draws on the actors' background knowledge to authenticate the film's constructed reality through amending small plot details, or adding or amending specific words from the script. As such, the actors and supporting artists have a degree of agency beyond their actual performance. But what do these points amount to? They create an authenticity register which is thicker than the one that could be created by either the writer, or the writer and director working together. The approach, then, returns to the question of teams and leadership first discussed in Chapter 3. Here, the dynamic is different, but the principle, that more can be achieved through collaborative than individual ventures, is writ large, indicative of the filmmakers' political and philosophical perspectives. It further illustrates that Loach's filmmaking process is not characterised by easily definable and strict binaries, it is a process which is fluid with its component

---

[43] Victoria Coren (2012) 'Keep our curses in rude health', *The Guardian*, 27 May 2012, https://www.theguardian.com/commentisfree/2012/may/27/victoria-coren-ken-loach-wrong-on-oaths (last accessed 29 August 2020).

parts and contributors always already entangled. The BBFC's intervention highlights a further layer of entanglement which the filmmakers must negotiate, pointing to factors which emerge beyond their control, and to the world beyond the screen.

6

Politics beyond the screen

> For if we are serious about even political life we have to enter that world in which people live as they can as themselves, and then necessarily live within a whole complex of work and love and illness and natural beauty. If we are serious socialists, we shall then often find within and cutting across this real substance – always, in its details, so surprising and often vivid – the profound social and historical conditions and movements which enable us to speak, with some fullness of voice, of a human history.
> Raymond Williams[1]

Walking through Glasgow's Kelvingrove Park one spring morning in 2017, I receive a phone call from Tommy Breslin, a trade unionist and activist in Glasgow's radical film scene. During the call, Tommy explains that he is helping to organise the speakers for a forthcoming Glasgow May Day rally and, as such, is looking for Ken Loach's contact details. Eager to capitalise on the interest surrounding *I, Daniel Blake*, which had provoked considerable political commentary since its release the previous year, he hopes Loach will consider being the rally's keynote speaker. Details are exchanged and, as it transpires, Paul Laverty addresses the Glasgow event, with images associated with the film featuring prominently on publicity posters.[2]

This exchange is useful in indicating something of Loach's, and Laverty's, broader political activity. It also exemplifies how activists have utilised Loach's work, indicative of how it resonates beyond the screen with working-class organisations. My Certain Tendencies in Loach's Cinema started with politics, and it ends with politics, and in this chapter I deal with off-screen political engagement, exploring how Loach has

---

[1] Williams (1989a: 116)
[2] In the same week, Loach addressed the Scottish Trades Union Congress annual congress.

Figure 6.1 Glasgow May Day poster: illustration of Dave Johns as Daniel Blake, the film's eponymous hero, his left arm raised, fist clenched tight in defiance © Lorna Miller

utilised the platform provided by his films' success and his position on the international film community to intervene in political discourse. As such, and in the spirit of Raymond William's words above, I illustrate something of how Loach enters the world in which people live, not simply through the cinema screen, but through film-related political engagement.[3] I begin by analysing Loach's relationship with the Cannes Film Festival and my observations from attending *The Angels' Share*'s world premiere and associated events at the 65th festival in 2012. I spend some time discussing Cannes as it seems vital to understanding Loach's position in international cinema, and because it is from here that *The Angels' Share* was launched into the world. I then proceed to examine instances in which Loach has intervened politically on the international film festival circuit and film-related political

---

[3] I restrict my analysis to Loach's film-related political activity. More work could be done on his direct involvement with political campaigns, but space precludes a wider examination.

interventions closer to home.[4] As outlined in the Introduction, Loach's work has had significant political influence and the extent of this would merit a book itself. My aim in this chapter is to highlight something of how Loach and his work operates beyond the screen, and to suggest that a broader interpretive framework beyond conventional text-based analysis is required to analyse the films.

Cannes

Initiated in 1939 as an alternative to Venice Film Festival, which had been inaugurated under Mussolini's fascist regime in 1932, Cannes was political from the outset (Marijke de Valck 2007; Cindy Hing-Yuk Wong 2011). The start of the Second World War prevented all but the opening day's screenings from proceeding, and the festival took an extended sabbatical before reconvening in 1946. Thereafter, Cannes quickly became established as the world's pre-eminent film festival, focusing on art cinema but more than tinged with Hollywood glamour. The opulent wealth on display in the festival's French Riviera setting, exemplified by the ostentatious yachts docked in its harbour or the plentiful number of Rolls Royce limousines cruising through its streets, sits uncomfortably and incongruously alongside the programme's generally progressive politics. Drawing on Thomas Elsaesser's work on film festivals and Pierre Bourdieu's work on taste, Marijke de Valck and Mimi Soeteman (2010: 290–3) contend that film festivals add value and cultural capital to films through the distribution of awards and the media attention that they receive. De Valck also notes (2007: 87–8) that film festivals provide an alternative to the studio system's vertical integration model. As such, festival success, for instance, a positive critical reception or winning awards, can boost a film's distribution and subsequent commercial prospects. These are commonly held understandings in the film industry, though underexplored in film studies. Examining Loach's relationship with Cannes allows us to place some empirical flesh on theoretical bones and industry assumptions, and to illustrate how Loach utilises the festival circuit platform to advance his political perspectives, which in turn influences the films' critical reception and the interpretive frameworks through which they might be analysed.

---

[4] A useful bibliography on film festivals is updated regularly by the Film Festival Research Network: http://www.filmfestivalresearch.org/index.php/ffrn-bibliography/ (last accessed 20 August 2020).

Loach's Cannes curriculum vitae includes fourteen films screened in the official competition: *Looks and Smiles* (1981), *Hidden Agenda* (1990), *Raining Stones* (1993), *Land and Freedom* (1995), *My Name is Joe* (1998), *Bread and Roses* (2000), *Sweet Sixteen* (2002), *The Wind That Shakes the Barley* (2006), *Looking for Eric* (2008), *Route Irish* (2010), *The Angels' Share* (2012), *Jimmy's Hall* (2014), *I, Daniel Blake* (2016) and *Sorry We Missed You* (2019).[5] In addition, *Kes* (1970) screened in Critics' Week and *Family Life* (1972), *Black Jack* (1979) and *Riff-Raff* (1991) screened in Directors' Fortnight. *The Gamekeeper* (1980) was screened in Un Certain Regard and *Happy Ending* (2007), which was Loach's contribution to *Chacun son cinéma/To Each His Own Cinema*, an anthology of short films commissioned to mark the 60th festival, screened out of competition. Excluding the short, this represents a total of twenty-two features which have garnered the following awards: the Palme d'Or (*The Wind That Shakes the Barley, I, Daniel Blake*); the Jury Prize (*Hidden Agenda, Raining Stones, The Angels' Share*); the Prize of the Ecumenical Jury (*Land and Freedom, Looking for Eric*); the Prize of the Ecumenical Jury – Special Mention (*Looks and Smiles, Hidden Agenda*); the FIPRESCI Prize (*Riff-Raff* and *Land and Freedom*); the FIPRESCI Prize – Parallel Section (*Black Jack*); the Young Cinema Award (*Looks and Smiles*); Best Screenplay Award for Paul Laverty (*Sweet Sixteen*); and Best Actor Award for Peter Mullan (*My Name is Joe*). In addition, in 2004, Loach received the Ecumenical Jury's 30th Anniversary Award in recognition of his work until that point; by any measure, Loach's record at Cannes is unparalleled and extraordinary.

In interview at the festival, Rebecca O'Brien suggests that Cannes provides the best launch for a film, stating that it 'throws a spotlight on a film in such an extraordinary way'.[6] Prior to the awards being announced, O'Brien had stated: 'We really don't expect to win. We're well aware that we're not in the heavyweight department.' She added, however, 'There's always the outside chance that we might get a Jury Prize.' O'Brien's observations chime with those of Cindy Hing-Yuk Wong who notes (2011: 85) that major film festivals tend to favour weighty, artistic films, often associated with established or emerging directors who fit easily into *auteurist* discourses, and that comedies and musicals 'seem to violate the serious tone of the festival forum'. An analysis of the 2012 Cannes official competition programme,

---

[5] The bracketed years represent the year of the film's screening at the festival, not its cinematic release.

[6] Interview with the author (22 May 2012, the day following the competition screening). All subsequent quotes from O'Brien come from this interview.

which comprised twenty-two films dominated by serious subject matter, lends weight to this position. That *Amore/Love* (Haneke, 2012), with its focus on ageing and mortality, received the Palme d'Or and *După dealuri/Beyond the Hills* (Mungiu, 2012), an account of the traumatic experiences of two female Romanian orphanage occupants, won the Best Screenplay Award, reinforces the impression that serious films are more likely to be garlanded with the major awards. With *Reality* (Garrone, 2012), a comic critique of reality television, receiving the Grand Prix, and *The Angels' Share* receiving the Jury Prize (regarded as the festival's *de facto* second and third prizes respectively), it suggests that films lighter in tone can still be successful on these terms. *The Angels' Share*'s success in competition was reflective of wider appreciation of the film at the festival.

Press events

Two press screenings of *The Angels' Share* took place in the festival's early days. Discerning a communal mood amongst those assembled was difficult; nevertheless, considerable laughter, an audible gasp throughout the auditorium when the group's plan to liberate some expensive whisky appears to have been literally shattered, and extended applause at the conclusion indicated an enthusiastic response.[7] At a press conference the following day, attended by approximately 100 journalists along with various camera crews, film critic and event chair Henri Behar introduced Loach, O'Brien and Laverty as 'bona fide citizens of the Cannes Film Festival'. Two actors joined them on the platform, Paul Brannigan and Charles MacLean, while several other cast and crew members sat in the auditorium. Behar opened the conference with three questions dealing with whisky, comedy, and parallels between *The Angels' Share* and *Kes*. This was followed by nine questions from the floor from journalists from Belgium, South Africa, Sweden, the UK and the USA. The first three of these focused on Brannigan's acting plans and reports that he had worked with Scarlett Johansson: his status as a first-time actor with a similarly disadvantaged background to that of

---

[7] These initial impressions were confirmed by analysis of the film's early reviews, which were overwhelmingly positive in nature. In the British press the film received numerous four-star reviews and significant praise: for example, Peter Bradshaw in his *Guardian* review wrote, 'In many ways this is his [Loach's] most relaxed and successful screen offering for some time', https://www.theguardian.com/film/2012/may/21/the-angels-share-review (last accessed 17 December 2021). O'Brien in interview said that the reviews were better than they had anticipated.

his character offering a 'triumph over adversity' human-interest angle, a staple of journalistic (and Hollywood) production narratives.[8] Subsequent questions focused on the use of English subtitles (the film was screened with both English and French subtitles), similarities with the Dardennes brothers' films, casting, directing, comedy, how Loach has represented the working class over time, and political leadership. In the discussion over subtitles, O'Brien commented on the controversy over the use of 'cunt' as discussed in the previous chapter, adding, 'The language in the film is the language that these young people speak; it's completely natural and I think if they [the BBFC are] looking for diversity in Britain they need look no further than this film and Glasgow. There are different ways of speaking and that should be acceptable to all and should not be censored.' Loach added a class dimension to the discourse: 'The British middle class is obsessed by what they call "bad language". The odd oath, a word that goes back to Chaucer's time, they will ask you to cut but the manipulative and deceitful language of politics they use themselves.' This controversy received notable press coverage in the UK, indicating how discussion of the film moved beyond entertainment, into politics, which, in turn, moves coverage of the film from the arts pages and onto the news agenda.[9]

Responding to the *Kes*-related question, Loach suggested that while the film's central character, Billy, faced a future of dead-end employment in a Yorkshire coalfield, Robbie and his pals faced the prospect of long-term unemployment. Discussion over Robbie's search for gainful employment then segued into wider societal and political concerns. For instance, Laverty highlighted statistics from the International Labour Organisation 'Global Trends for Youth 2012' report, which the press had reported on that morning, and stated that 75 million young people were unemployed worldwide.[10] He added that in Spain, 5.6 million were unemployed

---

[8] This resulted in extensive coverage. For instance, Deirdre O'Brien, 'From a life of drugs on a tough housing estate to sharing a love scene with Scarlett Johansson – Britain's unlikely new movie star: Paul Brannigan's life story could make a Hollywood film on its own', *Daily Mirror*, 9 June 2012, http://www.mirror.co.uk/news/real-life-stories/from-a-life-of-drugs-on-a-tough-housing-estate-870119 (last accessed 20 December 2022). Brannigan featured alongside Johansson in *Under the Skin* (Glazer, UK/US/Switzerland, 2013).
[9] See, for instance, Charlotte Higgins, (2012) 'Ken Loach brands BBFC hypocritical over use of the c-word', *The Guardian*, 22 May 2012, http://www.guardian.co.uk/film/2012/may/22/ken-loach-bbfc-hypocritical (last accessed 5 March 2022).
[10] The full report is available at http://www.ilo.org/global/research/global-reports/youth/2012/lang--en/index.htm (last accessed 14 January 2022).

Figure 6.2 Loach is the main attraction for journalists at the Cannes press conference

and that the Spanish youth unemployment rate was 50 per cent. Loach responded to the question on political leadership in conventional Marxist terms: 'Our attitude to the working class doesn't change in that they are important because they are the agent of change. If there is to be change . . . it will come because of the organisation of the working class and for that you need political leadership.' This intervention marked a return to overt political discourse, and the concluding 10 minutes concentrated on the post-2008 economic crisis, the Arab Spring, and Occupy.[11] In this period, Loach also argued that media vilification of working-class people was being intensified as the economic crisis was deepening and that to campaign for employment, housing, sick care, and care for the elderly were, because of the nature of the crisis, 'revolutionary demands'. Such was the press conference's politicised nature that Behar, lightening the load somewhat, concluded by reminding the attendees that *The Angels' Share* was a comedy. I report these events in some detail to indicate how the filmmakers adopt a non-conventional approach towards the press, prioritising political over conventional entertainment discourse, which, in turn, bleeds into how the films are covered in the resultant press coverage.[12]

---

[11] Taking inspiration from the Arab Spring, Occupy was a loosely organised movement for social and political change. For more on Occupy, see Janet Byrne (2012).

[12] Whether this is an unconventional marketing strategy, or otherwise, the approach is effective in generating press attention and coverage.

The official premiere

If the press screenings are where Cannes' industrious side emerges, the glamour is attached to the official screenings: O'Brien comments, 'France doesn't have royalty, but films are the basis of their royalty substitute. That's how they treat you.' André Bazin (2009: 15) found parallels with another institution, arguing that at Cannes 'the Palace which rises up on *La Croisette* is nothing less than the present-day monastery of the moviemaker'. There was something unavoidably incongruous, therefore, about attending a screening of a film dealing with unemployed youngsters from Glasgow in such hallowed, illustrious surroundings. *The Angels' Share* competition screening took place during the evening of the day of the press conference. In advance, a forty-person 'Loach Party' assembled beforehand at a Creative Scotland reception on *La Croisette*'s Long Beach. In addition to Loach, Laverty and O'Brien, the group consisted of the leading cast and crew, co-producers, financers, close family members, and one academic with a notebook. The party, with men sporting obligatory black ties, some with optional kilts, and women in elegant evening dress, then walked the few hundred yards to the Carlton Hotel from where they were ushered into a cavalcade of black limousines provided (presumably gratis) by Renault, one of the festival's corporate sponsors. The cavalcade, escorted by motorcycle policemen, glided through Cannes' crowded streets to the festival's main cinema to be greeted by packs of press photographers. Here, to the sound of The Proclaimers' 'I'm Gonna Be (500 Miles)', the party ascended the red-carpeted steps to the Grand Théâtre Lumière. Inside the cinema, the entourage received an extended standing ovation before the screening and another at the film's conclusion, indicating not just support for the film, but for Loach's overall career. The group was then ushered out, guarded by a phalanx of red-sashed female ushers and burly male security guards, before descending the stairs and re-entering the limousines to be driven to a private party at Château de la Castre, a castle overlooking the city. It is all a far cry from Glasgow's impoverished East End, simply one more of Cannes' multifarious contradictions. Yet, it is precisely this contradiction – the images of working-class kids from Glasgow ascending the stairs to world cinema's grandest stage, enveloped in the festival's glamour and grandeur – which fuelled further press coverage and generated commercial interest.[13]

---

[13] See, for instance, Ali Howard, 'Binman bags star place at Cannes festival', *The Herald*, 16 May 2012. The focus here was on Gary Maitland. Maitland returned to his cleaning work after filming was completed and has not worked as an actor since.

Figure 6.3 Loach and team receive a lengthy standing ovation at Cannes

The press screening, photo-ops, and official competition screening provided countless marketing opportunities, and the response of journalists, the jury, and the official competition screening attendees indicated that *The Angels' Share* was well received: in addition to the press conference, during the festival the filmmakers and actors conducted twenty-eight interviews with television crews from eighteen countries and sixty-eight interviews with radio/newspaper/web outlets from nineteen countries.[14] In addition, three television interviews and one newspaper interview were conducted with international syndicated outlets.[15] Prior to the festival, the film had been pre-sold to several countries, including Germany, Greece, Italy, Benelux and Spain, and release dates had been scheduled in the UK and France.[16] During the festival, negotiations continued with several buyers, with O'Brien estimating that the film's positive reception would mean distribution in most if not all territories: 'It's really interesting how much more money is on the table now as opposed to two days ago because of the reaction.' Indeed, while interviewing O'Brien at the festival, our discussion was interrupted by telephone calls in which she discussed the details of competing bids for the film's US rights, lending weight to de

---

[14] Information from marketing report provided by Sixteen Films. This does not include any additional press interviews as a consequence of the film winning the Jury Prize, which was presented on the festival's final day.

[15] Ibid.

[16] Information from interview with O'Brien.

Valck's observation that film festivals add value, in this instance quite literal economic value, to the films that they screen. Cannes, then, provided a platform for the filmmakers to launch *The Angels' Share* into the wider commercial world, at the same time presenting a platform to discuss the film's broader thematic concerns, which significantly influenced how the press reported on it.

Turin

In contrast to how the filmmakers have utilised the official platforms afforded by film festivals, the exhibition of *The Angels' Share* on the international film festival circuit also threw up somewhat unorthodox events. Initially awarded a Gran Premio Torino lifetime achievement award at the 2012 Torino Film Festival, Loach declined the invitation to personally receive the award at the festival on the basis that Turin's National Film Museum, the festival's parent body, had outsourced cleaning and security contracts. This outsourcing had precipitated wage cuts for workers employed in these areas and when they had undertaken industrial action to improve their conditions several had been fired.[17] As Loach stated in the trade journal *Hollywood Reporter*: 'We made a film dedicated to this topic [the 2000 Cannes Palme d'Or-nominated *Bread and Roses*]. How could I not respond to a request for solidarity from workers who were fired for fighting for their rights? Accepting the award and confining myself to a few critical comments would be weak and hypocritical.'[18] In turn, the festival organisers withdrew *The Angels' Share* from the competition and Loach and Sixteen Films, working with the labour movement organisations and trades unions involved, organised a screening of *Bread and Roses* in Turin during the festival. Speaking at the screening attended by striking workers and their supporters, Loach offered solidarity to the workforce, pointing to generalised attacks on the working class internationally, the need to organise to resist neoliberalism, and for a new economic model based on planning and common ownership.[19] He also praised the assembled workers, 'You're showing us how to do it,' and directly addressed the question of

[17] Eric J. Lyman, 'Ken Loach Refuses Turin Fest Honor Over Alleged Abuses', *Hollywood Reporter*, 21 November 2012, https://www.hollywoodreporter.com/news/general-news/ken-loach-refuses-turin-film-393554/ (last accessed 20 December 2021).
[18] Ibid.
[19] Available to view at https://www.youtube.com/watch?v=4r2XB_6ZoBg (last accessed 14 December 2019).

refusing the award, 'Can I finish by saying it's very nice to get prizes from film festivals. I don't treat it lightly. It would be an honour for everyone involved in our film to have that; but there's one prize we all share and that's to be part of this struggle.'[20] Although the festival has a history of screening films related to labour issues and, in keeping with many international film festivals, sits broadly on the left of the political spectrum, Loach was seen to side with the workforce against the festival organisers, leading to further supportive press coverage. For example, the *New Statesman* noted, 'As the Italian cultural establishment walks the tightrope of diplomacy, Loach has decided to stand shoulder to shoulder with those who can barely afford to buy a festival ticket.'[21] In more active circumstances than at Cannes, the Turin events highlight instances in which Loach intervenes on the festival circuit, with this act of physical solidarity generating further press interest, including from the trade journal *Screen Daily*, the British newspaper *The Independent*, and France 24's website, indicating the reach of this activity.[22] It is further evidence of how Loach utilises the international film festival circuit as a platform for extra-political activity, which, although motivated by political desire, also functions to raise awareness of the films, and Loach's international profile.

Festival boycotts

A long-standing champion of Palestinian rights, Loach has supported Boycott, Divestment and Sanctions (BDS), a non-violent campaign established in 2005 aimed at focusing international pressure on the Israeli state.[23] Loach has also directly intervened in the international film festi-

---

[20] Ibid.
[21] Celluloid Liberation Front, 'Ken Loach Turns Down An Award: The director shows solidarity with festival workers'. *New Statesman*, 29 November 2012.
[22] Michael Rosser, 'Ken Loach rejects Turin award over worker dispute', *Screen Daily*, 22 November 2012, https://www.screendaily.com/festivals/ken-loach-rejects-turin-award-over-worker-dispute/5049288.article; Uncredited (2012) 'Ken Loach snubs Italian film prize after workers sacked', https://www.france24.com/en/20121123-loach-protest-italian-film-prize-workers; Nick Clark, 'Director Ken Loach refuses Italian award after row over wage and staff cuts', *The Independent*, 23 November 2012, https://www.independent.co.uk/arts-entertainment/films/news/director-ken-loach-refuses-italian-award-after-row-over-wage-and-staff-cuts-8347138.html (all last accessed 20 December 2021).
[23] The BDS movement developed out of the Palestinian Campaign for the Academic and Cultural Boycott of Israel which was launched in 2004. For more on the BDS move-

val circuit to support the campaign, including calling for a boycott of the Edinburgh International Film Festival when it was deemed to have broken the boycott.[24] This activity has earned Loach praise from pro-Palestinian voices: for instance, Omar Barghouti (2012: 27) argues that Loach has, as he puts it, 'played a distinguished role in promoting the cultural boycott and popularizing its criteria and guidelines'. He also, however, joined an extensive list of prominent anti-racist activists, artists and filmmakers who in supporting BDS and/or voicing criticism of the Israeli government's actions on Palestine have been denounced as anti-Semitic, including Archbishop Desmond Tutu, Angela Davis, Penelope Cruz, Javier Bardem and Emma Watson.[25] These names can be added to the list of organisations who have been charged with similar accusations, including B'Tselem: The Israeli Information Center for Human Rights in the Occupied Territories and Amnesty International.[26] This controversy is a useful one in indicating that involvement in politics can damage the participants' reputation and Loach's support for the Palestinian struggle has not been without its

---

ment, see their website: https://bdsmovement.net/pacbi (last accessed 18 August 2020).

[24] See Archibald and Miller (2011) 'From Rennes to Toronto: Anatomy of a Boycott', *Screen*, 52 (2) for a discussion of the controversy which Loach was involved in on these matters at the Edinburgh and Melbourne International Film Festivals.

[25] For more on the allegations against Archbishop Desmond Tutu see Uncredited (2011) '"Anti Semitic" attack on Tutu backfires', *The Times*, 13 January 2011, https://www.thetimes.co.uk/article/anti-semitic-attack-on-tutu-backfires-27zgdh28mtj (last accessed 17 December 2021); on Angela Davis see Uncredited (2019) 'Angela Davis Says She's "Stunned" After Award is Revoked Over Her Views on Israel', *The New York Times*, 8 January 2019, https://www.nytimes.com/2019/01/08/us/angela-davis-israel-civil-rights-institute.html (last accessed 19 December 2021); on Javier Bardem and Penelope Cruz see Uncredited (2014) 'Jon Voight Slams Penelope Cruise, Javier Bardem for Signing anti-Israel Letter', *Haaretz*, 5 August 2021, https://www.haaretz.com/life/television/jon-voight-slams-spanish-stars-over-anti-israel-letter-1.5258067 (last accessed 17 December 2021); on Emma Watson see Richard Spencer (2022) 'Emma Watson accused of antisemitism over post supporting Palestinians', *The Times*, 4 January 2022, https://www.thetimes.co.uk/article/emma-watson-labelled-antisemitic-over-palestinian-tweet-x68f8vwck (last accessed 4 January 2022).

[26] For more on B'Tselem see Tovah Lazaroff (2021) 'B'Tselem, for first time, labels Israel an apartheid state', *Jersusalem Post*, 12 January 2021, https://www.jpost.com/israel-news/btselem-for-first-time-labels-israel-an-apartheid-state-655109 (last accessed 20 December 2021); for Amnesty see James Rothwell (2021) 'Israel labels Amnesty International 'anti-semitic' over 'apartheid' report', *Daily Telegraph*, 30 January 2022, https://www.telegraph.co.uk/world-news/2022/01/30/israel-labels-amnesty-international-antisemitic-apartheid-report/ (last accessed 8 February 2022).

costs.[27] Loach has also intervened in other boycott campaigns, including at the 2010 Fajr Film Festival, at which he invoked a similar rationale for supporting a boycott when he announced that they would be withdrawing *Looking for Eric* from the festival line-up:

> It is the request first and foremost from the Iranian film makers that makes you think, and makes you want to support them. There are many repressive regimes and you can't go on individual boycotts. But when the people themselves say, 'Don't come because you will be endorsing the regime that is perpetrating the violence,' you have to stop and think carefully.[28]

This broader festival activity has led to press coverage which has not been as positive as the aforementioned coverage, suggesting that it is the desire to intervene politically rather than to be in receipt of positive press coverage that is the dominant driver.

Back to Britain

In 2020, *Somerset Live* published an article headed '*I, Daniel Blake* director Ken Loach blasts plans to turn Bath hospital into a hotel'.[29] There are four points worth pulling out from this headline: first, it indicates that

[27] For instance, in March 2020, Loach was pressurised to withdraw as a judge on a Show Racism the Red Card schools competition. In response, Sixteen Films issued the following statement: 'The allegations made against Ken Loach lean heavily on a deeply controversial International Holocaust Remembrance Alliance document that attempts to redefine antisemitism so as to conflate it with criticism of Zionism and of Israel's treatment of the Palestinians', https://www.sixteenfilms.co.uk/news/2020/3/18/show-racism-the-red-card-and-ken-loach-a-statement-from-his-supporters (last accessed 31 July 2020). Loach has drawn on the Glasgow Media Group's work to support his political position, notably providing an approving blurb for their 2019 book, *Bad News for Labour: Anti-Semitism, The Party & Public Belief*, and participating in their workshops which have explored how the British media has represented the Israel/Palestine conflict. See Philo, Berry, et al. (2011: 313–4) for commentary from Loach on the Israel/Palestine conflict and news reporting.

[28] Quoted in Katherine Butler (2010), 'British directors lead boycott of Iran's cultural showpiece', *The Independent*, 23 January 2010, https://www.independent.co.uk/news/world/middle-east/british-directors-lead-boycott-of-irans-cultural-showpiece-1876487.html (last accessed 20 August 2020).

[29] Stephen Sumner (2020) '*I, Daniel Blake* director Ken Loach blasts plans to turn Bath hospital into a hotel', Somerset Live, 21 August 2020, https://www.somersetlive.co.uk/news/somerset-news/i-daniel-blake-director-ken-4447360 (last accessed 21 August 2020).

Loach's political interventions are not restricted to such glamorous contexts as the international film festival circuit; second, they have not all focused on global concerns but are often connected to local campaigns; third, as the headline carries the film title, it illustrates how it is Loach's status as a filmmaker that has afforded him the platform; and, fourth, it indicates how Loach utilises the films themselves to intervene politically. As is well established, in the early years of his career, *Cathy Come Home* led to questions in the House of Commons about the state of homelessness in Britain, and the release of *I, Daniel Blake* five decades later led once more to extensive House of Commons discussion about the plight of the most disadvantaged sections of the working class. As an indication of how the films have influenced British parliamentary political discourse, Hansard includes 162 references to *Cathy Come Home* and 49 references to *I, Daniel Blake*.[30] The films also often feature heavily in popular discourse, as evidenced by a LexisNexis database search for *I, Daniel Blake* which returns 1,084 results from a search of UK national newspapers.[31] Although this includes numerous items discussing the film's cinematic aspects, most of the articles deal with the film's subject matter, including accounts of individuals suffering circumstances akin to the film's lead character. A lead story in the British tabloid, *the Daily Mirror*, headlined 'Real-life Daniel Blake who suffered heart attack after leaving Job Centre has benefits slashed to just £20 a week' is indicative of the coverage that the film received.[32] A small glimpse of how the film was distributed beyond the commercial exhibition sector is that the Unite union organised 120 community screenings across the UK, 60 of which were in Scotland; Head of Unite Community Liane Groves states, '*I, Daniel Blake* was a game changer for campaigners on the cruel changes the Tories have made to our welfare system.'[33] The screenings organised by activists forces reflection on the assertion that films such as *I, Daniel Blake* are politically pessimistic, and highlights the capacity of political campaigners to identify more positive uses for the films than many professional film critics. The impact of *I, Daniel Blake* was not restricted to the UK: for instance, the leader of the French trade union federation, Confédération générale

---

[30] https://hansard.parliament.uk/ (last accessed 6 March 2022).
[31] https://www.lexisnexis.co.uk (last accessed 6 March 2022).
[32] Scarlet Howes (2018) 'Real-life Daniel Blake who suffered heart attack after leaving Job Centre has benefits slashed to just £20 a week', *Daily Mirror*, 19 January 2018, https://www.mirror.co.uk/news/uk-news/real-life-daniel-blake-who-11881128 (last accessed 21 January 2018).
[33] Email to author, 23 August 2017.

du travail, cited the film as an important critique of society, indicating both the reach of the film and the positive response of some representatives of the workers' movement.[34] These indicative, certainly far from exhaustive, examples illustrate that Loach's films are entangled in broader political contexts and it is within these contexts that they might best be understood.

Wider analysis

In film studies' formative years, its critical focus remained bound within the parameters of the film itself and, although the discipline has moved into significantly wider terrain since, much criticism remains locked within the text.[35] A useful example here is Martin Hall's (2020: 149) article, which suggests that Loach's films present the idea of revolutionary transformation as locked in the past and are downbeat about the possibilities for even minor political change in the present. He states (137), 'The films of the director considered to be the most left-wing in Britain show no faith in a contemporary transformative paradigm.' Hall's use of close textual analysis is a valid scholarly approach; however, when dealing with engaged filmmakers such as Loach it fails to comprehend activity beyond the frame, either of the filmmaker, or of the films. Given Loach's political interventions, the films and the surrounding political activity are best understood as linked and imbricated, rather than discrete and separate. In contrast to Hall's textual fetishism, one might reflect on how actually existing audiences, and activists, might engage with Loach's work. Jacques Rancière (2009: 13) challenges the perceived dichotomy between the active performer

[34] Evie Burrows Taylor (2018) 'French Trade Union Chief slams UK and US over lack of workers' rights', The Local, 12 January 2018, https://www.thelocal.fr/20180112/french-union-chief-slams-workers-rights-in-uk-and-us (last accessed 20 January 2018).

[35] It is noticeable, for instance, that more academic articles on *I, Daniel Blake* have been published in non-film studies journals than in those of the discipline itself. See, for instance, Nick O'Brien (2018) 'Administrative Justice in the Wake of *I, Daniel Blake*,' *The Political Quarterly*, 89 (1), January–March 2018 on how the film deals with questions of administrative justice and Amanda M. L. Taylor (2017) for how it highlights the negative impacts of digital technology on claimants, written from a social work studies perspective: '*The unintended impacts of I Daniel Blake*', blog post, https://amltaylor66.wordpress.com/2017/06/02/the-unintended-impacts-of-i-daniel-blake/ (last accessed 14 January 2022).

and the passive spectator, suggesting that the emancipation of the spectator

> begins when we challenge the opposition between viewing and acting ...It begins when we understand that viewing is also an action that confirms or transforms this distribution of positions. The spectator also acts, like the pupil or scholar. She observes, selects, compares, interprets.

If we accept the spectator's capacities as advanced by Rancière, then they never remain within singular texts, but are always already making connections between texts and contexts. As such, Loach's films should be judged not simply in aesthetic or political terms fixed within the frame, but in wider contextual frameworks. In the closing paragraph of John Hill's monograph on Loach he argues (2011: 221) that it could be 'an urge to provoke audiences to "step back" from the drama, and reflect on the film's relationship to the social world it addresses, that has been a recurring feature of Loach's work since the beginning of his career'. Loach's cinema might then be best understood through relational, not simply textual practices. Nicolas Bourriaud has coined the term 'relational aesthetics', which he defines as 'A set of artistic practices which take as their theoretical and practical point of departure the whole of human relations and their social context, rather than an independent and private space' (2002: 113). If we understand criticism to be a part of this practice, then Loach's work demands a 'relational criticism', one which moves beyond the text into the world. While we might not be able to finitely measure their capacity to instigate change, by analysing how the filmmakers have intervened in contemporary political discourse, and how the films have been appropriated for political purposes, we can develop a fuller picture of how they function and thence of their value as artistic objects.

Conclusion

This chapter has given some indication of the extent to which Loach has utilised his work to engage with extratextual political discourse on a range of domestic and international political topics across his career. In doing so, the chapter has also sought to illustrate that rather than viewing the films as discrete textual entities, they are consumed and understood within broader political contexts, and it is from within these contexts that critical takes on the films themselves should be developed. In some ways the films can be viewed as an adjunct to Loach's political activism, and his solidarity with a plethora of national and international campaigns. That the political controversies provoked by his work often move press coverage of the films from the arts pages to the news sections, generating significantly greater coverage than the film might otherwise receive, ensures that the films themselves become further enmeshed and entangled within wider, politicised extratextual discourse and activity. As such, although I have separated out on-screen politics and off-screen political engagement as separate entities bookending the Certain Tendencies in Loach's Cinema, they might well be viewed as one and the same.

Epilogue: Revolutionary respair

> A writer or painter cannot change the world. But they can keep an essential margin of non-conformity alive. Thanks to them, the powerful can never affirm that everyone agrees with their acts. That small difference is very important. When power feels itself totally justified and approved, it immediately destroys whatever freedoms we have left, and that is fascism. My ideas have not changed since I was 20. Basically, I agree with Engels. An artist describes real social relationships with the purpose of destroying the conventional ideas about those relationships, undermining bourgeois optimism, and forcing the public to doubt the tenets of the established order.
>
> Luis Buñuel[1]

As I write this Epilogue in March 2022, Loach and Sixteen Films are preparing to shoot a new fictional feature film, provisionally titled *The Old Oak*. Covid difficulties mean that its production is uncertain, adding to the uncertainty over the director's future output. Perhaps Loach will follow a similar path to that of Portuguese director Manoel de Oliveira who continued making films even when he had surpassed the ripe age of 100. Even if he did not add to his extensive list of films, however, Loach's contribution to cinema over almost six decades would still be remarkable in terms of scale and success.

What I hope to have laid out in the preceding chapters is an appraisal of this work, on-, behind- and off-screen. In charting and theorising his working methods in general and analysing how they are implemented

---

[1] Quoted in Carlos Fuentes (1973) 'Spain, Catholicism, surrealism, anarchism', *New York Times*, 11 March 1973, https://www.nytimes.com/1973/03/11/archives/the-discreet-charm-of-luis-bunuel-spain-catholicism-surrealism.html (last accessed 20 December 2021).

in the production of one film, I have sought to contribute to a broader understanding of the films, building on existing film and television scholarship and studies by academics across various disciplines interested in his work and its influence. At the same time, I hope that the fieldwork I conducted has enabled a more evidenced-based contribution to current debates on the collaborative nature of filmmaking, and highlighted production studies' opportunities for enriching the study of film more broadly. My contention is that the methodological approach I have adopted allows us to understand Loach's cinema in new ways, and that 'ethnografilmic analysis' allows fresh insights into *The Angels' Share* itself and Loach's wider *oeuvre*. I also hope that it has brought forward a concrete understanding that Loach's approach to realism is a practice as much as an aesthetic, that it deconstructs some of the mythology around auterism and how films actually get made and, in studying how Loach intervenes beyond the screen, connects this off-screen activity with the films themselves. As indicated previously, there are relatively few detailed academic production studies of filmmakers at work and perhaps this book might encourage other film scholars to pursue similar paths.

I have attempted to indicate something of the reach of Loach's work, and this might also be measured by his influence on other filmmakers. Loach has been cited as a major influence by several prominent filmmakers: actor and director, Icíar Bollaín, who appeared as the militia fighter, Maite, in *Land and Freedom*, also wrote *Ken Loach: un observador solidario* (which might translate as 'sympathetic observer') based on her experience of observing the making of *Carla's Song*. Loach's influence finds expression in her directorial style, particularly her earlier films, *Hola, ¿estás sola?* (Spain, 1995), *Flores de otro mundo* (Spain, 1999), *Tey doy mis ojos/Take My Eyes* (Spain, 2003) and *Mataharis* (Spain, 2007). Other filmmakers who cite Loach's influence include Diego Quemada-Díez, who worked as part of the camera crew on *Land and Freedom*, *Carla's Song* and *Bread and Roses*. Most well-known for *La juala de oro/Golden Dream* (Mexico/Spain, 2013), Quemada-Díez states, 'Ken's method is incredible and I applied a lot of it to this film.'[2] Other international filmmakers who have cited

---

[2] Paul MacInnes (2014) 'The Golden Dream: "I wanted to convey brotherhood beyond races, beyond nationalities"', *The Guardian*, 21 January 2014, https://www.theguardian.com/film/2014/jun/21/diego-quemada-diez-the-golden-dream (last accessed 23 January 2018).

Loach's influence include Wes Anderson,[3] Sean Baker,[4] Luc Dardenne,[5] Bong Joon-Ho[6] and Gaynor Preston.[7] In addition to filmmakers, numerous prominent actors have cited Loach as a major influence on their careers, including Daniel Day-Lewis[8] and Jake Gyllenhaal.[9] Regardless of the status of Loach's career, its afterlife will be measured not only in the films he has created but also in the films he has influenced thus far and those that will be made by filmmakers who are yet to discover his work.

In concluding, however, it seems apposite to return to politics and social change. Buñuel's words in this chapter's epigraph fit comfortably alongside Loach's method, which has involved tempering the political content of his work to the political mood, as he sees it. In doing so, seeking moments of revolutionary potential in the past is not a retreat into history as critics have suggested. Rather, it might be best described as an act of 'revolutionary respair', that is, trying to find hope after a period of defeat by recourse to moments of revolutionary inspiration in the past.

No filmmaker has so consistently, and for such a lengthy period, utilised cinema to champion socialist ideas, and consequently Loach has suffered a sustained assault on his work and his character. It is perhaps worth recalling that the release of *The Wind That Shakes the Barley* in 2006 provoked

---

[3] Kevin Jagernauth (2012) 'Wes Anderson Says Francois Truffaut's "Small Change" Ken Loach's "Black Jack" & Alan Parker's "Melody" Are Influences On "Moonrise Kingdom"', *Indiewire*, 10 April 2012, https://www.indiewire.com/2012/04/wes-anderson-says-francois-truffauts-small-change-ken-loachs-black-jack-alan-parkers-melody-are-influences-on-moonrise-kingdom-252623/ (last accessed 20 December 2021).

[4] Sophie Monks Kaufman (undated) 'Sean Baker: "If you're a filmmaker in the 21st century, it's hard not to be a social activist", *Little White Lies*, http://lwlies.com/interviews/sean-baker-the-florida-project/ (last accessed 20 December 2020).

[5] Various (2011) 'On Ken Loach', *Sight & Sound*, October 2011, http://old.bfi.org.uk/sightandsound/feature/49773 (last accessed 29 December 2020).

[6] Victor Stepien (2020) '*Parasite* Review: An unmitigated triumph for South Korea's Ken Loach', *Catholic Herald*, 13 February 2020, https://catholicherald.co.uk/parasite-rev iew-an-unmitigated-triumph-for-south-koreas-ken-loach/ (last accessed 13 November 2021).

[7] See Estella Tinknell (2007: 75).

[8] Andreas Wiseman (2018) 'Daniel Day-Lewis reveals what he loves most about working with Paul Thomas Anderson', *Screen Daily*, 29 January 2018, https://www.screendaily.com/news/daniel-day-lewis-reveals-what-he-likes-most-about-working-with-paul-thomas-anderson/5126049.article (last accessed 20 December 2020).

[9] Baltasar Kormakur (2015) 'Jake Gyllenhaal', *Vogue Italia*, September 2015, http://www.vogue.it/en/uomo-vogue/cover-story/2015/09/jake-gyllenhaal (last accessed 20 December 2020).

Figure E.1 Kim raises her fist aloft after emptying a handful of collectivised Spanish earth into her grandfather's graveside

newspaper headlines such as 'Top Cannes film is most pro-IRA ever', 'Why does Ken Loach loathe his country so much?' and even 'More poison from Loach the Leech'.[10] The end of Loach's career, whenever it arrives, will be welcomed by his critics and opponents: jaded scribes in the British tabloids and broadsheets; Tory and right-wing Labour MPs; those striving to sustain ruling class power and privilege. Loach's cinema, however, will remain with us in its moments of on-screen solidarity: in a trench in revolutionary Spain, a prison cell in Ireland, a benefits office in Newcastle, a flat in Glasgow's East End, sitting astride the political discourse and activism that it fosters. In these moments, on- and off-screen, lie the seeds of another world.

---

[10] Harry Macadam (2006) 'Top Cannes film is most pro-IRA ever', in *The Sun*, 30 May 2006; Ruth Dudley Edwards (2006) 'Why does Ken Loach loathe his country so much?' *Daily Mail*, 30 May 2006; Simon Heffer (2006) 'More poison from Loach the Leech', *Daily Telegraph*, 5 June 2006.

Appendices

Appendix I: *The Angels' Share*: Scene breakdown utilised by Sixteen Films

SEQ
1. Flashback: Station: Albert on the track
2. Sheriff's Court: Community Service orders
3. Flashback: City Centre: Rhino on horseback
4. Sheriff's Court: The steps: Clancy threatens Robbie
5. East End streets: Vans pick up conscripts, inc Robbie
6. Community Centre: painting: Robbie hears Leonie is in labour
7. Van to Hospital: Robbie asks Harry to go into hospital with him
8. Hospital: Robbie is intimidated by Matt and others
9. Harry's flat: they toast the new baby
    – Harry arranges for Robbie to see Leonie
10. Hospital: Robbie sees the baby
11. Flat: Robbie returns – others in flat are stoned
12. Park: Robbie tells Leonie he has to meet his victim
13. Meeting Room: Robbie meets Anthony and his family
14. Flashback: Robbie's attack in city centre
15. Cafe: Robbie is ashamed – tells Leonie of feud with Clancy
16. Harry's van in countryside: Harry takes gang to visit distillery
    – they stop by a field of cattle
17. Distillery: tour by Mairi
    – Robbie gets the bug
18. Tasting Room: they sample whiskies

19 Car park: Mo has stolen some miniatures
20 Park: Clancy's intimidation
21 Flat: Gang try out various whiskies
     – Robbie has been getting books from library
22 Snooker Hall: gang play snooker
     – Clancy chases him through streets
     – Matt rescues him
23 Road to Robbie's flat: Matt's car
     – Matt offers Robbie money to leave Glasgow
24 Sighthill Cemetery: Harry offers to take them to Edinburgh
25 Edinburgh: Waverley Station: Harry and gang on way to hotel
26 Hotel: whisky tasting
     – Robbie nearly gets it right
     – Rory, Grand Master, tells of rare cask
     – Robbie meets Thaddeus, collector and dealer
     – Mo steals Rory's notes
27 Waverley Station: Mo tells Robbie she has details of cask
28 Tenement flat: Robbie, Leonie and Luke see flat
     – family friend offers them the flat
29 Outside flat: Sniper has followed Robbie
     – Sniper has told Clancy where Robbie will live
30 Bar: Robbie see Harry
     – Robbie intends to take Matt's money and leave
     – instead borrows £500
31 Flat: they read Rory's tasting notes
     – they decide to go to the auction
32 Hitch-hiking
     – French girl students chat them up
33 By the sea: Albert's lagging behind
     – Robbie still not describing his plan
34 Distillery visitor's office: they ask to go to auction
35 Field by distillery: Robbie explains plan
     – phone call to Robbie: Clancy has smashed up flat
36 Dunnage: Rory conducts the tasting
     – Robbie hides behind barrels
37 Tent: they see local bar in distance, get text from Robbie
38 Dunnage: Robbie siphons whisky out. Dobie declines Thaddeus' plan
39 Dunnage: morning light
40 Dunnage: the auction: bought by American

41 Visitor's centre: Thaddeus taste sampling bottle
     – Robbie wants money and a job
42 East end Glasgow: police stops the gang
     – search – nothing
     – bottles clash, 2 break
     – Clancy phones
43 East End streets to Tanning Salon: Robbie confronts Clancy
     – tells him feud is over
44 Bar: Robbie does deal with Thadeus
45 Harry's flat: Harry finds bottle
46 Leonie's house: Robbie, Leonie and Luke drive off
     – rest of gang go to get wasted
47 Robbie drives into sunset

Appendix II: *The Angels' Share*: Production schedule 18 May 2011

2011

Jan – March	Locations and casting
7th March	Pre-production starts
18th April	2 days flashback shooting
25th April	First day Principle Photography, Glasgow
14th May	Re-start Principle Photography
24th June	Principle Photography complete
3-week break	
18th July	Post Production Start
12th September	First Cut
26th September	Paul/Rebecca/Roger viewing Sound Editor Starts
17th October	Exec Screening
24th October	Fine Cut, Film to George Fenton
21st November	Record Music
5th December	Dub (3 weeks – 1st week pre-mixes, 2nd week finals, 3rd week delivery items)

2012

January	Neg Cut
February	Grading and Prints
March	Delivery

Appendix III: *The Angels' Share*: Draft schedule

Pre-Shoot Week
Sun	1	Albert on track
Fri	14	Robbie's attack
	2	Rhino on horseback

Week 1
Sun	2	Sheriff's Court INT
Mon	3	Sheriff's Court Cont'd EXT
Tue	4	Vans pick offenders
	5	Community centre: painting
Wed	6	Van to Hosp
	7	Hosp
Thu	9	Harry's flat
Fri	10	Hosp. Robbie sees baby INT blackout

Week 2
Mon	12	Park: Robbie has to meet victim
	11	Flat: Robbie returns EVE – LATE DAY
Tue	13	Mtg
	15	Cafe
Wed	16	Harry's van – trip
Thu	17	Distillery tour
Fri	18	Tasting room
	19	Van home

Week 3
Mon	20	Park: Leonie's idea
	21	Flat: trying whiskies
Tue	23	Snooker Hall: pursuit
	24	Matt's car
Wed	25	Sightwell Cemetery: trip to Edinburgh
Thu	27/28	Edinburgh Princes St/ Hotel Tasting
Fri	26/28	Arrival and return to Edinburgh

Week 4
Mon	29	Flat: Robbie and Leonie are offered home
Tue	30	Outside
	31	Bar: Robbie sees Harry
Wed	32/33	Flat: Read tasting notes/Hitching outside Glasgow
Thu	33	Hitch-hiking

	33	(Cont'd) Ferry
Fri	34	Islay: by sea

Week 5

Mon	35	Distillery office
	36/37	Field by sea: the plan
Tue	38	Dunnage: tasting
	39	Outside hotel LATE
Wed	40	Dunnage: siphoning LATE
	42	–
Thu	43/44	Dunnage: the auction
Fri	45	Hotel: Robbie's deal with Thadeus

Week 6

Mon	46	East End: police search
Tue	47/48	Tanning salon
Wed	49	Bar: Robbie delivers to Thadeus
Thu	50/52	Harry's flat
Fri	51/53	Leonie's house – leaving

Filmography

Loach filmography

Catherine (BBC, *Teletale*, 1964)
Z-Cars (BBC, series episodes, 1964)
Diary of a Young Man (BBC, series episodes, 1964)
A Tap on the Shoulder (BBC, *The Wednesday Play*, 1965)
Wear a Very Big Hat (BBC, *The Wednesday Play*, 1965)
Three Clear Sundays (BBC, *The Wednesday Play*, 1965)
Up the Junction (BBC, *The Wednesday Play*, 1965)
The End of Arthur's Marriage (BBC, *The Wednesday Play*, 1965)
The Coming Out Party (BBC, *The Wednesday Play*, 1965)
Cathy Come Home (BBC, *The Wednesday Play*, 1966)
In Two Minds (BBC, *The Wednesday Play*, 1967)
Poor Cow (UK, 1967)
The Golden Vision (BBC, *The Wednesday Play*, 1968)
The Big Flame (BBC, *The Wednesday Play*, 1969)
Kes (UK, 1969)
Family Life (UK, 1971)
Talk About Work (A Central Office of Information Film, UK, 1971)
The Rank and File (BBC, *Play for Today*, 1971)
Save the Children Fund Film (LWT, 1971)
After a Lifetime (LWT, *Sunday Night Theatre*, 1971)
A Misfortune (BBC, *Full House*, 1973)
Days of Hope (BBC, *Play for Today*, 1975)
The Price of Coal (BBC, 1977)
Black Jack (UK, 1979)
The Gamekeeper (ATV, 1980)
Auditions (ATV, 1980)
A Question of Leadership (ATV, 1981)
Looks and Smiles (UK, 1981)
The Red and the Blue: Impressions of Two Political Conferences – Autumn 1982 (Channel 4, 1983)
Questions of Leadership (Channel 4, 1983, untransmitted)

Which Side Are You On? (Channel 4, 1985)
End of the Battle... Not the End of the War (Channel 4, *Diverse Reports*, 1985)
Fatherland (UK, Germany, 1986)
Time to Go (BBC, *Split Screen*, 1989)
The View from the Woodpile (Channel 4, 1989)
Hidden Agenda (UK, 1990)
The Arthur Legend (Channel 4, *Dispatches*, 1991)
Riff-Raff (UK, 1991)
Raining Stones (UK, 1993)
Ladybird Ladybird (UK, 1994)
Land and Freedom (UK, Spain, Germany, Italy, France, 1995)
A Contemporary Case for Common Ownership (UK, 1995)
Carla's Song (UK, Spain, Germany, 1996)
The Flickering Flame: A Story of Contemporary Morality (BBC, 1996)
Another City: A Week in the Life of Bath's Football Club (HTV, 1998)
My Name Is Joe (UK, 1998)
Bread and Roses (UK, Germany, Spain, 2000)
The Navigators (UK, Germany, Spain, 2001)
Sweet Sixteen (UK, 2002)
11'09"01 September 11 (segment United Kingdom) (UK, France, Egypt, Japan, Mexico, Iran, US, 2002)
Ae Fond Kiss... (UK, Belgium, Germany, Italy, Spain, 2004)
Tickets (Italy, UK, Iran, 2005) (with Ermanno Olmi and Abbas Kiarostami)
McLibel (UK, 2005) (with Fanny Armstrong)
The Wind That Shakes the Barley (UK, Ireland, Italy, Germany, France, Spain, Switzerland, 2006)
It's a Free World... (UK, 2007)
Looking for Eric (UK, France, Belgium, Italy, Spain, 2009)
Route Irish (UK, France, Belgium, 2010)
The Angels' Share (UK, France, Belgium, Italy, 2012)
The Spirit of '45 (UK, 2013)
Jimmy's Hall (UK, Ireland, France, Belgium, Japan, 2014)
I, Daniel Blake (UK, France, 2016)
In Conversation with Jeremy Corbyn (UK, 2016)
Sorry We Missed You (UK, France, Belgium, 2019)
The Old Oak (in pre-production)

Additional television and film titles discussed in this book

Acqua e zucchero: Carlo Di Palma, i colori della vita/Water and Sugar: Carlo Di Palma, the Colours of Life (Kamkari, Italy, 2016)
Les Bien-aimés/The Beloved (Honoré, France/UK/Czech Republic, 2011)
Brigadoon (Minnelli, US, 1954)
Cargo (Gordon, Spain/UK/Sweden, 2006)
Casting By (Donahue, US, 2012)
Citizen Kane (Welles, USA, 1941)
La Commune (Paris, 1871) (Watkins, France, 2000)

Country (Eyre, BBC, 1981)
Culloden: Making Reel History (BBC Scotland, 1996)
Distilling The Angels' Share (McArdle, UK, 2012)
Fish Tank (Arnold, UK, 2009)
Flores de otro mundo (Bollaín, Spain, 1999)
Ginger and Rosa (Potter, UK/Denmark/Canada, 2012)
Groundhog Day (Ramis, USA 1993)
Hola, ¿estás sola? (Bollaín, Spain, 1995)
Hoří, má panenko/The Firemen's Ball (Forman, Czechoslovakia, 1967)
How to Make a Ken Loach Film (BFI, 2016) Online interactive film.
The Hurt Locker (Bigelow, USA, 2008)
If. . . (Anderson, UK, 1966).
Ivanovo detstvo/Ivan's Childhood (Tarkovsky, USSR, 1962)
La juala de oro/Golden Dream (Quemada-Díez, Mexico/Spain, 2013)
Just A Boys' Game (Mackenzie, director/MacDougall, writer, BBC, 1979)
Katmandú, un espejo en el cielo/Katmandu Lullaby (Bollaín, Spain, 2012)
Ken Loach in Conversation with Cillian Murphy (BBC Four, 2015)
Lásky jedné plavovlásky/A Blonde in Love, (Forman, Czechoslovakia, 1965)
Loach on Location: Making Land and Freedom (Boulting, UK, 1995)
Local Hero (Forsyth, UK, 1983)
Mataharis (Bollaín, Spain, 2007)
El olivo/The Olive Tree (Bollaín, Spain, 2016)
Oranges and Sunshine (Jim Loach, UK/Australia, 2010)
Ostře sledované vlaky/Closely Observed Trains (Menzel, Czechoslovakia, 1966)
Ratcatcher (Ramsay, UK, 1999)
The Red Badge of Courage (Huston, USA, 1951)
Red Road (Arnold, UK/Denmark, 2006)
River City (BBC, 2002–present)
Rocky (Avildsen, US, 1976)
Rome, Open City (Rossellini, 1945).
The Searchers (Ford, USA, 1956)
Secret People (Dickinson, UK, 1952)
The Shipping Forecast: the audiovisual poetics of Ken Loach (Greene, 2015) (audiovisual essay)
Shoah (Lanzmann, France, 1985)
The South Bank Show (LWT, 1978–2010)
Summer (Glenaan, UK, 2008)
También la lluvia/Even the Rain (Bollaín, Spain/Mexico/France, 2010)
Tey doy mis ojos/Take My Eyes (Bollaín, Spain, 2003)
Under the Skin (Glazer, UK/US/Switzerland, 2013)
El verdugo/The Executioner (Berlanga, Spain, 1963)
Versus: The Life and Films of Ken Loach (Osmond, UK, 2014)
Whisky Galore! (Mackendrick, UK, 1949)
The Wire (HBO, USA, 2002–8)
You Were Never Really Here (Ramsay, UK/US/France, 2017)
Young James Herriot (BBC, 2010–11)
Yuli/Yuli: the Carlos Acostas Story (Bollaín, Germany/UK/Cuba/Spain, 2018)
World in Action (Granada Television, 1963–88)
Wuthering Heights (Arnold, UK, 2011)

Bibliography[1]

Adams, Tim (2021) 'John Cooper Clarke: "There's three food groups I draw the line at – flapjack, falafel and tripe"', *The Guardian*, 19 September 2021, https://www.theguardian.com/food/2021/sep/19/john-cooper-clarke-poet-punk-manchester-ken-loach

Aita, Sean (2014) 'Toward a Contemporary Screen Actor Training', in Aaron Taylor (ed.), *Theorizing Film Acting*, New York and London: Routledge.

Alcoff, Linda (1991/2) 'The Problem of Speaking for Others', in *Cultural Critique* (20) (Winter, 1991/2).

Ancelotti, Carlo (2016) *Quiet Leadership: Winning Hearts, Minds and Matches*, London: Penguin.

Anderson, Lindsay (1999) *About John Ford*, London: Plexus.

Antonioni, Michelangelo (2007), *The Architecture of Vision: Writings and Interviews on Cinema*, Carlo di Carlo, Giorgio Tinazzi and Marga Cottino-Jones (eds), Chicago, IL: University of Chicago Press.

Archibald, David (2002) 'Match Made in Heaven', *Sunday Herald*, 29 September 2002.

Archibald, David (2006) 'Republic Opinion', *Sunday Herald*, 25 June 2006.

Archibald, David (2007) 'Correcting Historical Lies: An Interview with Ken Loach and Paul Laverty', *Cineaste*, 32 (2).

Archibald, David (2011) 'Reeling From Injustice', *Financial Times*, 26 August 2011.

Archibald, David (2012) '*The Angels' Share* at the 2012 Cannes Film Festival', NECSUS: European Journal of Media Studies, 1 (2), Autumn 2012.

Archibald, David (2012) *The war that won't die: The Spanish Civil War in cinema*, Manchester: Manchester University Press.

Archibald, David (2017a) 'Loach and Acting: Seven Fragments', *The Drouth* (60).

Archibald, David (2017b) 'Revolution, my arse', in *Three Films by Ken Loach: Riff-Raff, Raining Stones, Ladybird Ladybird*, British Film Institute.

Archibald, David (2017c) 'Team Loach and Sixteen Films: Authorship, Collaboration, Leadership (and Football)', in Ewa Mazierska and Lars Kristensen (eds), *Contemporary Cinema and Ideology: Neoliberal Capitalism and Its Alternatives in Filmmaking*, New York and London: Routledge.

Archibald, David and Mitchell Miller (2011) 'From Rennes to Toronto: Anatomy of a Boycott', *Screen*, 52 (2).

---

[1] In instances in which there is a significant gap between the date of writing and the date of publication I have added both.

Archibald, David and Finn Daniels-Yeomans (2020) 'Dialogical encounters on the cinema of revolution: *Save the Children Fund Film* and *Metalepsis in Black*', in Ewa Mazierska and Lars Kristensen (eds), *Third Cinema, World Cinema and Marxism*, London: Bloomsbury Academic.
Arendt, Hannah (1958) *The Human Condition*, Chicago, IL: University of Chicago Press.
Aristotle (2004/5 BC) *The Nicomachean Ethics*, London: Penguin.
Atkinson, Sarah (2018) *From Film Practice to Data Process: Production Aesthetics and Representational Practices of a Film Industry in Transition*, Edinburgh: Edinburgh University Press.
Auslander, Philip (2002) 'Just Be Yourself: Logocentrism and difference in performer theory', in Phillip B. Zarrilli (ed.), *Acting (re)considered: a theoretical and practical guide*, New York and London: Routledge.
Banks, Mark and David Hesmondhalgh (2009) 'Looking for work in creative industries policy', *International Journal of Cultural Policy*, 15 (4).
Barad, Karen (2007) *Meeting the Universe Halfway: Quantum Physics and the Entanglement of Matter and Meaning*, Durham, NC: Duke University Press.
Barghouti, Omar (2012) 'The Cultural Boycott: Israel vs South Africa', in Andrea Lim (ed.), *The Case for Sanctions Against Israel*, London and New York: Verso.
Baron, Cynthia and Sharon Marie Carnicke (2008) *Reframing Screen Performance*, Ann Arbor: University of Michigan Press.
Bazin, André (1967) *What is Cinema? Volume 1*, transl. Hugh Gray, Berkeley, Los Angeles and London: University of California Press.
Bazin, André (2009) 'The Festival Viewed as a Religious Order', in Richard Porton (ed.), *Dekalog 3: On film festivals*, London and New York: Wallflower.
Beckett, Samuel (1974) *Texts for Nothing*, London: Calder & Boyars.
Benjamin, Walter (1974) 'Left-Wing Melancholy (On Eric Kästner's new book of poems)' *Screen* 15 (2).
Benjamin, Walter (1999/various) 'Chaplin in Retrospect', in *Selected Writings: Volume 2, 1927–34*, Cambridge, MA: The Belknap Press of Harvard University Press.
Benjamin, Walter (2007/various) *Illuminations: Essays and Reflections*, Hannah Arendt (ed.), New York: Schocken Books.
Bindel, Julie (2014) 'Dick-swinging filmmakers like Ken Loach constantly write real women and our struggles out of history', *The Spectator*, 2 June 2014, https://www.spectator.co.uk/article/dick-swinging-filmmakers-like-ken-loach-constantly-write-real-women-and-our-struggles-out-of-history
Bohrer, Ashley J. (2020) *Marxism and Intersectionality: Race, Gender, Class and Sexuality under Contemporary Capitalism*, New York: Columbia University Press.
Bollaín, Icíar (1996) *Ken Loach: un observador solidario*, Madrid: El País Aguilar.
Bordwell, David, Janet Staiger and Kristin Thompson (1985) *The Classical Hollywood Cinema: Film Style and Mode of Production to 1960*, New York: Columbia University Press.
Born, Georgina (2000) 'Inside television: television studies and the sociology of culture', *Screen*, 41 (4).
Born, Georgina (2005) *Uncertain Vision: Birt, Dyke and the Reinvention of the BBC*, London: Vintage.
Bourdieu, Pierre (1993) *The Field of Cultural Production: Essays on Art and Literature*, Polity Press: Cambridge.
Bourriaud, Nicolas (2002) *Relational aesthetics*, transl. Simon Pleasance and Fronza Woods with the participation of Mathieu Copeland, Dijon: Les presses du réel.

Bourriaud, Nicolas (2016) *The Exform*, transl. Erik Butler, London, Paris and New York: Verso.
Bradley, Kate (2019) 'Ken Loach, sex work and paternalism', RS21, 9 October 2019, https://www.rs21.org.uk/2019/10/09/ken-loach-sex-work-and-paternalism/
Bradshaw, Peter (2012) 'Cannes 2012: The Angels' Share – review', *The Guardian*, 21 May 2012, https://www.theguardian.com/film/2012/may/21/the-angels-share-review
Brady, Tara (2012) '*The Angels' Share*', *The Irish Times*, 1 June 2012, https://www.irishtimes.com/culture/film/the-angels-share-1.1063293
Brecht, Bertolt (1977/1938) 'The Popular and the Realistic', in David Craig (ed.), *Marxists on Literature: An Anthology*, Harmondsworth and New York: Penguin.
Brecht, Bertolt (1978/various) *Brecht on Theatre: The Development of an Aesthetic*, John Willet (ed.), New York: Hill and Wang; London: Methuen.
Breton, André and Leon Trotsky (1938) 'Manifesto: Towards a Free and Revolutionary Art', in *Partisan Review* 6 (1).
Brewer, John D. (2000) *Ethnography*, Buckingham and Philadelphia, PA: Open University Press.
Brown, Ian (2012) *From Tartan to Tartanry: Scottish Culture, History and Myth*, Edinburgh: Edinburgh University Press.
Burns, James M. (1978) *Leadership*, New York: Harper & Row.
Burrows Taylor, Evie (2018) 'French Trade Union Chief slams UK and US over lack of workers' rights', *The Local*, 12 January 2018, https://www.thelocal.fr/20180112/french-union-chief-slams-workers-rights-in-uk-and-us
Butler, Katherine (2010) 'British directors lead boycott of Iran's cultural showpiece', *The Independent*, 23 January 2010, https://www.independent.co.uk/news/world/middle-east/british-directors-lead-boycott-of-irans-cultural-showpiece-1876487.html
Byrne, Janet (2012) *The Occupy Handbook*, New York: Back Bay Books.
Caldwell, John Thornton (2013) 'Para-Industry: Researching Hollywood's Blackwaters' in *Cinema Journal* 52 (3), Spring 2013.
Caldwell, John Thornton (2008) *Production Culture: Industrial Reflexivity and Critical Practice in Film and Television*, Durham and London: Duke University Press.
Cardullo, Bert (2010) *Loach and Leigh, Ltd: The Cinema of Social Conscience*, Newcastle: Cambridge Scholars Publishing.
Cardullo, R. J. (2016) 'Work, Family and Politics: Ken Loach's *Riff-Raff*', in *Teaching Sound Film: A Reader*, Rotterdam: Sense Publishers.
Carnicke, Sharon Marie (2012) 'The Screen Actor's "First Self" and "Second Self": John Wayne and Coquelin's Acting Theory', in Aaron Taylor (ed.), *Theorizing Film Acting*, New York and London: Routledge.
Carringer, Robert L (1985) *The Making of Citizen Kane*, Berkeley: University of California Press.
Caughie, John (1980) 'Progressive Television and Documentary Drama', *Screen*, 21 (3).
Caughie, John (ed.) (1981) *Theories of Authorship*, London: Routledge.
Caughie, John (1982) 'Scottish Television: What Would It Look Like?' in Colin McArthur (ed.), *Scotch Reels*, London: BFI Publishing.
Caughie, John (2000) *Television Drama: Realism, Modernism and British Culture*, Oxford and New York: Oxford University Press.
Caughie, John (2007) 'Authors and auteurs: the uses of theory', in J. Donald and M. Renov, (eds), *The SAGE Handbook of Film Studies*, London: Sage.
Celluloid Liberation Front (2012) 'Ken Loach Turns Down an Award: The director shows solidarity with festival workers', in *New Statesman*, 29 November 2012.

Chambers, Jamie (2014) '"On the Side of the Angels?": Ken Loach, *The Angels' Share*, and the pursuit of new forms of politically engaged cinema', *International Journal of Scottish Theatre and Screen*, 7 (1).

Chen, Anna (2013) 'People of colour like me have been painted out of working-class history', *The Guardian*, 16 July 2013, https://www.theguardian.com/commentisfree/2013/jul/16/people-of-colour-working-class-history

Clark, Nick (2012) 'Director Ken Loach refuses Italian award after row over wage and staff cuts', *The Independent*, 23 November 2012, https://www.independent.co.uk/arts-entertainment/films/news/director-ken-loach-refuses-italian-award-after-row-over-wage-and-staff-cuts-8347138.html

Clarke, Romy (1999) 'From text to performance: interpretation or traduction? Trevor Griffiths' *Fatherland*, as directed by Ken Loach', in *Language and Literature: International Journal of Stylistics*, 8 (2).

Conroy Scott, Kevin (2005) 'Paul Laverty: *Sweet Sixteen*', in *Screenwriters' Masterclass: Screenwriters Talk About Their Greatest Movies*, London: Faber and Faber.

Cook, John, R. (2010) '"Don't forget to look into the camera!": Peter Watkins' approach to acting with facts', *Studies in Documentary Film*, 4 (3).

Coren, Victoria (2012) 'Keep our curses in rude health', *The Guardian*, 27 May 2012, https://www.theguardian.com/commentisfree/2012/may/27/victoria-coren-ken-loach-wrong-on-oaths

Corliss, Richard (2008) 'Notes on a Screenwriter's Theory, 1973', in Barry Keith Grant, *Auteurs and Authorship: A Film Reader*, Malden: Blackwell.

Corrigan, Timothy (1990) 'The Commerce of Auteurism: A Voice without Authority', in *New German Critique*, Winter 1990.

Cowan, Philip (2012) 'Authorship and the Director of Photography: A Case Study of Gregg Toland and Citizen Kane', in *Networking Knowledge*, 5 (1).

Crenshaw, Kimberlé (1991) 'Mapping the Margins: Intersectionality, Identity Politics, and Violence Against Women of Color', *Stanford Law Review* 43 (6).

Curtin, Michael and Kevin Sanson (eds) (2017) *Voices of Labor: Creativity, Craft, and Conflict in Hollywood*, Oakland: University of California Press.

Dave, Paul (2006) *Visions of England: Class and Culture in Contemporary Cinema*, Oxford and New York: Berg.

Davidson, Neil (2001) 'Marx and Engels on the Scottish Highlands', in *Science & Society*, 65.

Davies, Luke (2018) 'Precarious Living in the Films of Ken Loach', in Chiara Briganti and Kathy Mezei (eds), *Living with Strangers: Bedsits and Boarding Houses in Modern English Life*, London: Routledge.

Debord, Guy (2009) *Panegyric: Volumes 1 & 2*, London and New York: Verso.

Deleuze, Gilles (1985) *Cinema 2: The Time Image*, London and New York: The Athlone Press.

Deleuze, Gilles (1992) 'Postscript on the Societies of Control', in *October*, 59.

Derrida, Jacques (2006) *Specters of Marx: The State of the Debt, the Work of Mourning and the New International*, transl. Peggy Kamuf, New York and London: Routledge.

Deutscher, Isaac (2005) *The Prophet: The Life of Leon Trotsky*, London and New York: Verso.

De Valck, Marijke (2007) *Film Festivals: From European Geopolitics to Global Cinephilia*. Amsterdam: Amsterdam University Press.

De Valck, Marijke and Mimi Soeteman (2010) '"And the Winner is . . ." What Happens Behind the Scenes of Film Festival Competitions', in *International Journal of Cultural Studies* 13 (3).

Dudley Edwards, Ruth (2006) 'Why does Ken Loach loathe his country so much?' *Daily Mail*, 30 May 2006.
Eagleton, Terry (2011) *Why Marx Was Right*, New Haven, CT, and London: Yale University Press.
Eleftheriotis, Dimitris (2010) *Cinematic Journeys: Film and Movement*, Edinburgh: Edinburgh University Press.
Engels, Friedrich (1977/1845) *The Condition of the Working Class in England*, Oxford: Oxford University Press.
Engels, Friedrich (1977/1888) 'Letter to Margaret Harkness (April 1888)', in David Craig (ed.), *Marxists on Literature: An Anthology*, Harmondsworth and New York: Penguin.
Ezra, Elizabeth (2000) *Georges Méliès: The Birth of the Auteur*, Manchester: Manchester University Press.
Faiers, Jonathan (2008) *Tartan*, London: Bloomsbury.
Ferguson, Alex (2015) *Leading*, London: Hodder & Stoughton.
Fielding, Steven (2020) 'Socialist Television Drama, Newspaper Critics and the Battle of Ideas During the Crisis of Britain's Post-War Settlement', *Twentieth Century British History*, 31 (2), June 2020.
Forrest, David (2013) 'Twenty-first-Century Social Realism: Shane Meadows and New British Realism', in Martin Fradley, Sarah Godfrey and Melanie Williams (eds), *Shane Meadows: Critical Essays*, Edinburgh: Edinburgh University Press.
Forrest, David (2019) 'Art Cinema and the British Poetic Realist Tradition', in Paul Newland and Brian Hoyle (eds), *British art cinema: creativity, experimentation and innovation*, Manchester: Manchester University Press.
Forrest, David (2020) *New Realism: Contemporary British Cinema*, Edinburgh: Edinburgh University Press.
Forrest, David and Sue Vice (2017) *Barry Hines: Kes, Threads and beyond*, Manchester: Manchester University Press.
French, Philip (2012) '*The Angels' Share* – Review', *The Observer*, 3 June 2012.
Fuentes, Carlos (1973) 'Spain, Catholicism, surrealism, anarchism', *New York Times*, 11 March 1973, https://www.nytimes.com/1973/03/11/archives/the-discreet-charm-of-luis-bunuel-spain-catholicism-surrealism.html
Fuller, George (1998) *Loach on Loach*, London: Faber and Faber.
Gallagher, Mark (2013) *Another Steven Soderbergh Experience: Authorship and Contemporary Hollywood*, Austin: University of Texas Press.
Ganti, Tejaswini (2012) *Bollywood: Inside the Contemporary Hindi Film Industry*, Durham, NC, and London: Duke University Press.
Garnett, Tony (2016) *The Day the Music Died: A Memoir*, London: Constable.
Gaut, Berys (1997) 'Film Authorship and Collaboration', in Richard Allen and Murray Smith (eds), *Film Theory and Philosophy*, Oxford: Oxford University Press.
Genovese, T. R. (2019) 'Going Gonzo: Toward a performative practice in multimodal ethnography' *entanglements*, 2 (1).
Goffman, Erving (1959) *The Presentation of Self in Everyday Life*, New York: Anchor Books.
Golding, Simon, W. (2014) *Life After Kes: The Making of the British Film Classic, the People, the Story and Its Legacy*, Clacton on Sea: Apex Publishing.
Goss, Brian Michael (2009) *Global Auteurs: Politics in the Films of Almodóvar, von Trier, and Winterbottom*, New York: Peter Lang.
Gove, Michael (2006) 'A truly radical film would dare to tell the truth', *The Times*, 31 May 2006, https://www.thetimes.co.uk/article/a-truly-radical-film-would-dare-to-tell-the-truth-w3nf3xvbgj0

Grant, Barry Keith (2008) *Auteurs and Authorship: A Film Reader*, Blackwell: Malden.
Grant, Catherine (2000) 'www.auteur.com?', *Screen*, 41 (1).
Grant, Catherine (2008) 'Auteur machines? Auteurism and the DVD', in James Bennett and Tom Brown (eds), *Film and Television After DVD*, London: Routledge.
Grant, Nick (2018) 'Keeping it real: the brutal art of Ken Loach', in *International Socialism: A Quarterly Review of Socialist Theory*, 160.
Griffiths, Trevor (1974) *The Party*, London: Faber and Faber.
Hall, Martin (2020) 'The Future is Past, the Present cannot be fixed: Ken Loach and the Crisis', in Thomas Austin and Angelos Koutsourakis (eds), *Cinema of Crisis: Film and Contemporary Europe*, Edinburgh: Edinburgh University Press.
Hames, Scott (ed.) (2010) *Edinburgh Companion to James Kelman*, Edinburgh: Edinburgh University Press.
Havens, Timothy, Amanda D. Lotz and Serra Tinic (2009) 'Critical Media Industry Studies: A Research Approach', *Communication, Culture & Critique*, 2.
Havens, Timothy and Amanda D. Lotz (2012) *Understanding Media Industries*, New York: Oxford University Press.
Hayward, Anthony (2004) *Which Side Are You On? Ken Loach and His Films*, London: Bloomsbury Publishing.
Heffer, Simon (2006) 'More poison from Loach the Leech', *Daily Telegraph*, 5 June 2006.
Higgins, Charlotte (2012) 'Ken Loach brands BBFC hypocritical over use of the c-word', *The Guardian*, 22 May 2012, http://www.guardian.co.uk/film/2012/may/22/ken-loach-bbfc-hypocritical
Hill, John (2011) *Ken Loach: The Politics of Film and Television*, London: Palgrave/BFI.
Hilton, Matthew (2015) 'Ken Loach and the *Save the Children Fund Film*: Humanitarianism, Imperialism, and the Changing Role of Charity in Postwar Britain', in *The Journal of Modern History*, 87 (2), June 2015.
Hjort, Mette (2010) 'On the plurality of cinematic transnationalism', *World Cinemas, Transnational Perspectives*, Natasa Durovicová and Kathleen E. Newman, New York and London, Routledge.
Hoek, Lotte (2015) *Cut-Pieces: Celluloid Obscenity and Popular Cinema in Bangladesh*, New York: Columbia University Press.
Holloway, John (2010) *Crack Capitalism*, London: Pluto Press.
Howard, Ali (2012) 'Binman bags star place at Cannes festival', *The Herald*, 16 May 2012.
Howes, Scarlett (2018) 'Real-life Daniel Blake who suffered heart attack after leaving Job Centre has benefits slashed to just £20 a week', *Daily Mirror*, 19 January 2018 https://www.mirror.co.uk/news/uk-news/real-life-daniel-blake-who-11881128
Hunter, Aaron (2016) *Authoring Hal Ashby: The Myth of the New Hollywood Auteur*, London: Bloomsbury.
Ide, Wendy (2012) 'Cuddlier Ken loses his Gorbals', *The Times*, 1 June 2012.
Jagernauth, Kevin (2012) 'Wes Anderson Says Francois Truffaut's "Small Change" Ken Loach's "Black Jack" & Alan Parker's "Melody" Are Influences On "Moonrise Kingdom"', *Indiewire*, 10 April 2012, https://www.indiewire.com/2012/04/wes-anderson-says-francois-truffauts-small-change-ken-loachs-black-jack-alan-parkers-melody-are-influences-on-moonrise-kingdom-252623/
Jones, Huw D. (2016) 'UK/European Co-productions: The Case of Ken Loach', in *Journal of British Cinema and Television*, 13 (3).
Jones, Tobias (1998) 'How we met: Ken Loach and Jim Allen', *The Independent on Sunday*, 22 November 1998, https://www.independent.co.uk/arts-entertainment/how-we-met-ken-loach-and-jim-allen-1186744.html
Kelly, Lisa (2009) 'Casting The Wire: Complicating Notions of Performance, Authenticity,

and "Otherness"', *darkmatter: in the ruins of imperial culture*, 29 May 2009, http://www.darkmatter101.org/site/2009/05/29/casting-the-wire-complicating-notions-of-performance-authenticity-and-otherness/

Kelman, James (2008) *How Late It Was, How Late*, London: Vintage Books.

Kennedy-Martin, Troy (1964) 'Nats Go Home: First Statement of a New Drama for Television', *Encore*, March–April 1964, 11 (2).

Kirby, Michael (2005) 'On Acting and Non-Acting', in Philip B. Zarrilli, *Acting (Re)Considered: A Theoretical and Practical Guide* (2nd edn), London and New York: Routledge.

Klinger, Barbara (2006) *Beyond the Multiplex: Cinema, New Technologies and the Home*, Berkeley: University of California Press.

Kormakur, Baltasar (2015) 'Jake Gyllenhaal', in *Vogue Italia*, September 2015, http://www.vogue.it/en/uomo-vogue/cover-story/2015/09/jake-gyllenhaal

Lacey, Stephen (2012) *Tony Garnett*, Manchester: Manchester University Press.

LaFargue, Paul (2011/1883) *The Right to Be Lazy: Essays by Paul LaFargue*, Bernard Marszalek (ed.), Oakland, CA: AK Press.

Laverty, Paul (1997) *Carla's Song*, London and Boston, MA: Faber and Faber.

Laverty, Paul (2002) *Sweet Sixteen*, Ipswich: Screenpress Publishing.

Laverty, Paul (2012) *The Angels' Share*, Pontefract: Route.

Lawson, Dominic (2006) 'A hard-line Marxist distortion of history', *The Independent*, 10 May 2006.

Lazaroff, Tovah (2021) 'B'Tselem, for first time, labels Israel an apartheid state', *Jerusalem Post*, 12 January 2021, https://www.jpost.com/israel-news/btselem-for-first-time-labels-israel-an-apartheid-state-655109

Lefebvre, Henri (1991) *The Production of Space*, transl. Donald Nicholson-Smith, Oxford: Blackwell.

Leigh, Jacob (2002) *The Cinema of Ken Loach: Art in the Service of the People*, London: Wallflower.

Loach, Ken (2001) 'Rob Dawber: Radical rail worker and writer who sued his bosses over fatal illness', *The Guardian*, 23 February 2001, https://www.theguardian.com/news/2001/feb/23/guardianobituaries

López Hernández, Sofía (2017) 'La contribución de la música de George Fenton al cine de Ken Loach/The Contributions of the Music of George Fenton to the Films of Ken Loach', *Anuario Musical*, 72, enero-diciembre 2017.

Lukács, György (1970) *Writer and Critic*, London: Merlin Press.

Lyman, Eric J. (2012) 'Ken Loach Refuses Turin Fest Honor Over Alleged Abuses', *Hollywood Reporter*, 21 November 2012.

Macadam, Harry (2006) 'Top Cannes film is most pro-IRA ever', *The Sun*, 30 May 2006.

McArthur, Colin (ed.) (1982) *Scotch Reels: Scotland in Film and Television*, London: BFI.

McAuley, Gay (2010) *Space in Performance: Making Meaning in the Theatre*, Ann Arbor: University of Michigan Press.

McDonald, Paul (2000) 'Film Acting', in John Hill and Pamela Church Gibson (eds), *Film Studies: Critical Approaches*, Oxford: Oxford University Press.

McDonald, Paul (2013) 'IN FOCUS: Media Industry Studies – Introduction', *Cinema Journal*, 52 (3).

MacInnes, Paul (2014) 'The Golden Dream: "I wanted to convey brotherhood beyond races, beyond nationalities"', *The Guardian*, 21 January 2014, https://www.theguardian.com/film/2014/jun/21/diego-quemada-diez-the-golden-dream

McKnight, George (1997) *Agent of Challenge and Defiance: The Films of Ken Loach*, Trowbridge: Flicks Books.

Maclean, John (1920) 'All Hail, the Scottish Communist Republic' reproduced (1922) as 'All Hail, the Scottish Workers Republic!', https://www.marxists.org/archive/maclean/works/1922-swr.htm
Macnab, George (2016) 'Ken Loach: keeper of the flame', in *Screen Daily*, 13 June 2016.
Madden, Paul (1981) 'Jim Allen', in George Brandt (ed.), *British Television Drama*, Cambridge: Cambridge University Press.
Maley, Willy (1996) 'Swearing blind: Kelman and the curse of the working classes', *Edinburgh Review*, 95.
Martin-Jones, David (2013) '*The Angels' Share*: Ken Loach and Paul Laverty Lift Scotland's Kilts to Expose Its Darker Parts', *Senses of Cinema*, 66, March 2013.
Marx, Karl (1968/1843–4) *Contribution to the Critique of Hegel's Philosophy of Right: Selected Works*, London: Norton.
Marx, Karl (1973/1858) 'Fragments on Machines', in *Grundrisse*, transl. M. Nicolaus, London: Penguin Books – New Left Review.
Marx, Karl (1977/1868–83) *Capital: A Critique of Political Economy, Volume III*, Frederick Engels (ed.), London: Lawrence and Wishart.
Mason, Paul (2015) *Post-Capitalism: A Guide to our Future*, London: Allen Lane.
Mayer, Vicki, Miranda J. Banks and John Thornton Caldwell (2009) *Production Studies: Cultural Studies of Media Industries*, New York and London: Routledge.
Mazdon, Lucy and Katherine Wheatley (2010) *Je t'aimé moi non plus: Franco-British cinematic relations*, Oxford: Berghahn Books.
Mazierska, Ewa (2015) *From Self-Fulfilment to Survival of the Fittest: Work in European Cinema from the 1960s to the Present*, Oxford: Berghahn Books.
Mazierska, Ewa, and Lars Kristensen (eds) (2014) *Marx at the Movies: Revisiting History, Theory and Practice*, London: Palgrave Macmillan.
Mazierska, Ewa, and Lars Kristensen (eds) (2017) *Contemporary Cinema and Ideology: Neoliberal Capitalism and Its Alternatives in Filmmaking*, New York and London: Routledge.
Mazierska, Ewa, and Lars Kristensen (eds) (2020) *Third Cinema, World Cinema and Marxism*, London: Bloomsbury Academic.
McKnight, George (ed.) (1997) *Agent of Challenge and Defiance: The Films of Ken Loach*, Trowbridge: Flicks Books.
Meir, Christopher (2015) *Scottish Cinema: Texts and Contexts*, Manchester: Manchester University Press.
Monks Kaufman, Sophie (undated) 'Sean Baker: "If you're a filmmaker in the 21st century, it's hard not to be a social activist', *Little White Lies*, http://lwlies.com/interviews/sean-baker-the-florida-project/
Moss-Wellington, Wyatt (2017) 'Affecting Profundity: Cognitive and Moral Dissonance in Lynch, Loach, Linklater, and Sayles', *Projections: The Journal for Movies and Mind*, 11 (1).
Munton, Alan (2004) 'How gender serves Trotskyism: The Spanish Civil War in Ken Loach's Land and Freedom', in Angela K. Smith (ed.), *Gender and warfare in the twentieth century: Textual representations*, Manchester: Manchester University Press.
Nancy, Jean-Luc (2007) *Listening*, transl. Charlotte Mandell, New York: Fordham University Press.
Naremore, James (1990) *Acting in the Cinema*, Berkeley: University of California Press.
Neale, Stephen (1981) 'Art Cinema as Institution', *Screen*, 22 (1).
Nelmes, Jill (2011) *Analysing the Screenplay*, London and New York: Routledge.
Newland, Paul and Brian Hoyle (2016) 'Introduction: Post-millenial British Art Cinema', in *Journal of British Cinema and Television*, 13 (2).

Ngũgĩ wa Thiong'o (1986) *Decolonizing the Mind the Politics of Language in African Literature*, London: J. Currey.
Nichols, Bill (2001) *Introduction to Documentary*, Bloomington: Indiana University Press.
Nolas, Sevasti-Melissa and Christos Varvantakis (2018) 'Entanglements that matter', *entanglements*, 1 (1).
Nwonka, Clive James (2014) '"You're what's wrong with me": *Fish Tank*, *The Selfish Giant*, and the language of contemporary British social realism', *New Cinemas Journal of Contemporary Film*, 12 (3).
O'Brien, Deirdre (2012) 'From a life of drugs on a tough housing estate to sharing a love scene with Scarlett Johansson – Britain's unlikely new movie star: Paul Brannigan's life story could make a Hollywood film on its own', *Daily Mirror*, 9 June 2012, http://www.mirror.co.uk/news/real-life-stories/from-a-life-of-drugs-on-a-tough-housing-estate-870119
O'Brien, Nick (2018) 'Administrative Justice in the Wake of *I, Daniel Blake*,' *The Political Quarterly*, 89 (1), January–March 2018.
Orr, John (2004) 'New directions in European Cinema', in Elizabeth Ezra (ed.), *European Cinema*, Oxford and New York: Oxford University Press.
Ortner, Sherry, B. (2010) 'Access: Reflections on studying up in Hollywood', *Ethnography*, 11 (2).
Ostrowska, Dorota (2010) 'Magic, Emotions and Film Producers: Unlocking The "Black-Box" Of Film Production', *Wide Screen*, 2 (2).
Pandian, Anand (2015) *Reel World: An Anthology of Creation*, Durham, NC, and London: Duke University Press.
Petley, Julian (1982) 'An Interview with Ken Loach', *Framework*, 18.
Petley, Julian (1997) 'Ken Loach and Questions of Censorship', in George McKnight (ed.), *Agent of Challenge and Defiance: The Films of Ken Loach*, Trowbridge: Flicks Books.
Petrie, Duncan (2004) *Contemporary Scottish Fictions: Film, Television and the Novel*, Edinburgh: Edinburgh University Press.
Philo, Greg and Mike Berry (2011) *More Bad News from Israel*, London: Pluto Press.
Philo, Greg, Mike Berry, Justin Schlosberg, Antony Lerman and David Miller (2019) *Bad News for Labour: Anti-Semitism, The Party & Public Belief*, London: Pluto Press.
Pink, Sarah (2009) *Doing Sensory Ethnography*, London: Sage Publications Ltd.
Powdermaker, Hortense (1951) *Hollywood, The Dream Factory: An Anthropologist Looks at the Movies*, London: Secker and Warburg.
Presence, Steve and Andrew H. Spicer (2016) 'Autonomy and dependency in two successful film and television companies: An analysis of RED Production Company and warp Films', *Film Studies*, 14 (1).
Presence, Steve, Mike Wayne and Jack Newsinger (eds) (2020) *Contemporary Radical Film Culture: Networks, Organisations and Activists*, New York and London: Routledge.
Quart, Leonard (1980) 'A Fidelity to the Real: An Interview with Ken Loach and Tony Garnett,' *Cineaste*, 10 (4).
Rancière, Jacques (2009) *The Emancipated Spectator*, London and New York: Verso.
Rancière, Jacques (2011) *The Politics of Literature*, transl. Julie Rose, Cambridge: Polity Press.
Randle, Keith (2015) 'Class and exclusion at work: The case of UK film and television', in Kate Oakley and Justin O'Connor (eds), *The Routledge Companion to the Cultural Industries*, London: Routledge.
Rees, John (2016) 'Ken Loach talks Daniel Blake, Jeremy Corbyn and Leon Trotsky',

Counterfire, 4 October 2016, https://www.counterfire.org/interview/18543-ken-loach-talks-daniel-blake-jeremy-corbyn-and-leon-trotsky
Rickards, Carolyn (2018) 'An Ordinary Spectacle: Critical Responses to Fantasy and Whimsy in *Looking for Eric* and *The Angels' Share*', *Journal of British Cinema and Television*, September 2018, 15 (4).
Rose, Steve (2021) 'Why is British cinema so reluctant to tackle immigration', *The Guardian*, 26 July 2021, https://www.theguardian.com/film/2021/jul/26/why-is-british-cinema-so-reluctant-to-tackle-immigration
Ross, Kristin (2002) *May '68 and its Afterlives*, Chicago, IL: University of Chicago Press.
Ross, Kristin (2015) *Communal Luxury: The Political Imaginary of the Paris Commune*, London and New York: Verso.
Rosser, Michael (2012) 'Ken Loach rejects Turin award over worker dispute,' *Screen Daily*, 22 November 2012, https://www.screendaily.com/festivals/ken-loach-rejects-turin-award-over-worker-dispute/5049288.article
Rosten, Leo (1941) *Hollywood, the Movie Colony, the Movie Makers*, New York: Harcourt.
Rothwell, James (2021) 'Israel labels Amnesty International "anti-semitic" over "apartheid" report', *Daily Telegraph*, 30 January 2022, https://www.telegraph.co.uk/world-news/2022/01/30/israel-labels-amnesty-international-antisemitic-apartheid-report/
Schatz, Thomas (1988) *The Genius of the System: Hollywood Filmmaking in the Studio Era*, New York: Pantheon.
Schweiger, Daniel (2016) 'Interview with George Fenton,' *Film Music Magazine*, January 11, 2016, https://filmmusicinstitute.com/interview-with-george-fenton/
Sellors, C. Paul (2007) 'Collective Authorship in Film', *Journal of Aesthetics and Art Criticism*, 65 (3), Summer 2007.
Sellors, C. Paul (2010) *Film Authorship: Auteurs and Other Myths*, London: Wallflower.
Shoard, Catherine (2012) '*The Angels' Share*'s Paul Brannigan: "I've been slashed, stabbed and shot at"', *The Guardian*, 31 May 2012, https://www.theguardian.com/film/2012/may/31/the-angels-share-paul-brannigan
Solnit, Rebecca (2000) *Wanderlust: A History of Walking*, New York: Viking.
Spiegel, Jennifer Beth (2020) 'Amateur Performance and the Labour of Love or cultural reproduction "after" the collapse of capitalism', *Performance Research*, 25 (1).
Spencer, Richard (2022) 'Emma Watson accused on antisemitism over post supporting Palestinians', *The Times*, 4 January 2022, https://www.thetimes.co.uk/article/emma-watson-labelled-antisemitic-over-palestinian-tweet-x68f8vwck
Stanislavski, Konstantin (2008) *An Actor's Work*, transl. Jean Benedetti, Oxon and New York: Routledge.
Stepien, Victor (2020) '*Parasite* Review: An unmitigated triumph for South Korea's Ken Loach' *Catholic Herald*, 13 February 2020, https://catholicherald.co.uk/parasite-review-an-unmitigated-triumph-for-south-koreas-ken-loach/
Streeck, Wolfgang (2016) *How Will Capitalism End? Essays on a Failing System*. London and New York: Verso Books.
Street, Sarah (2001) *Costume and Cinema: Dress Codes in Popular Film*, London and New York: Wallflower.
Street, Sarah (2018) 'The Colour of Social Realism', *Journal of British Cinema and Television*, 15 (4).
Sumner, Stephen (2020) '*I, Daniel Blake* director Ken Loach blasts plans to turn Bath hospital into a hotel', Somersetlive.co.uk, 21 August 2020, https://www.somersetlive.co.uk/news/somerset-news/i-daniel-blake-director-ken-4447360

Tarkovsky, Andrei (2003) *Sculpting in Time: Reflections on the Cinema*, transl. Kitty Hunter-Blair, Austin: Texas University Press.
Taylor, Amanda, M. L. (2017) 'The unintended impacts of *I Daniel Blake*', blog post, https://amltaylor66.wordpress.com/2017/06/02/the-unintended-impacts-of-i-daniel-blake/
Thatcher, Margaret (1975) Speech to Conservative Party Conference, 17 October 1975, http://www.margaretthatcher.org/document/102777
Thorp, Margaret (1946) *America at the Movies*, London: Faber
Tinknell, Estella (2007) 'Between the Personal and the Political: Feminist Fables in the Films of Gaylene Preston', in Ian Conrich and Stuart Murray (eds), *New Zealand Filmmakers*, Detroit, MI: Wayne Street University Press.
Traverso, Enzo (2017) *Left-Wing Melancholia: Marxism, History and Memory*, New York: Columbia University Press.
Trotsky, Leon (1930) *My Life: An Attempt at an Autobiography*, New York: Dover.
Trotsky, Leon (1973/1923) 'The Struggle for Cultured Speech,' *Pravda*, 15 May 1923, in *Problems of Everyday Life and Other Writings on Culture and Science*, New York and London: Pathfinder Press.
Trotsky, Leon (1991/1923) *Literature and Revolution*, London: RedWords.
Trotsky, Leon (2002/1938) *The Transitional Program*, https://www.marxists.org/archive/trotsky/1938/tp/transprogram.pdf
Trotsky, Leon (2009/1931-9) *The Spanish Revolution 1931–39*, (eds) George Breitman and Naomi Allen, New York: Pathfinder Press.
Tulloch, John (1999) 'John Tulloch in conversation with Rona Munro, "Whose stories you tell": writing Ken Loach', in Jonathan Bignell (ed.), *Writing and Cinema*, Harlow: Longman.
Tulloch, John (2011) *Trevor Griffiths*, Manchester: Manchester University Press.
Uncredited (2011) '"Anti Semitic" attack on Tutu backfires', *The Times*, 13 January 2011, https://www.thetimes.co.uk/article/anti-semitic-attack-on-tutu-backfires-27zgdh28mtj
Uncredited (2011) 'Support the SSP', *Scottish Socialist Voice* (372), 20 April 2011, https://issuu.com/scottishsocialistparty/docs/socialistvoice372
Uncredited (2012) 'Ken Loach snubs Italian film prize after workers sacked', *France 24*, 23 November 2012, https://www.france24.com/en/20121123-loach-protest-italian-film-prize-workers
Uncredited (2014) 'Jon Voight Slams Penelope Cruz, Javier Bardem for Signing anti-Israel Letter', *Haaretz*, 5 August 2021, https://www.haaretz.com/life/television/jon-voight-slams-spanish-stars-over-anti-israel-letter-1.5258067
Uncredited (2019) 'Angela Davis Says She's "Stunned" After Award is Revoked Over Her Views on Israel' *The New York Times*, 8 January 2019, https://www.nytimes.com/2019/01/08/us/angela-davis-israel-civil-rights-institute.html
Vallejo, Aida and María-Paz Peirano (eds) (2017) *Film Festivals and Anthropology*, Newcastle upon Tyne: Cambridge Scholars Publishing.
Vaneigem, Raoul (2012/1967) *The Revolution of Everyday Life*, transl. Donald Nicholson-Smith, Oakland, CA: PM Press.
Various (2011) 'On Ken Loach', *Sight & Sound*, October 2011, http://old.bfi.org.uk/sightandsound/feature/49773
Wacquant, Loïc (2003) 'Ethnografeast: A progress report on the practice and promise of ethnography', *Ethnography*, 4 (1), March 2003.
Wallerstein, Immanuel, Randall Collins, Michael Mann, Georgi Derluguian and Craig Calhoun (2013) *Does Capitalism Have a Future?* Oxford: Oxford University Press.

Wayne, Mike (2019) *Marxism Goes to the Movies*, New York and London: Routledge.
Weber, Max (1948) *From Max Weber: Essays in Sociology*, transl. and ed. Hans Gerth and Charles Wright Mills, New York and London: Routledge and Kegan Paul.
Whitworth, Damian (2012) 'Movie stardom in *The Angels' Share*? I'll drink to that', *The Times*, 22 May 2012.
Williams, Raymond (1977) *Marxism and Literature*, Oxford: Oxford University Press.
Williams, Raymond (1980) 'The Welsh Industrial Novel', in *Problems in Materialism and Culture*, London: Verso.
Williams, Raymond (1989a) 'Cinema and socialism', in *Politics of Modernism: Against the New Conformists*, London: Verso.
Williams, Raymond (1989b) *Resources of Hope: Culture, Democracy, Socialism*. London: Verso.
Willis, Andy (2009) 'Jim Allen: Radical Drama Beyond *Days of Hope*', *Journal of British Cinema and Television*, 5 (2).
Wiseman, Andreas (2018) 'Daniel Day-Lewis reveals what he loves most about working with Paul Thomas Anderson', *Screen Daily*, 29 January 2018, https://www.screen daily.com/news/daniel-day-lewis-reveals-what-he-likes-most-about-working-with-paul-thomas-anderson/5126049.article
Wong, Cindy Hing-Yuk (2011) *Film Festivals: Culture, People, and Power on the Global Screen*, New Brunswick and London: Rutgers University Press.
Young, Graham (2014) 'Film Director Ken Loach dismisses Steven Knight's plan for sound stage in Birmingham', *Business Live*, 20 October 2014, https://www.birming hampost.co.uk/business/creative/film-director-ken-loach-says-7965069
Zarrilli, Phillip B. (1995) 'General Introduction: Between Theory and Practice', in Phillip B. Zarrilli, (ed.), *Acting (Re)Considered: Theories and Practices*, London and New York: Routledge.
Zinn, Howard (2006) *A Power Governments Cannot Suppress*, San Francisco, CA: City Lights Publishers.

Index

11'09"01 (United Kingdom), n142
Abbott, Paul, 93
Ackroyd, Barry, 68, 80n, 95
Addison, Bruce, 9, 113, 133–4
Ae Fond Kiss ..., 5, 6, 37, 42, 55, 56, 56n, 61n, 95, 100, 101, 141, 142n
After a Lifetime, 91
Aita, Sean, 122
Alcoff, Linda, 156
Allam, Roger, 9, 22, 112, 112–13n, 120, 129, 134
Allen, Jim, 26, 27n, 28, 37, 37n, 87, 88
Ancelotti, Carlo, 90
Anderson, Lindsay, 15, 21
Andrea, Arnold, 72n
Angels' Share, The, 1–2, 5–21, 23–5, 32n, 36, 39–49, 50, 51, 54, 55–83, 84, 85, 86, 88, 95, 97–100, 102, 105, 106–38, 139–59, 161–70, 178, 181–6
Antonioni, Michelangelo, 7, 51n
Arendt, Hannah, 120
Aristotle, 21, 39
Arnheim, Rudolf, 137
Astruc, Alexander, 84
Atkinson, Sarah, 114
Auslander, Philip, 106

Banks, Miranda, 89
Barad, Karen, 10
Barghouti, Omar, 171
Baron, Cynthia, 125n, 137
Barratt, Joss, 8, 95, 100
Barthes, Roland, 85
battaglia di Algeri, La/The Battle of Algiers, The, 30
Bazin, André, 70, 83, 90n, 167

BBC, 1, 3, 12, 53, 91, 96, 107, 144
BBFC (British Board of Film Classification), 154–6, 159, 165
Beckett, Ray, 8, 10n, 70, 80–1, 96, 123, 123n, 134
Beckett, Samuel, 139
Benjamin, Walter, 29, 31, 56, 69, 103, 124–5
BFI (British Film Institute), 4, 17, 91, 142
BFI Ken Loach archive, 5, 91–2, 107, 108, 135–6n, 144–5
Bien-aimés, Les/Beloved, The, 92
Big Flame, The, 9, 19, 25n, 26, 28, 30, 34, 36, 39, 102
Bindel, Julie, 37n
Birchard, Paul, 22, 148
Black Jack, 37, 88, 91, 92, 95, 140, 163
Bollaín, Icíar, 141n, 178
Bordieu, Pierre, 90–1
Bordwell, David, 13, 89n
Borher, Ashley, 38n
Born, Georgina, 12n, 15n,
Bourriaud, Nicolas, 5, 175
Bradley, David, 107
Brannigan, Paul, 9, 22, 106, 107, 107–8n, 111, 125–7, 134, 139, 146, 164–5
Bray, Camilla, 94n
Bread and Roses, 30, 35, 36, 37, 95, 102, 108, 163, 169
Brecht, Bertolt, 52–3, 106, 110, 129
Breslin, Tommy, 160
Breton, André, 28
Brewer, John, D., 10
Brigadoon, 43
Brody, Adrien, 108
Brotherston, Karen, 8, 65, 125–6
Brown, Ian, 45

Brown, Jas, 8, 97
Buñuel Luis, 177, 179
Burns, James, 97

Cabezas, Oyanka, 115
Caldwell, John Thornton, 8, 12, 12n, 144
Cannes Film Festival, 3, 7, 8, 20, 84, 108n, 145, 161–9
Cantona, Eric, 25, 47, 93, 103
Capra, Frank, 89
Cardullo, Bert, 16, 81n
Cargo, 6
Carla's Song, 30, 35, 37, 42, 43, 55, 56, 88, 95, 101, 108, 114, 141, 178
Carlyle, Robert, 108
Carnicke, Sharon Marie, 125, 126, 127, 137
Carringer, Robert, L., 12, 13
Casey, James, 57, 120
Casting By, 108
Catherine, 145
Cathy Come Home, 3, 5, 24, 33, 36, 50, 53, 88, 101, 141, 173
Cattrall, Ann, 94n
Caucheteux, Pascal, 98
Caughie, John, 3n, 16n, 45, 51, 53n, 69n, 78n, 85, 87, 103
Certain Tendencies in Loach's Cinema, 18–21
Chambers, Jamie, 46, 52, 82
Channel 4, 91
Chen, Anna, 38
cinematography, 18, 20, 24, 34, 50, 54, 58, 66–72, 73, 77, 79, 80, 89, 95, 97, 106, 118, 119, 121–5, 129–31, 133, 134, 136
Citizen Kane, 79
Clegg, Fergus, 8, 61–3, 64, 95, 98, 132
Clegg, Paul, 8, 124n
Cocteau, Jean, 70
Cole, Andy, 8, 72–3, 95–6
Comedians, 135
Coming Out Party, The, 26, 141
Commune (Paris, 1871), La, 14, 136
Compston, Martin, 107
Conversation with Cillian Murphy, 139
Cook, John, 14, 14n, 136
Cooper Clarke, John, 22, 48
Coquelin, Benoît-Constant, 126
Corliss, Richard, 88
Corrigan, Tim, 85
Country, 135
Cowan, Philip, 89n
Cowie, Roderick, 128

Crawford, Kahleen, 8, 65n, 95, 108, 109–14, 134n
Creative Scotland, 142
Crenshaw, Kimberlé, 38n
Curtin, Michael, 9

Daniels-Yeomans, Finn, 37n
Dave, Paul, 33, 96
Davidson, Neil, 44
Davies, Luke, 36
Dawber, Robb, 141
Days of Hope, 16, 22, 28, 30, 31, 36, 39, 61n, 63, 69n, 78, 95, 135
De Valke, Marijke, 162
Debord, Guy, 41
Deleuze, Gilles, 32, 106–7
Derrida, Jacques, 39n
Diary of a Young Man, 53
Distilling The Angels' Share, 17, 66n
Dunn, Nell, 141
Durgan, Andy, 31n
Dymond, Scott, 113

Eagleton, Terry, 40
editing, 7, 18, 20, 50, 51, 53, 77–80, 81, 88, 124, 136, 137, 153
Eleftheriotis, Dimitris, 71
End of Arthur's Marriage, The, 66
Engels, Friedrich, 34, 39n
ethnografilmic analysis, 12–15, 138, 178
ethnography, 6, 9–15
Evets, Steve, 103
Ezra, Elizabeth, 85

Faiers, Jonathan, 45
Fajr Film Festival, 172
Family Life, 36, 56, 91, 163
Fatherland, 55, 88, 92, 95, 134, 144–5
Fenton, George, 81, 95
Ferguson, Alex, 90
Flickering Flame: A Story of Contemporary Morality, The, 34, 95
Ford, John, 21, 89, 108
Forrest, David/Dave, 28n, 52, 71, 88, 88n
Fraser, Carole, 8, 63, 65
Friell, Vincent, 113
Fuller, Graham, 16, 101, 120, 131, 140

Gallagher, Mark, 86
Gallagher, Peter, 8, 100, 108, 122, 142n, 145n, 154
Gamekeeper, The, 37, 54, 78, 88, 163
Ganti, Tejaswani, 13, 13n

Garnett, Tony, 9, 9n, 17, 26n, 27n, 58, 84, 88–9, 91, 96, 106, 108, 116, 118, 124n, 140, 140n, 147, 153
Gaut, Berys, 89
Genovese, Taylor, R., 11n
Getino, Octavio, 54
Gilchrist, David, 8, 98, 121
Gillette, William, 118
Ginger and Rosa, 14
Godard, Jean-Luc, 54
Goffman, Erving
Golden Vision, The, 101
Golding, Simon, W., 17
Gonzalez, Mike, 99n
Grant, Catherine, 85
Grant, Nick, 52
Greene, Liz, 16n
Grierson, John, 51
Griffiths, Trevor, 26n, 27n, 88, 134–6, 140, 144–5, 146
Grotowski, Jerzy, 106
Groundhog Day, 81

Hall, Martin, 174
Happy Ending, 163
Hawks, Howard, 89
Hayman, David, 110
Hayward, Anthony, 1n, 17, 99
Heasman, Paul, 151
Henshaw, John, 22, 111n, 112, 112–13n
Hibbin, Sally, 91
Hidden Agenda, 4, 28, 35, 38, 91, 95, 108, 163
Higson, Michael, 2, 8, 59–60, 63, 64, 98
Hill, John, 3n, 16, 25, 28, 42, 52, 82, 86, 91, 109n, 142, 175
Hines, Barry, 52, 88, 140, 141, 144
Hing-Yuk Wong, Cindy, 162, 163
Hitchcock, Alfred, 89
Hjort, Mette, 98
Hoek, Lotte, 13
Holloway, John, 35
Hoří, má panenko/The Firemen's Ball, 67
How to Make a Ken Loach Film, 17
Hoyle, Brian, 25
Hunter, Aaron, 86, 89
Hunter, Barry, 113
Hurt Locker, The, 80

I, Daniel Blake, 32, 36, 37, 84, 93, 95, 142, 143, 163, 172, 173
It's a Free World, 25, 36, 101, 102, 142, 142n

Jameson, Fredric, 33
Jimmy's Hall, 37n, 95, 142
Johnson, Martin, 61n, 95
Jones, Huw, 92
Just A Boys' Game, 151

Kazan, Elia, 108
Kelly, Lisa, 109n
Kelman, James, 156–7
Kennedy, Anne-Marie, 129
Kennedy Martin, Troy, 53
Kes, 4, 5, 17, 28, 37, 53, 54, 64, 67, 68, 82, 83, 88, 101, 102, 107, 140, 150, 163, 164
Kestrel Films, 88, 91
Kiarostami, Abbas, 42
Kiernan, Ford, 116
Kirby, Michael, 127
Klinger, Barbara, 8n
Kristensen, Lars, 33n, 94n
Kyle, Scott, 23, 115, 151–2

Lacey, Stephen, 89
Ladybird Ladybird, 25, 36, 56, 56n, 69n, 95, 99, 107, 110
LaFargue, Paul, 41
Land and Freedom, 5n, 6, 28, 29–31, 35, 37n, 39, 49, 55, 56, 59, 64, 69n, 102, 109n, 119, 163, 178
Lanzmann, Claude, 98
Lásky jedné plavovlásky/A Blonde in Love, 67
Laverty, Paul, 4, 5n, 6, 8, 48, 56, 78, 88, 94n, 95, 108, 109, 111, 112n, 121, 140, 141–3, 145–7, 149, 160, 165–6, 167
Lawson, Emma, 94
Lefebvre, Henri, 58–9
Leigh, Jacob, 16, 28, 68
Leigh, Mike, 16
Leiper, Neil, 151–2
Lenton, Susanna, 8, 115n, 119
Lighting, 10, 18, 20, 51, 61n, 68, 72–4, 122
Littlewood, Joan, 50
Loach, Jim, 121
Loach on Location: Making Land and Freedom, 17
Local Hero, 43
Looking for Eric, 25, 47, 88, 92, 93, 98, 101, 103, 112, 142, 163, 172
Looks and Smiles, 88, 91, 163
López Hernández, Sofía, 81
Lukács, György, 52–3

McArthur, Colin, 45n
McDonald, Paul, 110, 136

McDormand, Frances, 108
McGinnes, Alison, 128
McKnight, George, 16, 28
MacLean, Charles, 9, 22, 65, 105, 113, 120, 125–32, 147, 164
Maclean, John, 43–4
McMahon, Eimhear, 8, 92, 94n
Maitland, Gary, 9, 22, 112, 116n, 119, 167n
Maley, Willy, 157–8
Martin, Gilbert, 22, 113
Martin-Jones, David, 45, 57
Marx/Marxism, 26, 30, 33n, 36, 38, 40, 42, 43–4, 49, 52, 55, 69n, 88, 166
Mayer, Vicki, 89
Mazdon, Lucy, 92n
Mazierska, Ewa, 25n, 33n, 94n, 191n
Meadows, Shane, 93
Meir, Christopher, 142
Menges, Chris, 67, 68, 89, 95
Metz, Christian, 137
Meyerhold, Vsevolod, 121
Michael Goss, Brian, 85
Misfortune, A, 140
Mitchell, Campbell, 8, 120, 123, 130, 151
Molière, 129
Morris, Jonathan, 9, 77–80, 81, 95, 97, 98
Moss-Wellington, Wyatt, 55
Mullan, Peter, 108
Munro, Rona, 99, 101
Murphy, Cillian, 108, 110
Murphy, Pete, 123
My Name is Joe, 25, 32, 33, 35, 36, 37, 42, 43, 44, 56, 64, 95, 101, 108, 110, 122, 141, 163

Nancy, Jean-Luc, 150
Naremore, James, 118, 119, 124
Navigators, The, 32, 36, 88, 91, 100, 102, 141
Neale, Steve, 85
Nelmes, Jill, 153–4
Newland, Paul, 25
Ngũgĩ wa Thiong'o, 38
Nichols, Bill, 73
Nolas, Savasti-Melissa, 11
Nwonka, Clive, 36

O'Brien, Rebecca, 1–2, 5n, 7, 8, 17, 19, 65n, 78, 84–104, 109, 110n, 121, 133, 145, 149, 163, 164, 165, 167–9
Occupations, 134
O'Connor, John, 141
Old Oak, The, 4n, 43, 177
Olmi, Ermanno, 42

Ondříček, Miroslav, 67, 68
Oranges and Sunshine, 94
Orr, John, 4n, 59
Ortner, Sherry, B., 12n
Ostrowska, Dorota, 14

Palestine, 170–2
Pandian, Anand, 13
Parallax Pictures, 91
Peirano, María-Paz, 12n
performance, 7, 14, 20, 58–9, 66, 69, 96, 105–38, 146, 148, 150, 158
Petrie, Duncan, 32
Pink, Sarah, 6
Pirandello, Luigi, 137
Pontecorvo, Gillo, 30
Poor Cow, 3, 36, 53, 64, 67, 108, 140, 141
Potter, Sally, 14
Powdermaker, Hortense, 12, 15, 86, 89, 99–100
Presence, Steve, 93–4
Price of Coal, The, 32, 56, 88
Proclaimers, The, 24, 46, 79, 82, 156n, 167
Pudovkin, Vsevolod, 137

¡Queimada!/Burn!, 30
Quemada-Díez, Diego, 178
Question of Leadership, A, 28, 87
Questions of Leadership, 4, 28, 87

Rae, Alastair, 80n
Rahman, Habib, 94
Raining Stones, 22, 28, 32, 34, 35, 56, 70, 95, 163
Rancière, Jacques, 157, 174–5
Rank and File, The, 26, 30, 34, 35, 36, 39, 102
Ratcatcher, 70
realism, 16, 20, 39, 51–3, 59–60, 79, 82, 106, 124, 129, 140, 153, 177, 178
Red and the Blue: Impressions of Two Political Conferences – Autumn 1982, The, 79
Red Badge of Courage, The, 15
Reilly, Siobhan, 22, 107, 112
respair, 177–80
revolution, 6n, 19, 26, 27, 28, 30–2, 34, 35, 37, 38, 39, 40–1, 43, 49, 54, 46, 128, 166, 174, 177–80
Rickards, Carolyn, 25n
Riff-Raff, 5, 31, 36, 37, 56, 56n, 91, 102, 163
Riggins, Jasmine, 9, 23, 112, 116, 118, 151–2
River City, 126
Road Movies, 92
Rock, Chrissie, 107

Rocky, 79
Rome, Open City, 58
Rose, Steve, 52
Ross, Kristin, 31, 39–40
Ross, Lilian, 15
Route Irish, 37n, 56, 142, 163
Ruane, William, 9, 22, 105, 112, 118, 146–7
Ryan, Robbie, 9, 66n, 68, 68n, 71–2, 95, 97–8, 100, 121, 130

Sandford, Jeremy, 141
Sanson, Kevin, 9
Save the Children Fund Film, 3, 34, 37, 91
Schatz, Thomas, 89, 100
Schein, Edgar, 94, 95
Scorsese, Martin, 108
Scottish Socialist Party, 5, 5n
Screen, 5, 16n, 55n
screenplay, 18, 20, 40, 55, 56, 83, 88, 113, 118, 139–59
Searchers, The, 70, 127
Sellors, C. Paul, 90
Shankly, Bill, 101
Shoah, 98
Sixteen Films, 7, 8, 17, 34n, 60n, 84–104, 109, 112, 133, 142, 144, 169n, 169, 177
Smith, Roger, 78, 145
socialism, 22, 27, 29–30, 33, 34, 35, 37n, 41, 49
Soetman, Mimi, 162
Solanas, Fernando, 54
Solnit, Rebecca, 43, 46
Sorry We Missed You, 3, 18, 33, 35, 36, 37, 41, 69n, 95, 101, 102, 142, 143, 163
sound, 10n, 70, 74–5, 80–2, 123, 124, 128, 131, 134
soundtrack, 80–2
South Bank Show, The, 115
Spicer, Andrew, 93–4
Spiegel, Jennifer Beth, 107–8
Spirit of '45, The, 38, 93n
Staiger, Janet, 13, 89n
Stamp, Terence, 108
Stanislavski, Konstantin, 106, 110, 124n
Stein, Jock, 101
Street, Sarah, 64, 64n
Summer, 94
Sweet Sixteen, 5, 6, 32, 36, 37, 42, 48, 56, 100, 102, 107, 112, 113, 139, 141, 142, 145, 155, 163

Tap on the Shoulder, A, 25, 102, 141
Tarkovsky, Andrei, 105, 106, 144

Teitelbaum, Irving, 91n, 92n
That Sinking Feeling, 24
Thatcher, Margaret, 22
Thomas-O'Brien, Jack, 94
Thompson, Kristin, 13, 89n
Tickets, 42, 101, 112, 141
Torino Film Festival, 169–70
Tornasol, 92
Traverso, Enzo, 29–30, 33
Trotsky, Leon/Trotskyism, 20, 25n, 26–9, 30, 40, 41n, 87, 128, 158
Truffaut, Francois, 18

Under the Skin, 126
Up the Junction, 3, 26, 36, 47, 50, 53, 78n, 82, 141

Vallejo, Aida, 12n
Vaneigem, Raoul, 41
Varvantakis, Christos, C., 11
Verdugo, El/Executioner, The, 56
Versus: The Life and Films of Ken Loach, 17
Vive, Sue, 88n

Wacquant, Loïc, 9
Watkins, Peter, 14n, 51, 136
Wayne, John, 127
Weber, Max, 99
Welles, Orson, 12
Wenders, Wim, 15
Wheatley, Katherine, 92
Which Side Are You On?, 4
Whisky Galore!, 43
Whitworth, Damian, 149–50
Why Not Productions, 92
Wild Bunch, 92
Williams, Raymond, 13, 30, 48, 160
Willis, Andy, 87
Wind that Shakes the Barley, The, 3, 5, 5n, 6, 27n, 30, 35, 38, 56, 61n, 64, 79, 88, 93, 95, 105, 108, 110, 112, 129, 132, 150, 163, 179
Winstone, Ray, 110
Wonderland, 64
World in Action, 50, 51

You Were Never Really Here, 92
Young James Herriot, 109n

Zarrilli, Philip, B., 106
Zinn, Howard, 48
Žižek, Slavoj, 34

EU representative:
Easy Access System Europe
Mustamäe tee 50, 10621 Tallinn, Estonia
Gpsr.requests@easproject.com

www.ingramcontent.com/pod-product-compliance
Lightning Source LLC
Chambersburg PA
CBHW070354240426
43671CB00013BA/2501